JEAN MAYER, Ph.D. (Yale), D.Sc. (Sorbonne), A.M. (hon.) (Harvard), is one of the world's foremost authorities on nutrition. He has served on a number of United Nations committees on nutrition requirements, and on the editorial boards of six professional journals in the fields of physiology, medicine, and nutrition. He is a Fellow of the American Academy of Arts and Sciences and a member or fellow of a number of other professional and honorary societies. Since 1950, he has been on the faculty of Harvard University and is now Professor of Nutrition, Lecturer on the History of Public Health and Member of the Center for Population Studies at Harvard. He is also consultant in Nutrition to the Children's Hospital of Boston. Dr. Mayer has held honorary lectureships at a number of academic and medical institutions and given many named lectures, in particular at the Jubilee of the Royal College of Physicians of Australia and at that of the American Dietetic Association. He is the author of 400 research articles and reviews, most of which deal with the problems of hunger and obesity in experimental animals and in men, women, and children. In June 1969 Dr. Mayer was appointed Special Consultant to the President of the United States and placed in charge of organizing the 1969 White House Conference on Food, Nutrition and Health.

OVERWEIGHT
Causes, Cost, and Control

JEAN MAYER

A SPECTRUM BOOK

PRENTICE-HALL, Inc.
Englewood Cliffs, N. J.

To Harry E. Wheeler, Jr.

Without whose friendly but steady prodding, invaluable criticism, and help, this book would probably never have seen the light of day.

Hygiene is as much a virtue as a science.

Jean-Jacques Rousseau

Consumers Union Edition
First printing, May 1969
Second printing, August 1969

Copyright © 1968 by PRENTICE-HALL, Inc.,
Englewood Cliffs, N. J.

PRINTED IN THE UNITED STATES OF AMERICA

Current printing (last digit):
10 9 8 7 6 5 4 3 2

PRENTICE-HALL INTERNATIONAL, INC., *London*

Foreword to the Consumers Union Edition

Too many Americans weigh too much. But what to do about it? A host of "cures"—fad diets, reducing pills, vibrating machines—tempts the overweight American to waste his money and sometimes injure his health. The medical profession itself is not without quacks—"fat doctors" who prescribe, among other things, dangerous drug combinations. Even if one succeeds in resisting the lures of charlatans, the countervailing truths the overweight individual needs in order to help himself are hard to find. Too often they come dressed up with meaningless tables of "ideal" weights, or theories that fail to consider complicating factors; or they come tainted by leftover folklore. Small wonder, then, that the average American, buffeted by a mass of misinformation, finds it difficult to establish any effective program for weight control. In this comprehensive work, Jean Mayer replaces the myths about obesity, its causes and its control, with sound, scientifically based knowledge.

"The goal of any reducing program," says Mayer, "is not merely to lose weight, but to keep it off." He then explains how—for many individuals—weight *can* be reduced *and* controlled. But Mayer makes no attempt to minimize the difficulty of the task. He examines the complex mix of physiological, psychological and environmental factors that may contribute to obesity. His discussion ranges from simple tests for assessing fatness to advanced analyses of nutritional factors, from the role played by exercise to the role played by genetics. Although one of the world's foremost authorities on obesity, Mayer doesn't hesitate to note: "After close to twenty years of research in the somatic, the psychologic, and the social aspects of obesity, I am as aware as any man of the gigantic gaps in our knowledge—and of the likelihood that many of our present concepts may be erroneous." But he is meticulous in distinguishing between scientifically accepted fact and scientifically based speculation. The result of this broad exploration is a book that can't be skimmed. It must be read slowly and with care. CU believes that anyone seriously concerned about overweight can derive from this book benefits well worth the effort.

As with all CU Special Publications not of CU's own making, "Overweight" represents the thinking of its author; it should not be assumed that CU concurs with all his views. For example, in considering a program of weight control, Mayer insists that the physician remain the cornerstone of therapy for the obese individual. CU agrees with Mayer in principle. The management of obesity is and will remain a medical problem. Decisions about a weight control program—who, when, how much—should be made by a physician, and the program executed under his guidance or with his knowledge. But, as Mayer himself states, many health professionals, including physicians, are poorly trained in nutrition and in the management of obesity. And, we must emphasize, physicians willing to treat obesity can range from the conscientious and well-informed doctor to the doctor who simply hands out a diet sheet—and even to the doctor who specializes in lucrative but questionable and sometimes dangerous procedures. We believe one of the best defenses against inadequate medical care of obesity is a careful study of this book. As a matter of fact, CU's medical consultants believe many practicing physicians and medical students will also benefit from the information contained in "Overweight."

Obesity is a major public health problem with no certain methods of control in sight. Jean Mayer notes, "Knowledge is not sufficient for cure, but its acquisition is a necessary step." It is in that spirit that CU makes available to readers of *Consumer Reports* this special, low-cost edition of "Overweight." THE EDITORS OF CONSUMER REPORTS

CONSUMERS UNION
MOUNT VERNON, NEW YORK
APRIL 1969

Foreword

Originally, I had planned to include the word "obesity" in the title of this book. Obesity, or the state of being too fat, is really what it is about. While the term "overweight," merely the state of weighing more than the average for one's height and age, is by no means equivalent to the more accurate "obesity," it is a word which people who are too fat will more easily identify with. They tend to think of obesity as denoting a degree of adiposity far more extreme than their own, and, in fact, take it as an insult. The subtitle, "Causes, Cost, and Control," was added because the book focuses on the condition's etiology and modes of development, its penalties in terms of health and social acceptance, and finally, the ways in which it can be minimized. Unfortunately, there is as yet no "cure" for obesity.

The book grew out of a dual source: articles I wrote for the general public in the *Atlantic Monthly, Harper's,* and the *New York Times Sunday Magazine,* and articles I wrote for general practitioners in *Postgraduate Medicine,* a journal of which I have been nutrition editor for a number of years. It is my hope that this book will be intelligible to educated laymen, but informative to physicians, dietitians, and other health professionals at the same time. That it is written from one man's viewpoint I do not for a minute deny. I justify it to myself on the grounds that I have been immersed in the subject of control of appetite and obesity as deeply and as continually as anyone and have been particularly lucky in the company I have kept and the means I have been given. In the last two decades, I have had the great good fortune of being able to attract to my laboratory in the Department of Nutrition at the School of Public Health, Harvard University, a succession of distinguished young research workers and clinicians—representing such varied fields as anthropology, histology, physiology, neurophysiology, endocrinology, metabolism, biochemistry, animal behavior, human psychology, sociology, internal medicine, pediatrics, and psychiatry—who were interested in working with me on problems of food intake control and the etiology and treatment of obesity. So as not to burden unduly the style of this volume, I have mentioned only a fraction of their number by name in the text. To do justice to their contributions, I had planned to include in the Appendix a list of some 250 research papers from my laboratory, which not only documented my statements, but also gave for the corresponding phase of the research the name of each of my collaborators. Limitation of space has forced me to eliminate this list. Only a number of my former and present co-workers will therefore see their names mentioned in the book, but I want all who have worked with me to know how much I have appreciated their help and fellowship and how often I thought of them with particular affection and gratitude while this book was being prepared.

Regretfully I have had to eliminate also a list of research articles by scientists in other institutions who have contributed greatly to our knowledge of the control of food intake and obesity. Many of these research workers are my old friends. Their openness and generosity in discussing problems of common interest have been a consistent source of pleasure through the years of my professional life. I am sorry that omission of important names in the text is no longer in part compensated by their inclusion in a more complete bibliography.

Contents

introduction

Obesity:
Quackery and Questions

Obesity has become in our time a national problem, if not, indeed, a national obsession. Newspaper and magazine articles, radio and television programs, and advertisements of various kinds all stress the theme that an ever-increasing proportion of Americans are overweight and that overweight carries the penalty of increased sickness and earlier death. Generally, in this barrage of propaganda, obesity is equated with overeating. Noncommercial health education material treats overeating as gluttony. The old view of medicine, that patients are sick because of their sins, including their lack of self-restraint—a view which has been generally abandoned in the Western world even in the matter of alcoholism—still dominates as far as obesity is concerned. Obesity, almost alone among all the pathologic conditions, remains a moral issue. Therapists and propagandists, conscious of their own lower weights and presumably purer natures, adopt either a sternly censorious or a pityingly superior attitude toward their more chubby charges. Not infrequently, usually dispassionate physicians and dietitians speak of their puffy patients in almost the terms used by proponents of lily-white supremacy for allegedly inferior ethnic minorities.

Such a mood has, of course, the useful corollary (from the professional weight-reducer's point of view) that it makes possible projection on the patient of full responsibility for the failure of the particular treatment being advocated. And, regrettably, it is true that "weight control programs" meet with only very limited success.

A study conducted in Boston illustrates this debacle only too vividly. Four similar groups were constituted, each of a hundred patients recognized as overweight. The first group was left untreated; the second group was referred to the dietary clinic of a university hospital; the third group was treated by group psychotherapy; and the fourth by individual psychotherapy. Three years later the individuals involved in the experiment were again examined. Although the various treatments had yielded some measure of temporary success, the long-term result was about equally dismal for all four groups. At the conclusion of the three-year period, a small minority in each group had lost weight, a somewhat larger number—again in each group—had gained weight, and the majority of the patients were in about the same position they had occupied before the experiment commenced. Their weight had bobbed up and down as a result of their practicing what I have called "the rhythm method of girth control." None of the three therapeutic approaches led to effective improvement over the untreated group.

In the peculiarly vindictive world in which the overweight individual moves, the responsibility is declared to be the patient's and the patient's alone. All his avenues of escape are carefully blocked. The guilty one is told that his lack of self-restraint, and *only* his lack of self-restraint, is the cause of his plight. Hunger, appetite, and the drive for food are dissociated from any but intellectual connotations, as though they represented errant entities suspended in mid-air, unconnected to the bodily machine which, after all, they serve.

Heredity as a possible contributing factor is dismissed: "Genes have nothing to do with obesity." Hormones are also eliminated from legitimate consideration: ". . . in less than one per cent of the cases are hormones concerned with overweight." The debit side of the caloric balance sheet is minimized: "Exercise is of no value as a reducing aid." The practices of animal husbandry, usually offered as models in "nutrition education," are spurned. In animal husbandry, of course, when the production of fat animals is desired, one first of all selects genetically obese strains of hogs, cattle, etc. This is certainly a procedure based upon heredity. Oxen and capons are brought into being by the process of castration. Other animals are injected with estrogens (female sex hormones), as in the case of chickens; or estrogen pellets are implanted, a practice recently introduced in the fattening of cattle. All these measures are certainly based upon the assumption that, at least in the domestic species, hormonal factors contribute to obesity. Finally, when the farmer has his heart set on bacon or on pâté de foie gras, the first step he takes is to "coop up" or "pen up" the animals selected. The farmer knows full well that if his pigs and geese are permitted to exercise at will, their rate of fat accumulation is going to be curtailed. In these species then, it is recognized that exercise has an important role in weight control. And while such significant phenomena as those just listed are ignored or irrationally contradicted, the sufferers from obesity are offered treatments which are either sheer moonshine or only fragmentarily scientific.

The paradox has not escaped the attention of that dedicated commentator on our mores, Mr. Al Capp. With the vigorous injunction, "Eat like a swine and stay slim as a snake," the some forty million readers of the spirited comic strip were introduced to a new—and fortunately nonexistent—commercial product. Called "Mockeroni," its perpetrators declared that "the more you eat, the thinner you get." In the accompanying panels, a spry advertising man named Rock Hustler demanded of a plump female gourmand, "How do you like that ad? Every word the truth!" The lady, however, objected: "But you didn't tell 'em once they start eating Mockeroni, they can't stop! And once they start getting thinner, that doesn't stop until they (shudder) float away!" Rock's answer to that was, "A smart advertising man knows how much of the truth to leave out!"

The broad burlesque of Mockeroni has its all-too-widespread counterparts on the American scene well outside of comic strips.

Ferguson's Formula—new, delightfully-flavored, relaxing chewing gum. Fat and Flab fade fast. . . . Clinical tests show an average weight loss of 3½ pounds the first week, 11½ pounds the first month . . . without special diet, without exercise.

Ferguson's Formula ($2.98 for 80 pieces, $5.49 for 160 pieces, the economy size) was claimed by its promoters to be "so unique" that it was offered a patent by the United States Government. One visualizes a battery of bureaucrats so stunned by the splendors of this product that they pleaded with the reluctant manufacturers to protect their own precious interests.

Less exotic than chewing gum is the formula that can be reduced to words with or without decorative charts. "Take weight off safely," went an ad a few years ago in a popular newspaper, "up to ten pounds a month. Forget calories. The secret is in the combinations." And the copy went on to celebrate the "phenomenon of low-protein diets without restriction as to calories." Later, the same newspaper, exhibiting the traditional open-mindedness of our press, hired out the full back cover of one of its Sunday sections to an incitement of the American public to sample the wonders of *Calories Don't Count,* offering to help the buyers of that book lose weight by eating an unrestricted high-protein, high-fat diet.

Nonprescription drugs by the hundred are also pressed upon obese people who don't want to change their food intake or physical activity habits or who, having tried and failed, are convinced that they can't. These are different from the prescribed amphetamines, which, properly used, have a limited efficacy through their temporary appetite-depressing effect. They usually lose their potency in less than six weeks and may have undesirable side-effects. That some day a better drug may be devised which acts specifically on hypothalamic centers—again to be sold by prescription and used under tight medical supervision—is a possibility this writer, himself a student of the central nervous mechanism of food intake regulation, would be the last to discount. More on this later.

At present, however, such a compound does not exist. Patients unwilling to diet or exercise or—ideally—do both are left with recourse only to magic. Du-Dol "reducing cocktail" (a "regular" supply, $3.00; a "giant double," $5.00) exults: "Now, for the first time, DRINK YOUR

FAT AWAY. Reduce up to 5 ounces per drink with each fabulous no-diet reducing cocktail." The term "no-diet" usually means to the reader that he or she can continue to eat as has been customary. But the ad, which describes Du-Dol as a "small bottle of liquid reducing medication," enjoins reverently "you put a couple of drops of that precious concentrated liquid into a glass of water, fruit juice, vegetable juice, even liquor." What happens after this mystic act? "Down comes your horrible craving for food, down comes caloric intake. . . ." One discovers that you go on a diet with "No-diet" Du-Dol. "You burn off those ugly pounds, lose up to 7 pounds the first 7 days, up to 14 pounds the first two weeks—you don't strain your heart with brutal exercise." The suggestion that weight reduction by the expenditure of energy is a matter of such fearful violence as to endanger life itself is a leitmotif of such ads.

A few months later, this "scientific formulation of safe, tested ingredients proved in doctor-supervised clinical tests" claimed, in an ad co-sponsored by a Boston department store, "Lose up to 9 pounds the first week, up to 24 pounds the first month." To lose one pound of fat, incidentally, you have to expend 3,500 calories more than you consume. Losing 9 pounds of fat a week would mean, for the average obese person, running a modest daily marathon plus a complete abstinence from food. Some time later, the Federal Trade Commission was in a position to approve a consent order requiring the makers of Du-Dol to stop making these claims in their advertising.

The reader may think that the examples I have selected are extreme. Unfortunately, this is not the case. A Post Office release declares that "medical frauds are today more lucrative than any other criminal activity. . . . Reducing schemes are perhaps the most lucrative of such schemes." The American Medical Association estimates the yearly yield of such ventures at 100 million dollars. One single company grossed eight million in ten months on one single worthless "drug"; the net was two million. Most of the sales cost was consumed by advertising, two million dollars on TV spots alone, with some of the best-known shows selected. It was long afterwards that a Federal court—before which this writer testified—put an end, one hopes, to over-the-counter sale of the main ingredient of this product, one of the least active amphetamine derivatives. And then there are the "miracle foods": low-calorie bread, low-calorie beer, "slimming" yoghurt, and blackstrap molasses—all offered to those who want to "enjoy their food" while losing weight.

Enterprises such as this drain away money which ought to go to legitimate food and medical channels. Some of the weirder regimens may be dangerous: girls placing themselves on low-protein diets, obese men of middle age switching to extremely high-fat diets, or even chronically constipated older patients attempting to sustain themselves on roughage-free, all-liquid diets. Many of these programs—certainly the low-protein and the carbohydrate-free diets—mean, in practice, the avoidance of entire classes of foods and hence, the likelihood of deficiencies in the nutrients which these foods supply. The very existence of these regimens and preparations shows that the great majority of our obese contemporaries, tens of millions of them, have not been sufficiently instructed in the basic elements of the science of nutrition and are thus easily misled by oversimplification and deception. Oddly enough, official health information has sometimes contributed to the explosive development of this type of quackery by assuming that all is known about obesity and that there are no problems left. In spite of the results of twenty years of concentrated research by this writer and others, all of which shows the extreme complexity and the multicausal etiology of obesity, persistent oversimplifications stressing that "obesity is due to overeating and all it takes is self-control to correct it" are, I believe, partly responsible for the exploitation of the public. If authoritative pronouncements, supposedly based on science, are at obvious variance with experience, then the door is open for the introduction of witchcraft. To a large extent the acceptance of quackery is an effort to avoid unmerited guilt.

Surely, recent experimental work does raise questions which make the "flagrante delicto" verdict, in the case of society versus the obese, untenable. If we can make animals obese rapidly by damaging various parts of the central nervous system, cannot similar, perhaps much slighter, lesions cause a slow development of obesity in man? I have shown that a certain chemical destroys certain brain cells which monitor food intake. The animals so treated become obese. Can certain diseases cause a similar effect in man? In the mouse alone we have been able to cause obesity by twelve different experimental procedures. Is it not likely that equally dissimilar events may cause obesity in man? Is man indeed unique as far as normal—and pathological—fat accumulation is concerned?

There are some even more urgent questions, none of them calculated to support the position of the addicts of oversimplification. For example, who is overweight? Is overweight the same thing as obesity? The 6-foot, 225-pound guard of the varsity football team is as much at variance from the life insurance "ideal" or "desirable" standard as is a 6-foot, 225-pound, inactive, sedentary paterfamilias. The fat content of both men can be determined by a number of methods, such as weighing them under water, measuring their subcutaneous fat with the aid of calipers, diluting injected heavy water, and by other procedures which will be reviewed in a later chapter. Such determinations reveal that, while the young athlete is "overweight," he is "underfat." His surplus weight is made up of muscle. By contrast, the chair-tied father is both "overweight" and "overfat." His deviation from the normal height-weight relation is due to the excessive development of his adipose tissue. Are both types of overweight equivalent from the point of view of health? Should attempts be made to correct them both, and by the same methods?

Further, there is our old acquaintance "overeating." Overweight individuals are often derided for their assertion, "But I eat like a bird." It is usually taken for granted that they are more or less knowingly lying. Another assumption, hardly more generous, is that they do not possess the wit to observe and judge the quantity of food that they consume. Is it not conceivable that these—the too easily and too frequently condemned—are, in terms of the urgent appetites which drive them, heroes of rigorous self-mastery?

It is known that excessively thin men and women often boast of *their* Gargantuan eating feats. Perhaps these slender ones have an equally valid right to brag. Might not they, in a presumably praiseworthy effort to put on weight, be stretching their abnormally restricted appetites to and beyond the limits of their capacities? If the merely mental aspects of appetite are, as here suggested, often unreliable, it is because they constitute only the conscious part of an enormous, otherwise unconscious, physiological mechanism, very much as the visible bulk of a passing iceberg represents only the small tip of a much greater submerged mass.

The compulsion of hunger feelings drove hitherto pious and law-abiding pioneers crossing this continent to cannibalism when their supplies were consumed. It destroyed the self-respect of some of our century's bravest men when they were systematically starved by the Nazis in concentration camps. These examples should prove that there is an inexorable underlying somatic regulator which can crush almost any mental resistance. And, if this is the case, ought we not to know, before passing glib and deprecatory judgments, just what this physical mechanism is?

It stands to reason that if all or some of the obese victims are as compulsively regulated for their excessive intakes and weights as average individuals are for their "normal" intakes and weights, the problem of cutting down the caloric rations of the overweight becomes extremely difficult. Underfeeding a normal-weight individual in the presence of food would obviously be unsuccessful in the long run. Even though for a while it might succeed, as it did with such a high-morale group as the volunteers studied at the University of Minnesota during World War II, it can be accomplished only at considerable physiologic and psychologic cost.

In the case of compulsively regulated obese individuals, powerful counter-balancing drives, such as the terror of impending death or an overriding desire for sexual fulfillment, may for a period successfully check the passion to overeat. But for how long? Clearly we must understand something of the variety of relationships possible between the bodily machine and the hunger drive in normal individuals and in the obese before we can justifiably or even plausibly make pronouncements on the causes of overeating.

Overeating, certainly, is not done *in vacuo*. One eats and one overeats a specific diet. However, when we read what has been—and, lamentably, is still being—written on the relation of food habits to obesity, we discover that anything goes. People are said to become obese because they eat too many "sweet" or "starchy" foods; because they eat too much or too little protein. The obese have been characterized as constantly nibbling, skipping meals, eating vast amounts of food at a single sitting, or doing much of their eating, like a well-known character in the comics, at night. Have any of these assertions been tested? Where, when, and by whom? What, if anything, has been found?

If psychologic factors are involved, as has been frequently affirmed, how do they intervene—directly or through functional disturbances of the body? Desire for pregnancy, fear of pregnancy, arrest of personality at the "oral" stage, desire for importance, timidity, sublimation, masochism, displaced aggression . . . all have been implicated by various authors. Has the validity of these devout and dogmatic statements been assayed on a statistical basis?

All this interrogation of ours, admittedly, simmers down in the end to the question: What are the causes of obesity? To attribute obesity to "overeating," as is almost obsessively fashionable, at best only pushes back the difficulty. As an explanation, this is as meaningful as to account for alcoholism by ascribing it to "overdrinking." If one presses on, however, and looks for the factors which cause energy intake to be greater than energy expenditure, is it not possible—indeed probable—that, considering the complication of physiologic and psychologic mechanisms involved, one will find not a single cause, but a multiplicity of interactions leading to this caloric imbalance? To phrase it another way, is it not likely that obesity is the common symptom of a large number of different conditions? And, if obesity does represent a symptom common to various and dissimilar somatic and emotional abnormalities, does not its cure, in each individual case, depend upon the deeper underlying conditions that prevail in each individual, and must it not vary with his changing nature?

This book will attempt to answer some of these questions. I will review present-day knowledge (as opposed to contemporary mythology) concerning body fat, its measurement and its significance. The reader will see what humblingly complicated mechanisms are concerned with the synthesis of fat, with its mobilization from the fat depots, and with its utilization. Together we will examine the concepts of appetite and hunger, discover whether food intake and body weight are regulated, and—if they are—how well and by what devices. We shall get on to a study of the abnormalities of these devices, and how they may lead, when it so suits them, to obesity or to extreme leanness. The influence of genes, their mode of transmission and of action will also be considered. Malfunction of hunger and satiety brought about by functional or by structural disturbances of the central nervous system (in particular, the frontal lobes and midbrain), and by certain chemical agents used in research, by endocrine imbalance, and by psychologic traumas, will be examined.

Finally, we will recognize that the human organism does not function independently of its environment. The nature of the diet, exposure to heat or to cold, the necessity for physical work or the availability of facilities for exercise, the social customs, the emotional involvements, are also important. I shall try to sum up what is known, to indicate areas of possible future progress, and to see what practical measures can be taken at the present time. It is hoped that this popular, highly emotional subject can thus be viewed with the dispassionate experimental attitude necessary for constructive action and that obese people who should reduce and who can reduce will be helped to identify their plight and to do something effective about it. At the same time, I hope that the reader will remember, as I point out the gigantic areas of ignorance which occupy most of the field, that through the centuries, the difference between scientists and physicians on the one hand and quacks and promoters on the other has been that the former attempted to show what they knew and what they didn't know, while the latter always had all the answers (and saw the questions as simple and obvious). The contrast is still there and is nowhere more obvious than in nutrition. This book will have served one of its purposes if it has illustrated this proposition as regards obesity.

chapter 1
The Physiology
of Hunger and Satiety

Hunger is one of mankind's giant words. It is the label we give to the need for food on its most desperate and demanding level. The mention of hunger suggests, and properly, the monstrous experience of castaways on barren islands, the calculated sufferings of prisoners in concentration camps, the slow terrible dehumanization of so many members of the Donner Party.

Most of us who write and read such books as this have rarely encountered hunger in others or experienced it in ourselves to any extreme degree or for any period of time painful to endure. For we, in this generation and in the United States, are the pampered of our planet. We are able, even compelled, to give thought to that uncommon mocker of hunger, surfeit, and to its inevitable grotesque expression, obesity. We are the fat of the land: never in history, nowhere else in the world have such huge numbers of human beings eaten so much, exerted themselves so little, and become and remained so fat. We have come suddenly into the land of milk and honey, and we look it. And we suffer because of it.

But, despite the astonishing—to most of the rest of the world and to a part of our own population—availability of nourishment, all of us do not become obese. Among those who do are certainly the self-indulgent, those who find in the excessive consumption of food a fulfillment more appropriately discovered in love and in the rewards of successful productive effort. There are a number of persons who, because of metabolic disturbances (or slight but consistent differences in the relative importance of various metabolic pathways) or because of dysfunction (or lack of sensitivity) of the brain centers regulating food intake, will experience unusual difficulties in reducing their food intake. A larger number, for a variety of reasons, find it impossible to perform the minimum amount of daily exercise necessary to control their weight without having to "starve" themselves. Finally, among the obese, there are also a number who could control their food intake and their exercise habits relatively easily, but are uninstructed and—often elaborately—misinformed.

Among the obese *and* the nonobese are millions who do not know or have forgotten that inside each of us is an animal of ancient origin. In the long processes attendant to its survival, it developed techniques of dealing with its environment—including that part which it consumed—which involve the mediation of consciousness either little or not at all. It is important that the obese who aspire to become less so, and the nonobese who are determined to remain so, acquire some understanding of the machinery of this complicated animal and how it functions. For activities are taking place inside us that have much to do with how frequently we feel like eating, how much we are likely to eat, and how difficult it is for so many of us to stop eating when our judgment feebly assures us that we've had enough.

We take it for granted that the behavior of those whom it pleases us to call the lesser animals is the result not of contemplation, evaluation and decision, but the automatic response to certain signals which, apart from the will of the beast, pop up inside or outside it and bring about the activity that dumb experience has established as appropriate. Thus the bird, at nesting time, prowls for sticks and piles them in a tree-crotch. Thus the wasp secretes at mating a hormone which induces it to sting and, thereby, paralyze a spider, which it places in a hole to provide food on that day in the future when its egg becomes a larva.

It has never suited our pride to welcome the awareness that many of our common impulses and powerful drives have their origins in our body chemistry. We are all much like the posthypnotic subject who, having under hypnosis been instructed to go in five minutes and open the window, goes in five minutes and opens the window—and then explains to his satisfaction and that of nobody else *why*. But in each of us there is an apparatus, cousin to that of the bird and the wasp, which has its own plans for us and its own ways of making us regard those intentions as our precious own.

Fortunately, as far as such matters as hunger and satiety are concerned, knowledge is accumulating. The diffusion of that knowledge—a major goal of this chapter—should lead to an increase in understanding for all, a greater measure of control for a good many, and the dissipation of much unmerited guilt for some. It should also be a protection against honest misinformation, misleading simplifications, and an infinity of quackery.

Students have long made it clear that there are differences between *appetite* and *hunger* beyond the obvious one of intensity. They have pointed to the differences in psychic associations. The terribly hungry man wants food, not a specific kind of food, though his cultural standards may compel him at least for a time to starve in the presence of food which human beings otherwise conditioned would find acceptable, even attractive. But, usually, the hungrier a man becomes, the less particularized become his demands. Only a few brief days of deprivation in the foodless individual separate a yearning for steak from a prayerful eagerness to devour any substance, however aesthetically and morally repulsive it had seemed before.

Appetite, even in the grossest feeder, is certainly a more civilized matter than hunger. Appetite has conspicuous nuances of taste, sight, and smell. And these considerations may make it seem that both hunger and appetite are sensations which occur when, and only when, it is environmentally appropriate, and are not amenable to any regulating mechanism inside the body. This statement appears obvious to the lay observer. George, otherwise well and customarily active, hasn't eaten in two days; he's hungry. Charley, accustomed to a variety of attractive dishes, has been on K-rations for a month; he'd like a rare chop. In other words, it's the lack of food that creates George's hunger, just as it's the monotony of K-rations that creates Charley's appetite for the chop. Regrettably, however, our "common-sense" data here are inadequate. Physiological research shows that intake *is* regulated from inside the human organism; there *are* a multiplicity of internal factors involved in determining whether, at a given moment, a person or other animal will or will not eat.

Today we are better equipped to discuss these factors than we were a short quarter of a century ago. For, in the course of those twenty-five years, considerable research has been done, many experiments have been conducted, and an appreciable amount of clinical material has been put in the record. At the same time, there has grown a realization that many of the often-repeated "common-sense" generalizations about hunger, satiety, and their abnormalities make hardly any sense at all.

Further, the terms appetite, hunger, satiety, regulation of food intake, obesity, overweight, and anorexia have all been used with a variety of meanings. This semantic confusion has often created apparent contradictions where basic agreement in fact prevailed. Words such as hunger, appetite, and satiety represent sensations and as such tend to take on highly personal colorations. Studies which I conducted with one of my students revealed great differences in the sensations of mild as well as extreme hunger in man and in the reasons given by subjects for stopping eating. Nevertheless, I will give a series of working definitions of the major terms used in this chapter.

Appetite: the complex of sensations, up to a point pleasant, or at least not unpleasant, by which one is aware of desire for and the anticipation of ingestion of palatable food. Specific appetites relate, of course, to desires for specific foods.

Hunger: the complex of unpleasant sensations, felt after prolonged deprivation, which will impel a man to seek, work or fight for immediate relief by ingestion of food. The passage from appetite to hunger is dependent on the duration of deprivation, the rate of energy expenditure, and other factors.

Satiety: the complex of sensations which drive the organism to stop eating because hunger and appetite have been satisfied, even though food is still available.

Regulation of food intake: the mechanism or mechanisms whereby the body adjusts ingestion of food to requirements for maintenance of health and the proper functioning of the body and, in the case of the young, for growth.

Limitation of food intake: the complex of sensations which lead to cessation of eating, even though food is still available, and whether energy requirements for maintenance and growth have or have not been met.

Obesity: excessive accumulation of body fat.

Overweight: weight in excess of normal range (which may, as we shall see in the case of many athletes, not involve obesity at all).

Homeostasis: a word coined at the beginning of this century by Walter Cannon, the Harvard physiologist, indicating the tendency of the body "to keep things the way that they are," despite a constant turnover of body substance and a constant flux of energy throughout the body.

Anorexia: pathological absence of appetite or hunger when either or both are clearly appropriate.

Leaving aside temporarily the conscious aspects, such as awareness of sensations of hunger, appetite, and satiety, and lining man up with the aforementioned bird and wasp, let us examine the manner in which homeostasis—the maintenance of form and function in the organism—is provided and the expected pattern of growth achieved. Let us do this by reformulating the problem into a four-fold question:

(1) Is there a regulation (a controlling process), or are there regulations, of caloric intake?
(2) What exactly is regulated?
(3) How well does this regulation work?
(4) By what steps does it work?

In short, is there in the human body a governing device or are there governing devices, which—independent of consciousness and will—strive to determine what and how much a person will eat and at what point he will stop?

The first answers to these questions were provided in the 1930's by this writer's father, Professor André Mayer of the Collège de France in

Paris. He did not attempt to analyze the internal regulatory mechanisms which control food intake, but limited himself to a very careful consideration of the amount of food animals ate every day and how this varied in relation to the weight and the composition of the body of the animals. Analysis of the large number of data he obtained enabled him to conclude (and his conclusions have been upheld by all succeeding work) that there were three types of regulation operating simultaneously in mammals. He called them respectively the "biometric regulation," the "adaptation of daily intake to daily output," and the "mechanism of correction by successive compensations." These difficult-sounding terms are actually simple to define.

The *biometric regulation* is not, properly speaking, a mechanism. It simply implies that an animal or a person, because of its very structure and physiological state, has to operate within definite limits, both in terms of food intake and in terms of energy expenditure. Your metabolism cannot be below so many calories per hour. (If you have not had breakfast, are lying on a couch in the morning after a good night's sleep, are resting at a comfortable temperature, your energy expenditure is at a low point called "basal metabolism.") Conversely, you cannot raise your energy expenditure beyond a point which is characteristic of your physical condition ("summit metabolism"). This is obviously higher for trained athletes than for sedentary unexercised individuals. Similarly, your food intake can go down to zero, but it cannot go above a certain value characteristic of your capacity.

The *adaptation of daily intake to output,* or *short term regulation,* is perhaps the most important mechanism. A number of studies in various animals, from insects to fish to mice to men, have examined how well intake matched energy expenditure as modified by cold, by exercise, by growth, pregnancy, lactation, and other variables. Some workers, this writer in particular, have also examined to what extent the nature of the diet and its bulk influenced this matching of calories eaten and calories spent. André Mayer showed that while the principle has many notable exceptions, animals (and most people) tend to eat each day approximately as much as they need (and no more) while they live and work under "normal" conditions.

The *mechanism of correction by successive compensations* is that system which, over a long period, compensates for the fact that an animal or a person does not, in fact, eat exactly as much every day as is necessary to make up for the energy and substance expended but does, in fact, eat sometimes more and sometimes less. The deficit or the excess is compensated for by eating less or eating more in the successive days so that over a longer period—say two weeks or more for a man—the weight and "body reserves" stay essentially "in balance," that is at a constant level. André Mayer showed the existence of this mechanism by demonstrating that the greater the excess of normal intake on a given day, the greater the chances of compensation by smaller than usual intakes in the following days and vice versa.

How well do these regulations function? Again André Mayer set the stage for succeeding work in this field by defining the *precision* of the regulations (that is how exactly the food we eat compensates for the energy we expend) and the *sensitivity* of the regulations (that is how well food intake responds to small increases or decreases in expenditure). He illustrated these concepts by studying the way in which the organism responds to changes in environmental temperature. I have found that exercise (or physical work) gives another striking illustration which, as we will see in subsequent chapters, is heavy with practical consequences in the matter of weight control. Within a certain range of physical activity (which I have called the range of "normal activity" or of "proportional response") the regulation of food intake is both precise and sensitive. Any increase in physical activity is followed by a corresponding increase in food intake. If activity, hence energy expenditure, is below this range (in what I call the "sedentary range") the precision and the sensitivity fall off. The regulation becomes so inaccurate that if the animal is very inactive, the food intake is actually greater than it is for a slightly higher activity (and some degree of obesity ensues). Above the range of normal activity the regulation becomes again highly imprecise and inaccurate, with the food intake first increasing too slowly, then at very high levels dropping (and the person or the animal loses weight).

The next phase of research in this field was a logical development. We knew that food intake was regulated. We knew how well it was regulated in various circumstances. We even knew that the mechanism was probably made of at least two control systems, one "a fine adjustment" equating food intake to needs on a day by day basis, the other "a very fine adjustment" compensating for the imprecision of the mechanism at the end of the day. In fact, for animals such as man, who eats a small number of meals every day, one could even distinguish between a coarse adjustment—the control of meal size, a fine adjustment —the control of daily intake, and a very fine adjustment—the correction of errors over a period of over several weeks. The obvious question was: what goes on inside? What are the components of the control system and how do they work? The scope of the answer to this question depends on one's curiosity and the time available. It could embrace what is known of the control of all chemical events by which food is eventually burnt or transformed into tissue—what we call metabolism. I have chosen to limit myself to describing what is known of the control of the intake of food as such and more particularly of those mechanisms whereby the body maintains its constancy or, as Walter Cannon called it, its "homeostasis." In other words we will be concerned not so much with all the factors, physiologic and psychologic, which *at a given time* on such and such a day, at such and such a meal, will determine whether you will eat more or less of a given dish, but with the factors which over a span of time lead you to eat the amount needed to maintain you as you are. (In Chapter 4 we shall, similarly, look at the possible errors in the body mechanisms which may, *over a span of time,* lead you to eat more than you require and thus become the victim of that condition which is the subject of this book.)

While the systematic study of the mechanisms by which the intake of food is controlled did not start until the early forties, some facts basic to our understanding of *hunger* had been established before that time. Haller, the great Swiss biologist, had suggested as early as 1777 that hunger was a complex of gastric sensations which we refer to (or feel is localized in) the stomach. For over a century the idea that hunger sensations were due to the excitation of stomach nerves was the most generally accepted theory. It was not until 1912 that it was tested experimentally by Walter Cannon, who showed that hunger sensations appeared whenever the empty stomach of a medical student, Mr. Washburn, contracted vigorously (on a rubber balloon linked by a thin tube to an outside pressure gauge). This phenomenon was further investigated by a Chicago physiologist, Anton Carlson, who found that during a prolonged fast the normal tension of the empty stomach as well as the frequency and intensity of its contractions become progressively more pronounced, at least until the fourth day. Carlson hypothesized that the vagus nerves were the main pathway for gastric impulses travelling from the abdomen to the brain and that the "primary hunger center" must be in the medulla, the posterior part of the brain from which these nerves arise.

Again before World War I, two French pathologists, Camus and Roussy, conducting autopsies of very obese patients, showed that some had brain lesions situated in or impinging on the hypothalamus, a part of the brain situated on the floor of the brain hemisphere, just above the pituitary (see Fig. 1). The hypothalamus has since been shown to be also involved in the control of water intake, body temperature, reproduction, and other basic functions. Experiments based on this pioneering observation and conducted on both sides of the Atlantic, notably by Hetherington in Chicago and by Brobeck (then at Yale), demonstrated that if two small centrally located areas of the hypothalamus of rats (the "ventromedial area") were destroyed, these rats overate and became obese. I was able, in the early fifties, to demonstrate that, by making minute symmetrical surgical lesions in the hypothalamus of the mouse, overeating was induced even in an animal which already had a food intake 30 times greater per unit weight than man. (Incidentally, of physiologic and possibly of economic interest were the production of obese chickens by Lepkovsky at Berkeley, and of the first hypothalamic obese ruminants —goats—by myself and my young associate, Clifton Baile.)

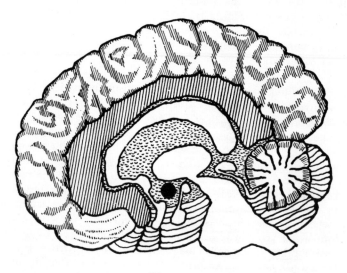

Figure 1

Schematic representation of vertical section of the brain. The black dot gives the approximate position of the hypothalamus. Copyright by *Nutrition Today*. Reproduced by permission.

The actual role of the ventromedial areas was elucidated by the use of behavioral techniques. Miller and his associates, working at Yale, showed that while animals with lesions in these areas overate (we say—in the Greek jargon of medical science—that they are "hyperphagic") they would not work as hard for food as normal animals, and might in fact be less hungry. My associates and I, using special cages (named after the Harvard psychologist, B. F. Skinner), trained "hypothalamic hyperphagic" mice as well as normal mice to press a lever so as to obtain small pellets of food. The rate at which the animals press the lever is a measure of hunger. Satiety supervenes as the animals slow down and stop. We found hunger unaffected after hypothalamic lesions, but satiety periods shortened. In other words, it appeared that the ventromedial areas are "satiety centers," brakes on an otherwise constantly activated feeding mechanism.

That the feeding mechanism may also be controlled by the hypothalamus was indicated when an Indian physiologist, Anand, working with Brobeck at Yale, showed that destruction of small "lateral areas"

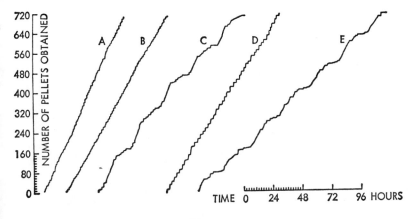

Figure 2

Cumulative records of pellets obtained on a schedule of reward that allows one pellet of food for every 25 lever-pressing responses. Records *A*, *B*, and *C* are from Swiss mice: *A*, goldthioglucose obese; *B*, hypothalamic obese; and *C*, normal. Records *D* and *E* are from two littermates: *D*, mouse with the obese hyperglycemic syndrome; *E*, normal littermate.

right and left of the satiety centers caused animals to stop eating and drinking. Morrison and I demonstrated that the cessation of eating in animals with these lesions was not a consequence of the cessation of drinking and resultant dehydration of the animal. Keeping the supply of body water normal through tube feeding did not automatically restore the eating. This brought support to the idea that the ventromedial areas ("satiety centers") act at various times as a brake on the lateral areas ("feeding centers") which otherwise keep the animals stimulated to eat. In 1967 Arees and I, using a recently developed technique for tracing fibers in the brain, were able to actually trace the fibers going from the "satiety" centers to the "feeding" centers thus giving a solid anatomical basis to the idea that the two centers are closely related and that what is regulated is not hunger but satiety.

With at least part of the central control system identified, the next problem was: to what stimuli does the satiety center respond? In other words, what determines satiety?

The oldest theory was that of Carlson. Struck by his observations on the presence of stomach contractions during fasting, and the disappearance of hunger pangs after meals, he felt that the consciousness of gastric phenomena was the kernel of the problem. While he did recognize that many normal persons experience in hunger, besides the gnawing pressure, pain sensation in the stomach, feelings of weakness, emptiness, headache, and sometimes nausea, he felt that such symptoms were of secondary importance, and called them "accessory hunger phenomena" because "they are not always present in hunger and their relative preponderance depends on the length of starvation and on some individual peculiarity in the person."

"It must be admitted," he continued, describing a phenomenon which should have been a warning, "that in some individuals these accessory phenomena appear to overshadow, if not entirely to suppress, the pressure pain from the stomach."

Carlson, struck by the fact that lowering blood glucose levels through injections of insulin leads to gastric contractions and hunger feelings, postulated that blood glucose levels *as such* determined the occurrence of hunger.

The theory received wide acceptance. Popular acceptance continued long after the scientific basis had been thoroughly undermined. A number of experiments, where food was diluted with inert (bulk) substances without substantially changing the caloric intake, cast doubt on the primacy of gastric phenomena. Observation of ulcer patients in whom the vagus nerves were severed surgically (thereby eliminating or modifying gastric hunger contractions) showed that hunger persisted, with the patients being guided by what Carlson had called "accessory phenomena," to consume their food in about the same amounts as they had when their vagus nerves were intact. Indeed gastrectomy itself did not eliminate hunger, only, understandably, its gastric component; it simply led patients to eat smaller but more numerous meals. The splanchnic nerves were shown to carry the consciousness of gastric contractions, limiting the the vagus to control of the contractions (and of the acid secretion). But again section of the splanchnic nerves, while it eliminated the gastric component of hunger, left the overall characteristics of the regulation of food intake (including daily overall intake, time it took after a standard meal for the subject to be ready to eat again, etc.) unaffected. The hypothesis that the regulation of food intake rests on gastric sensations thus proved inadequate. The existence of gastric hunger contractions remained, however, an undeniable fact; any theory which could not account for the occurrence of hunger pangs remained at best partial, at worst doomed from the outset. Actually it was to take almost fifty years before the pioneer observation of Cannon and Carlson on gastric contractions could become integrated, through work done in my laboratory (and none has given me greater satisfaction), into the overall scheme of food intake control.

But first let us dispose of two other theories which present not only definite historical interest but also illustrate the complexity and the number of factors which may be involved in the regulatory mechanism. Brobeck was struck by the fact that short term exposure to heat cuts down intake. He also knew that diets excessively high in protein also decrease food intake, a fact which he attributed to the supposed high specific dynamic action of such diets. The specific dynamic action (SDA) is the extra heat produced by the body when a meal is consumed. It is relatively low for pure carbohydrates—starches and sugars—and for fat, but high for pure protein. Actually in a mixed meal, that is one containing all three components, the SDA is quite low—on the order of 5 per cent of the calories ingested, and relatively insensitive to wide variations of protein content below levels so high as to be impossible of realization with ordinary foods. Brobeck also took into consideration the proximity in the hypothalamus of centers concerned with food intake, water intake, and temperature. To account for all this, he advanced a "thermostatic" hypothesis which essentially postulated that animals eat to keep warm and stop eating to prevent becoming overheated. The theory admittedly was not based on any direct measurement of hypothalamic temperatures before, during, and following meals; it did have the advantage of seeming to coordinate various hitherto unrelated body functions.

The thermostatic theory ran into trouble from the start. To begin with, it could not explain why diabetics have (until the disease reaches a point where life is in jeopardy) an enormous appetite; why patients with hyperthyroidism (and an elevated temperature) tend similarly to eat more than normal. Kennedy, of Cambridge University, showed that dehydration was probably responsible for the weight loss in acute exposure to heat; he also showed that sudden exposure to cold also caused an initial depression of food intake. I have shown that the lowering of intake by diets excessively high in protein was a "safety valve" effect, unrelated to the integrity of the ventromedial areas and thus obviously situated elsewhere than in the satiety centers. Dole, at the Rockefeller University showed that he could obtain spontaneous losses of appetite and weight on diets abnormally *low* in protein (an experimental procedure which, to his dismay, was popularized in magazines as "the Rockefeller diet").

More crucial was the fact that Baile and I at Harvard and workers in Brobeck's own department, demonstrated that the temperature of the hypothalamus is remarkably constant and does not go up as the animal stops eating nor go down as the animal becomes hungry. The failure of substantiating by direct measurement the central postulate of the "thermostatic theory" seems to eliminate definitively this theory as a basis for explanation of how the mechanism of control of food intake works (though at some ulterior stage in the development of physiology the regulations of food intake, water balance, and temperature will still have to be integrated).

The theory propounded by Souleirac, a professor of psychophysiology at the Sorbonne, was based on the sound observation that any modification of carbohydrate metabolism can affect appetite and even taste. He concentrated his efforts on interpreting observations where such factors influenced appetite for sugar and suggested that the desire for sugar was based on the rate at which this nutrient was absorbed through the intestinal wall. The implication was that hunger was a summation of selective hungers, and the regulation of food intake a summation of partial regulations. Again, while intestinal phenomena are probably most important, particularly in determining meal size (my associates and I are at present working on the possibility that already known or new gastrointestinal hormones may play a crucial role in the initiation of satiety as an animal or a person eats), the very basis of the theory could be shown immediately to be untenable. Selective appetites do exist and can be extremely compelling: the "salt wars" fought in Africa for surface salt deposits are bloody illustrations of their strength. But no one ever increases his food intake because the food is not salted enough. Man and animals do not eat excessive amounts of, say, a low protein diet or a low vitamin diet and become obese simply to satisfy a need for protein or a given vitamin. In fact they eat less than normal amounts of such diets. And the ease with which carbohydrate and fat are mutually substituted in the diet is another illustration of the fact that overall energy intake, not the sum of specific intakes of these two classes of nutrients, determines how much a person or an animal eats. Souleirac's theory, while original, never received much support, and seems to have been abandoned, even by its progenitor.

I have described an essential component of the mechanism by which the needs of the body make themselves felt in the satiety centers as "a glucostatic mechanism." The theory, sometimes known as the "glucostatic theory of regulation of food intake," has a great deal of solid experimental support and additional facts have recently enormously re-enforced its position. There are, however, still difficulties which must be cleared up and, as always, as science progresses, new orders of complexities are perceived which offer new challenges. I hope I shall not be accused of undue partiality if I say that it is the only theory which has permitted the uncovering of new and important facts (most notably, as we shall see, the description of the anatomical connections between the satiety and feeding centers, and between the feeding centers and the centers controlling the contractions and the secretory activity of the stomach). It is the only theory which enables us to integrate the hypothalamic and the gastric components of the regulation of food intake.

Basically, I postulated that there are in the hypothalamus receptors with a special affinity for glucose, which are activated by this blood component in the measure that they utilize it. The concept was based at the start on the fact that glucose is the almost exclusive fuel of the central nervous system. Its availability in turn determines the rate at which fat and protein are utilized: it therefore plays a central role in the economy of the body. It is stored (as glycogen) in small amounts and

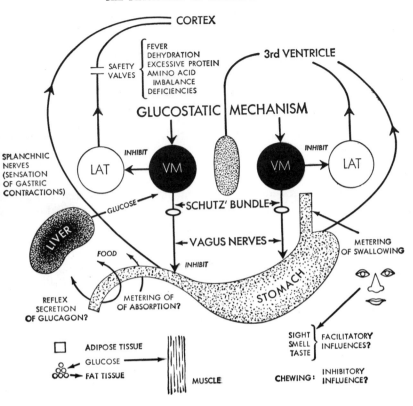

Figure 3

An overall schematic representation of the control of food intake, showing the interaction of the various functions and structures of the body. VM and LAT stand for the ventromedial and the lateral areas of the hypothalamus, respectively.

Copyright by *Nutrition Today*. Reproduced by permission.

the stores are depleted within a few hours, faster in the cold or when the subject is exercised. The utilization is influenced by various hormones, and is drastically decreased when insulin is lacking as in diabetics. (The hypothesis included the postulate that the hypothalamic receptors, unlike the rest of the brain, would be found to be influenced by the concentration of insulin).

The first experiments attempting to verify the theory were conducted in man. Van Itallie and I demonstrated a good correlation between utilization of glucose by the body generally and the state of hunger or satiety of the subjects studied: a large rate of utilization corresponded to satiety, a decreased rate to the reappearance of hunger (with psychological stimuli accelerating this reappearance when glucose utilization was low enough). Gastric hunger contractions also appeared when glucose utilization was low. In addition, Stunkard, Van Itallie, and Reiss found that a small injection of glucagon, a hormone secreted by the pancreas which releases glucose from liver stores quite reproducibly eliminated gastric contractions in hungry men. I found that in rats too, glucagon injection and the subsequent increase in blood glucose and in glucose utilization eliminated gastric hunger contractions. Particularly interesting was the observation that if the satiety centers were destroyed, glucagon no longer inhibited the stomach contractions of a hungry animal, which led me to conclude that the satiety center did control the motions of the stomach. I suggested that a system of nerve fibers, the bundle of Schutz, which were thought to originate in the general area of the satiety centers, might be carrying the satiety impulses to the root of the vagus nerves (and on to the stomach). Gastric acid secretion was subsequently also shown to be under the control of the ventromedial (satiety) centers. In 1967, Edward Arees and I, using the same staining procedure that we had used to show the existence of nerve fibers going from the satiety to the feeding centers were able to demonstrate that there are indeed

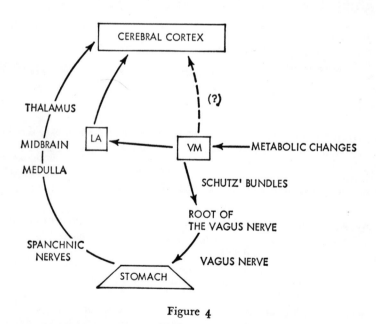

Figure 4

Integration of the hypothalamic, metabolic, and gastric factors in the phenomenon of hunger.

fibers which originate in the satiety area and travel down the bundle of Schutz.

Another important advance in our quest for the activation mechanism of the satiety center came when my co-workers, Norman Marshall and Russell Barrnett, and I found that the compound *goldthioglucose* destroyed part of the ventromedial area of the hypothalamus. Mice treated with this compound overeat and become obese, in a way similar to that I had observed in mice made obese by surgical lesions in the same area. The fascinating aspect of the finding is that the compound is made of a molecule of glucose attached to an atom of gold by an atom of sulphur. I found that if molecules of other common compounds were attached to gold by a sulphur bridge, they did not cause hypothalamic lesions or obesity. For example, if galactose, another sugar very similar to glucose, replaced glucose in the molecule, no effect on the satiety centers was seen. Nor were they seen with sorbitol, a compound differing from glucose only by the addition of two hydrogen atoms; nor with glycerol or various fatty acids; nor with other compounds I tried. It seemed that the affinity the receptors of the satiety centers held for glucose caused them to pull the poisonous gold atom if it was attached to glucose and not if it was attached to any other molecule, a conclusion later confirmed by Debons (at Brookhaven), who traced the gold by making it radioactive.

The goldthioglucose findings thus supported the concept that the satiety area contains glucoreceptors. Other findings confirmed other aspects of the glucostatic theory. Animals made obese by goldthioglucose were found to show only disturbances in the control of food intake, and not to show other disturbances such as inability to reproduce, heightened rage responses and troubles of water metabolism observed in surgical lesions where cells other than those involved in control of food intake are damaged. Diabetic animals were shown not to be susceptible to goldthioglucose lesions; the compound is not taken up by the satiety centers in the absence of insulin, verifying my hypothesis that this part of the brain, unlike the rest of the central nervous system, is influenced by insulin. And it was by staining the degenerating fibers (axons) issuing out of the glucoreceptors destroyed by goldthioglucose that Arees and I were able to stain the fibers going from the satiety centers to the feeding centers and from the satiety centers to the root of the vagus.

Using another type of technique, Anand, now working in New Delhi demonstrated that ingestion of a meal or glucose injections do not affect the electrical activity of the brain in general or of the hypothalamus in particular except for a drastic increase in the activity of the satiety area (and a corresponding decrease in that of the feeding area). Pursuing his analysis, he was able to correlate the electrical activity of single neurons (nerve cells) in the satiety and the feeding centers with glucose utilization: when utilization was high the satiety center cells were active, the feeding center cells correspondingly depressed; and vice versa when glucose utilization was low. He concluded that the satiety center is indeed activated by increased glucose utilization. While a number of difficulties remain to be solved (such as the possible influence of the physical state or configuration of the glucose presented, the microscopic structure of the glucoreceptors, the fate of impulses traveling from the feeding area to various brain areas), it appears that the existence of a "glucostatic" mechanism as part of the short term regulation of food intake is established. This is what we have referred to before as the "fine adjustment" knob.

Little is known at this point of the "coarse adjustment" knob, the control of meal size, the determination of immediate after-meal satiety. We are working on the possibility that receptors in the gastrointestinal tract may trigger some phenomena, nervous, hormonal or humoral, which will articulate with the hypothalamic mechanism to determine the cessation of eating. Such phenomena might accelerate the chain of events which result in the activation of hypothalamic satiety receptors. We have indications, for example, that changes in blood concentration of glucose and insulin may "anticipate" the actual absorption of the food.

While over a daily span, the stabler metabolic factors will take over and will activate the satiety centers in accordance with physiologic needs, the immediate satiety phenomena will of course interact with a variety of clues—appraisal of amount of food consumed, duration of meal, sensations of fullness—to determine the end of a particular meal. Different individuals may be unequally sensitive to such "external" clues. Recent work by Stanley Shackter on metering of food consumed and by Miriam Kelty and me on thresholds of taste perception suggests that certain obese subjects are particularly sensitive to external clues, less sensitive to the normally determinant internal clues. Certainly my studies of the hunger and satiety sensations of close to a thousand men, women, and children emphasize the tremendous apparent diversity in warning signs of hunger, with some individuals recognizing it through gastric pangs, others through throat or mouth sensations, others through feelings of "emptiness," weakness, or incipient headaches. Diversity as regards satiety is far less; the cessation of the desire to eat is hardly a sensory experience in most normal weight individuals. But there are varying degrees of abruptness in this cessation of desire for food. Some individuals, obese subjects in particular, "eat until their stomach feels full," but this is not the normal end-point in most people for most meals. And of course the taste of food, one's state of mind, the company we keep, and a myriad of other factors may influence at a given point whether one will go on eating. The fact that with all this apparent confusion, the enormous majority of people (and animals) regulate their food intake each day so as to stay approximately at the same weight is a measure of the adaptability of the hypothalamic mechanism which we have described above.

There also remains the problem of the nature of the very fine adjustment knob, the long term regulation of food intake which will over a span of several days and perhaps several weeks correct the errors of the short term mechanism. This is the mechanism which will make you regain the weight you lost after an illness, and which makes so difficult the maintenance of weight loss after an arduous weight reduction course. There are some indications that the state of the adipose tissue may influence the metabolism in such a way as to maintain a constant weight: fat synthesis seems speeded up after weight loss, becomes again slower as the "preferred weight" is re-established. It is possible that this long term mechanism works through the short term mechanism, with glucose more rapidly taken up whenever fat loss has occurred.

The wonder is that in most animals and men, with feeding behavior subject to so many influences, the mechanism of food intake regulation works so well. Certainly the existence of this complicated neurological and metabolic machinery governing food intake makes the easy "psychological" explanation of overeating look naive from a physiologist's viewpoint. Physiological signals still have to be interpreted and acted on; this certainly does leave room for psychological factors in the etiology of obesity; it has to be understood, however, that psychological factors operate within a complicated physiological framework. The realization of the complexity of the physiological machinery, and of the close interrelationship of the psychological and the physiological, should dispose once and for all of the oversimplifications, whether based on "common sense" or on Freud, which have hindered research in the past.

chapter 2
What Is Obesity?
How Prevalent Is It?

In theory, the question, "What is obesity?" is easily answered: obesity is present when the body is loaded with excessive fat. In practice, however, this question admits to no automatic answer. For many years, "standard" height-weight tables were commonly used in this country. In these tables, weights are given for each year of age from 15 to "55 and up," for men from 5 feet 2 inches in height to 6 feet 4 inches, and for women from 4 feet 8 inches to 6 feet. In these tables there is a steady increase of weight with age until age 55, after which, apparently, there is no further change. At the younger ages, the weights for women are considerably less than for men of the same age and height, but with increasing age, the weights for women increase faster than those for men; so that at about 50 years they are equal. These tables were based on average weights of some 200,000 men and women of the specified ages and heights who were accepted for life insurance between 1895 and 1900 for the men, and 1895 and 1908 for the women, the measurements being conducted in the subjects' street clothes including shoes. The significance of such tables can be questioned on several grounds: imprecision due to clothing and shoes; selection of a sample limited to policy-holders (especially for a period when life insurance policies were less widespread and, presumably, were in the hands of a more prosperous—and at that time smaller—segment of the community); lack of justification for the increase of weight with age to be considered as desirable, even if "standard"; and lack of appreciation of variability in shape and body composition of individuals of similar heights and weights.

In 1942–43 an attempt was made by the Metropolitan Life Insurance Company to correct some of these inadequacies. The age scale was abandoned, three classes of "frame size" were introduced, and ranges of weight rather than single figures were given. The figures in these "ideal" body weight tables are based on the same data as the "standard weight" tables (the term "ideal" was replaced a few years later by "desirable"), particular attention being now given to the weight of young adults. Insurance experience had shown that overweight policy-holders were poor mortality risks. Furthermore, it was recognized that weight gain after adult size has been reached could only be excess fat. Thus, all weight data after the age of 30 were discarded. The fact that even young adults have different shapes, different skeletal sizes, and different degrees of muscular development was dealt with by classifying the lightest third as "small frame," the middle third "medium frame," and the heaviest "large frame."

While the elimination of the age scale was logical and while the fact that human variability exists as regards height-weight relationship was acknowledged, these "desirable weight" tables, which have been the object of wide distribution and are quoted everywhere, still suffer from serious inadequacies. First, no definition was given of "frame size," thus leaving the patient or his physician with a great latitude of choice as regards the "desirable weight" of a particular person. Each could decide for himself what was meant by small, medium, or large. Secondly, mortality data themselves do not entirely agree with the qualification of "desirable" being applied to the same weight at all ages after 30. Thirdly, determinations of skinfold thickness by the caliper method (to be discussed later in this chapter) show that, while relative body weight and subcutaneous fat thickness tend to be correlated, the correlation between these two body characteristics is not very close, even in the wide range from 30 per cent underweight to 45 per cent overweight.

In a series of men studied by Ancel Keys, the well known Minneapolis physiologist, there were men 20 per cent underweight who were actually in the upper third of the distribution for fatness. And there were men 20 to 30 per cent overweight who were in the lower third of the fatness distribution. This latter finding was encountered particularly in men engaged in heavy manual work. When attention was confined to the people who were 10 to 30 per cent overweight by the "desirable weight" standards, it was almost impossible to predict fatness from relative body weight. This was particularly true when the subjects had a wide range of physical activity. As diagnosis of obesity in grossly overweight (over 30 per cent) subjects is no problem, results such as those of Keys and his co-workers cast doubt on the usefulness of such "desirable weight" tables.

Even the most recent insurance tables (which have appeared since Keys, this writer, and others have repeatedly called attention to the weaknesses of the older tables), are not free from similar confusion. The "Build and Blood Pressure Study, 1959" of the Society of Actuaries provided the basis for the latest (and currently most used) "average" and "desirable" weight tables. The "average" weight tables are based on data obtained by 26 United States and Canadian life insurance companies on several million policy-holders. Mortality in this population was followed for periods up to 20 years and analyzed for its relationship to "body build" (actually height and weight). The subjects' weight was recorded in ordinary indoor clothing and their height was measured with their shoes on. The authors of the study estimated that nude weights are seven to nine pounds less than recorded weights for men and four to six pounds less for women. Body frame was classified as small, medium, or large on the basis of chest breadth and hip width; no data or description of method was given. Furthermore, the significance of these measures for proper body-build assessment is extremely limited. In addition, the Metropolitan Life Insurance Company followed with a new table of "desirable" weights based on the pooled experience of greatest longevity. This table again suffers from the same inadequacies as its predecessors.

As in previous tables, it is obvious that if overweight (weight in excess of "average") is very marked, obesity (excessive fatness) is present. For moderate degrees of overweight, however, the relationship is not always clear. College football linemen are generally overweight; they are generally not obese. Conversely, some extremely sedentary persons can be obese without being markedly overweight. Without a more direct measurement of adiposity (the actual amount of fat in the body), the diagnosis of obesity cannot be certain.

The standards derived from the "Build and Blood Pressure Study, 1959" have additional weaknesses. First, there is some question as to how representative the insurance data are for the general population of the United States. My associate, Carl C. Seltzer, and I have shown that average weights in Metropolitan Life tables from which desirable weights are derived are nine to ten pounds less for men, and three to four pounds less for women, than the average values obtained in the National Health Examination Survey of the United States Public Health Service on a stratified, noninstitutionalized, random sample of men and women from all classes and areas of the country from 1960 through 1962. Secondly, the Metropolitan Life Insurance Company tables of 1959, like those of 1942–43, give no definition of frames, so that the user is unable to characterize his frame in the same way as the authors of the tables.

The results of recent studies on large groups of men and women have shown that properly defined variations in body structure are important not only in terms of defining obesity, but also possibly in terms of longevity. Analysis of the general background data of the "Build and Blood Pressure Study, 1959" tends to suggest this. In general, for each broad height category, mortality increased as weight increased. These data have been interpreted to mean that increased overweight is responsible for increased mortality. However, since, among those who are clearly not overweight by the definitions of the life insurance companies and by common sense, persons who have extremely low weight for height have the highest longevity, it appears that a lanky, not very muscular body type is associated with a longer-than-average life expectancy. The additional fact that obesity is usually associated with bones and muscles also larger than average—which has been demonstrated by Seltzer and myself in high school girls and in adult women in studies involving thousands of individuals—suggests that, at least among females, there may be an association between increased mortality and body type, irrespective of adiposity. A number of physical anthropologists, reviving Hippocrates' interest in the relation of "constitution" and disease, have also suggested the association of certain body types with specific illnesses. The ultimate answer to the question of the relation of obesity to mortality may lie in treating each type of body build separately and in correlating the extent of adiposity of each category of body build with mortality and disease manifestations.

While it is certainly not my intention to quarrel with the general concept that excessive weight gain after growth has ceased is bad for the individual, it appears questionable to base the diagnosis of obesity and the prescription of an ideal weight on height-weight tables, even those as seemingly sophisticated as the ones derived from the "Build and Blood Pressure Study, 1959." Dissatisfaction with such equation of obesity with overweight has led to the elaboration of a number of other methods to determine whether a given person is too fat and how fat he or she is. A knowledge of actual fatness is preferable, not only from the viewpoint of diagnosing obesity, but also because it emphasizes that component of body weight which can, in fact, be modified.

Among these other methods, let us first look at the "unscientific" methods of assessing fatness:

The mirror test: Looking at yourself naked in a mirror is often a more reliable guide for estimating obesity than body weight. If you *look* fat, you probably *are* fat. (This becomes a certainty if you also weigh appreciably more than you did at 25, if a man; at 21, if a woman, and if you looked your best then.)

The pinch test: If appearance does not give a clear answer, the pinch test usually will. It has been estimated that in persons under 50, at least half of the body fat is found directly under the skin. At many locations on the body—such as the back of the upper arm, the side of the lower chest, the back just below the shoulder blade, the back of the calf, or the abdomen—a fold of skin and subcutaneous fat may be lifted free, between the thumb and the forefinger, from the underlying soft tissue and bone. In general, the layer beneath the skin should be between one-fourth and one-half inch; the skinfold is a double thickness and should therefore be one-half to one inch. A fold markedly greater than one inch —for example in the back of the arm—indicates excessive body fatness; one markedly thinner than one-half inch, abnormal thinness.

The ruler test: This test has to do with the slope of the abdomen when an individual is lying on his back. If he or she is not too fat, the surface of the abdomen between the flare of the ribs and the front of the pelvis is normally flat or slightly concave and a ruler placed on the abdomen along the midline of the body should touch both the ribs and the pelvic area. It goes without saying that pregnancy and certain pathological conditions can interfere with this test.

The belt-line test: In men the circumference of the chest at the level of the nipples should exceed that of the abdomen at the level of the navel. If the latter is greater, it usually means that abdominal fat is excessive.

The more rigorous methods of assessing fatness are much more numerous; they can be direct or indirect. The only direct method is, of course, chemical analysis. Unfortunately, there is no means of measuring the fat content of the body directly in the living human being. Only in cadavers can such an analysis be done and the complications, both technical and legal, are such that only three or four reasonably "normal" cadavers have ever been analyzed. Ideally, we should directly analyze bodies on which previously indirect methods of fat determination have been conducted. Only then would we really know how well our indirect methods inform us of the fat content of the body.

The first and perhaps the best indirect method, the *densimetric* method, is based on the low specific gravity of adipose tissue. In other words, the fact that fat is lighter than water, muscle and blood slightly heavier, and bones much heavier, can be used to determine total body fat. Weighing people first in air and then in water is a procedure first hinted at by Archimedes. It was pioneered by a U. S. Navy medical officer, Captain Albert Behnke, Jr., who had previously served in submarines and thus had presumably given much thought to the behavior of submerged bodies. Further refinements have been devised by Ancel Keys and his associates. From the density of the individual underwater, that of fat, bone, and nonskeletal, nonadipose tissues, plus corrections for the air in the lungs, it is possible through appropriate formulas to determine the total amount of fat in the body. In our studies at Harvard, we have used the pool of the Children's Hospital in Boston and a portable pool, mounted on a truck loaned by the U. S. Army. An amusing and instructive application of the method was conducted by W. C. Welham and Behnke; their study, incidentally, confirms the fact that overweight and obesity are not synonymous. The average tackle or guard on a college or professional football team weighs 200 pounds or more. Even in relation to his height and even when he is considered as falling in the "large frame" class, the six-foot, 200-pound lineman is at least 10 per cent overweight according to the life insurance tables of "ideal" weight. Yet, when the Navy scientists measured the specific gravity of seventeen professional football players, several of them former All-Americans, they found them endowed with a greater than normal specific gravity, indicating an abnormally low fat content. These overweight men were underfat.

The other basic indirect method of arriving at an estimation of total body fatness is *hydrometry:* the measurement of total body water by injecting a diluting substance, the concentration of which can be determined after it has become distributed throughout the body.

In recent years, another method has been proposed as a means of evaluating the total fat of living man. It is based on the *determination of whole body potassium.* Almost all of this element is contained in cells, while fat contains almost none of it. Whole body potassium is determined by counting gamma rays emitted by the radioactive isotope of potassium which accompanies the nonradioactive potassium of the body in small and constant proportion. Obviously, the greater the amount of potassium in relation to the total size of the body, the greater the amount of living protoplasm and the smaller the amount of fat.

Finally, a series of assessments of body fat can be conducted by *anthropometric measurements* of skinfold thicknesses; circumferences and diameters of the trunk, chest, and abdomen, and of the limbs in various places, including bony diameters of the wrist and ankle; and (by means of soft-tissue X rays) widths of the skin plus subcutaneous tissue, of the muscle layer in limbs, and of bone.

Of these procedures to measure the fat content of the body and the degree of obesity, the most practical is the *use of calipers to measure skinfolds.* It is also apparently the most precise when tested against other methods, the densimetric method in particular. Because this is a simple method and one which I hope will be used more and more extensively, and because it has led Carl Seltzer and myself to propose new standards of obesity based on actual fatness, I believe that it may be useful to describe it in some detail.

The method, actually a scientific refinement of the pinch test referred to earlier, is based on the fact that about 50 per cent of the total fat is situated immediately under the skin. Certain sites, the triceps skinfold in particular, are representative of the fatness of the entire body. (The triceps is the skinfold which can be pinched on the back of the arm muscle, midway between the shoulder and the elbow). The skinfold measurements are made with a caliper so designed as to exercise a constant pressure, no matter how open the jaws (10 gm. per square millimeter with a contact surface of 20 to 40 square millimeters). The skinfold measurement to be obtained is the (doubled) thickness of the pinched "folded" skin plus the attached subcutaneous adipose tissue. The person making the measurement pinches up a full fold of skin and subcutaneous tissue with the thumb and forefinger of his left hand at a distance about 1 cm. from the site at which the calipers are to be placed, pulling the fold away from the underlying muscle. The fold is pinched up firmly and held while the measurement is being taken. The calipers are applied to the fold about 1 cm. below the fingers, so that the pressure on the fold at the point measured is exerted by the faces of the caliper and not by the fingers. The handle of the caliper is released to permit the full force of the caliper arm pressure; and the dial is read to the nearest 0.5 mm. Caliper application should be made at least twice for stable readings. If the folds are extremely thick, dial readings should be made three seconds after applying the caliper pressure.

Various investigators have used a number of sites, including the triceps, subscapular (under the shoulder), abdominal, hip, pectoral (in the chest), and calf areas. For the general population, the Committee on Nutritional Anthropometry of the National Research Council has recommended the triceps and the subscapular skinfolds as good indexes of an individual's overall fatness.

In the case of the triceps skinfold, the midpoint of the triceps is marked with the aid of a steel tape. The arm should hang freely during the skinfold measurement. Because of the gradation of subcutaneous fat thickness from shoulder to elbow, location of the midpoint is important.

In the case of the subscapular skinfold, the area measured is located just below the angle of the right scapula (shoulder and arm relaxed at the bottom of the back part of the shoulder). The fold is picked up in a line slightly inclined on the natural cleavage of the skin. Because the subcutaneous fat is fairly uniform in this region, precision of location is less critical.

My work as well as that of others leads me to believe that for obese individuals the triceps skinfold, which is the easiest to measure, is also the most representative of total body fatness. No special advantage is gained by utilizing any other skinfold in addition to the triceps.

Extensive data on the distribution of triceps skinfold values allow determination of the normal variation of such skinfolds in our population, at least for Caucasian subjects. The next step, setting up a cut-off point for obesity, is obviously arbitrary. Because of its association with certain body types, the distribution of fatness within the general population may be irregular; it does, however, represent a continuum, and any cut-off point would be a practical rather than a theoretically based selection. Furthermore, while this selection may represent a common fat content, it may not represent a common risk to health, because the significance of a given body fat content may differ with body type. Finally, it must be noted that the relation of skinfold thickness to body fat content is virtually independent of height. This permits giving a single value for each sex and age as a cut-off point.

With these considerations in mind, I have recommended that in the American population the qualification of obesity be reserved for those individuals less than 30 years old in whom the triceps skinfold is greater by more than one standard deviation from the mean. Furthermore, the standard established for subjects 30 years old should be applied to men and women in the 30-to-50-year age group, because, as previously noted, weight gain after adult size has been reached can only be excess fat. Table 1 shows the details of this definition in numerical terms; the minimal limits of our obesity criteria are shown graphically in Figure 5.

The very definition of standard deviation signifies that 16 per cent of the present American population less than 30 years of age are obese. My experience with obesity in children, adolescents, and young adults leads

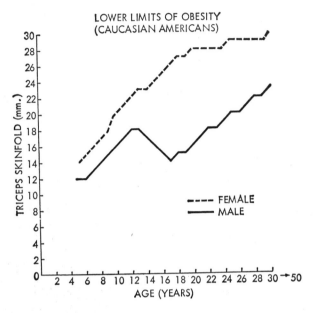

Figure 5

Lower limits of obesity for Caucasian Americans, based on measurements of skinfold thickness.

me to believe that competent pediatricians, other physicians, and physical anthropologists, whatever the basis for their criteria, would recognize at least a similar proportion as obese. (This does not mean that a physician may not consider some patients whose skinfolds are slightly below *our* cut-off points to be too fat for their body builds. Our criteria define unmistakable obesity.) For example, for 16-year-old girls the median skinfold thickness is 16 mm., corresponding to about 23 per cent of the body as fat. The suggested criterion for obesity is 25 mm., corresponding to 39 per cent of the body as fat. For persons more than 30 years old, the per cent considered to be obese, as defined by the criterion proposed here, would increase far above the 16 per cent for the population as a whole, in accordance with the general observation that obesity in middle age is more prevalent than it is in younger ages.

The results of the application of these methods of body fat de-

Table 1 OBESITY STANDARDS IN CAUCASIAN AMERICANS

Age (Years)	Minimum Triceps Skinfold Thickness Indicating Obesity (Millimeters)	
	Males	Females
5	12	14
6	12	15
7	13	16
8	14	17
9	15	18
10	16	20
11	17	21
12	18	22
13	18	23
14	17	23
15	16	24
16	15	25
17	14	26
18	15	27
19	15	27
20	16	28
21	17	28
22	18	28
23	18	28
24	19	28
25	20	29
26	20	29
27	21	29
28	22	29
29	22	29
30–50	23	30

From: Seltzer, C. C. and J. Mayer, "A Simple Criterion of Obesity," *Postgrad. Med.*, 38, 2 (1965), A-101.

termination have thrown new light on the nature of aging, as well as on the difference in fat content between the sexes. Whereas the tables of "normal" height-weight appeared to condone the progressive acquisition during maturity of surplus poundage, it can be made clear by these new techniques that weight accumulated after completion of muscular and skeletal growth is nothing but useless or dangerous fat.

Even if the same weight is maintained throughout adult life, active tissue is progressively replaced by fat. In other words, even if our body weight does not change, we become increasingly fatter as we grow older. Keys matched 33 younger (22 to 29 years) men and 33 older (48 to 57 years) men so that each young man was paired with an older man of the same height and weight. The fat content of the older men was found to be 50 per cent greater than that of the younger men. Women are proportionately fatter than men at all ages, but the evolution of their fat content shows an increase with age parallel to that of the leaner sex. Active individuals who continue to exercise into middle age maintain a proportionately greater lean body mass (that part of the body which excludes adipose tissue) than do sedentary people. Even in the active individuals, however, age inexorably infiltrates existing tissue with fat. For all of us, but perhaps particularly for highly muscular individuals who stop intensive exercising, it would appear that the only way we can decrease the rate of progressive accumulation of fat is (far from following the "normal" height-weight tables) to stop our weight gain at the age of twenty-two and, over the later years, slowly to lose weight. In other words, we should attempt to do what the French call *vieillir sec,* "to age dry."

Getting on now to a consideration of the subject as a whole, the description of obesity has to include the components of the body other than fat. If there is reason to suppose that, as has been said, "Inside every obese person there is a thin person struggling to get out," that person, however, does not necessarily look like the average person who is not trapped inside a large envelope of fat. Because it is well recognized that, outside of fatness, the body type is largely a matter of constitutional and generally inherited factors, what I shall say about body build and obesity is also relevant to the problem of heredity and obesity.

Although the importance of genetic and constitutional factors in animal obesities is well recognized and documented, surprisingly little information is available on the role of constitutional factors in human obesities. We need to know whether or not there are people who, under favorable environmental circumstances, are more predisposed than others to the development of obesity by their constitutional make-up and related genetic endowment. And it certainly would be a relief of sorts to many people afflicted with obesity to be assured that they, as they themselves had probably long suspected, were "naturally" obese. It would provide some degree of comfort for them to learn that their obesity was not entirely, or not at all, a result of their lack of character, but was due, in part or in whole, to forces that came with them at birth.

Because the expression of obesity is so conspicuously a matter of form and structure, any systematic approach to this problem must include a study of the structural constitution of obese subjects. Among many questions to be answered are the following:

(1) Do the obese differ from the nonobese in body features other than different amounts of fatty tissue?

(2) Does obesity occur among all varieties of physical types?

(3) Does obesity occur with greater frequency in some physical types than in others?

From a study conducted on data derived from a survey of a group of adolescent girls, our findings, perhaps, give the beginning of an answer to these questions.

The subjects were a group of healthy (if we do not regard their obesity as a disease), white, obese, young women. The majority of them were attending a summer weight-control camp whose purpose was to administer a reducing regimen consisting of diet, physical exercise, and psychological support. The remainder of the subjects (about a third) were obese patients of the outpatient clinic of the Adolescent Unit of the Children's Hospital Medical Center in Boston. The ages in both groups ranged from 11½ to 18¾ years. Ninety-five per cent of the girls were between 12 and 17. All were judged by the examining physician to be medically "normal," apart from their obesity.

Although they came from all over the United States, three-quarters of the group were residents of the Northeast with the New England and Greater Boston areas predominating. All but five per cent were native-born of native parents. Approximately 40 per cent were of Jewish background and the balance principally of ultimate English, Irish, Scottish, and German nationality origins. The group cannot be said, from a socio-economic view, to represent a random sample of the population at large. Those recruited from the summer weight-control camp were economically privileged. Those from the outpatient clinic, although not from families as prosperous as those of the campers, were on the whole somewhat above the economic level of the surrounding population in the community.

Skinfold measurements were taken to determine degree of fat content. The girls were weighed in pounds without clothing. Using photographs (front, side and back), somatotype ratings were made and later verified independently by another expert. "Somatotype" refers to the most useful and most widely used method of relating physique to disease in general. Sheldon, a well-known physical anthropologist who has tried to better describe the various body types for at least the last three decades, has classified human beings according to their physique as endomorphs, mesomorphs, or ectomorphs. The *endomorph* has a more or less large body and short arms and legs. The *mesomorph* is, at least for men, more aesthetically proportioned. The *ectomorph* has a relatively small body with long arms and legs. When *endomorphy* predominates, abdomen mass overshadows the bulk of that section of the body above it; all regions are notable for softness and roundness. When *mesomorphy* predominates, the chest is massive and muscular and dominates over the abdomen; body joints are prominent. When *ectomorphy* prevails, the individual tends to be slender, delicate in bone structure as well as stringy in muscular development (Figures 6 A, B, C). In the study we are discussing, the girls were rated as endomorphs, mesomorphs, and ectomorphs in a scale of 1 to 7. Each individual was thus characterized by three numbers. For example,

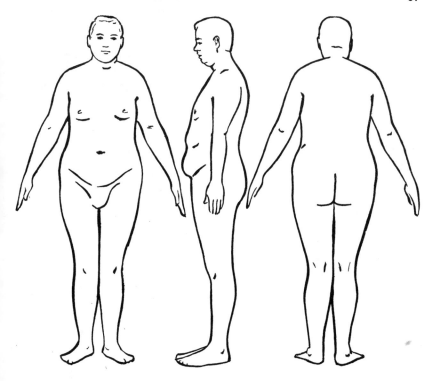

Figure 6A

Extreme endomorph (Somatotype 7-1-2)

a girl with very high endomorphy, fairly high mesomorphy, and very low ectomorphy would be 7-5-1. A "pure endomorph" would be 7-1-1, a "pure mesomorph" 1-7-1, and a "pure ectomorph" would be 1-1-7.

The prime criterion for the designation of obesity in these subjects was the amount of subcutaneous fat tissue, as indicated by the triceps and the subscapular skinfolds. The values for skinfold thickness arrived at were roughly between two and three times those of girls of the same age but of normal weight.

Although no precise data on the duration of obesity could be obtained from the subjects, the information available was sufficient to indicate that the overwhelming majority of the girls had been obese for a long time. Few, if any, appeared to be simply undergoing a stage of transient obesity of the "puppy fat" variety of very early adolescence. Most of the girls were beyond that stage. The average body weight of the subjects was 170 pounds. As a group they were 46 per cent "overweight," based on some of the most commonly used standards of weight for height, age,

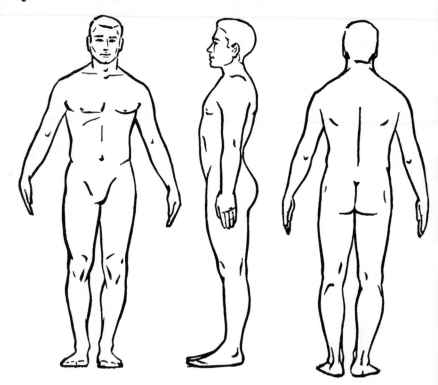

Figure 6B

Extreme mesomorph (Somatotype 1-7-1)

and sex. In more detail, 93 per cent were 20 per cent or more "over-weight"; 73 per cent were 30 per cent or more "overweight"; and 35 per cent were as much as 50 per cent or more "overweight." By any reasonable standards, then, these subjects may properly be designated as obese. However, I emphatically put the term "overweight" in quotation marks. This is done to indicate that there is, as I shall attempt to show, no universal equivalence between the degree of overweight and the degree of obesity. The selective nature of the subjects (approximately two-thirds were attending camp for the correction of their obesity) guaranteed the virtually exclusive dominance of endomorphy in the distribution of the somatotypes. Surprisingly, even when endomorphy was excluded, the obese were found not somatotypically homogeneous. In these obese adolescent girls, mesomorphy, indicative of substantial development of bone-muscle mass, was unexpectedly strong. These subjects were thus

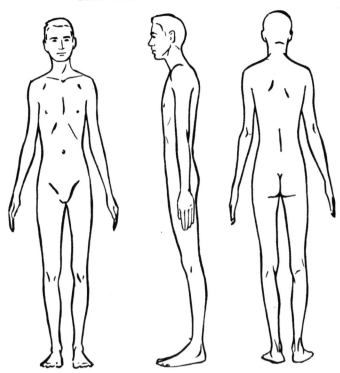

Figure 6C

Extreme ectomorph (Somatotype 1-1-7)

extreme in softness, roundness, and fatness, with the mass of fatty tissues covering a quite sturdy skeletal-muscular foundation.

The obese differed from the nonobese, thousands of whom had been examined in previous studies, in yet another respect. The obese were not only consistently higher in mesomorphy, they were also considerably lower in ectomorphy.

Let us first look at the difference between obese and nonobese in endomorphy. Granted, in a sense the obese subjects were selected for study largely because they were endomorphs, inasmuch as we know that roundness and a predisposition to fatness are characteristic of endomorphs. On the average, the obese adolescent group was about 40 pounds heavier than a large sample of college women (including both the obese and nonobese) and about one and one-third inches shorter. But how prevalent is endomorphy in the obese population as a whole? Is a high degree of endomorphy an inherent characteristic of obese subjects? Would obese subjects still remain endomorphic if they shed enough fat to be of normal weight for age, sex, and height?

It is true that endomorphy is highly correlated with amount of body fat, but the association in the general population between degree of endomorphy and amount of fatty tissue does not indicate complete mutual dependence. Investigators have found a variance of about 36 per cent to be accounted for by variables other than body fat. Furthermore, although the present form a given body takes is an expression of the state of nutrition, it is also, as Theodosius Dobzhansky of Columbia University has pointed out, an expression of underlying genetic influence. While nutrition may do its modifying work, the basic form and structure in an individual remains relatively stable. Endomorphs do not freely change into mesomorphs or ectomorphs, and so on, back and forth. I believe that, by and large, the obese subjects are inherently endomorphic, and that a reduction of the overweight state to a normal weight would not result in a major change in that component. Endomorphy, I think, would continue to remain strong in the overwhelming number of the obese adolescent subjects, but final proof of this must await more extensive studies.

It has already been pointed out that the mesomorphic component (bone-muscle development, ruggedness, hardness, coarseness) in the obese adolescent girls in our study was somewhat higher than in the general nonobese female population. This greater degree of mesomorphy in the obese is based, as described, on photographic somatotype ratings. Since it may be considered that, in the obese, the overlying mass of fat would tend to make tenuous such judgments of the strength of the mesomorphic component, confirmation has been sought in an analysis of available objective anthropometric dimensions. This analysis is principally designed to evaluate the relative size and robusticity of the skeletal structure of the obese and their degree of muscularity.

With respect to the skeletal structure, those measurements have been selected which are essentially unaffected by the degree of adiposity, such as wrist breadth, ankle breadth, and hand breadth. When the average values of these dimensions for the obese adolescent girls were contrasted with those of 15-year-old nonobese girls drawn from a comparable general population in the same geographical area, the differences were consistent, substantial, and statistically significant. Furthermore, relative to stature, these dimensions were all greater in the obese than in the nonobese girls. These data lend support to the assumption that there is a condition of greater skeletal size and robusticity in the obese over the nonobese; and they are consistent with the greater degree of mesomorphy obtained from the somatotype ratings. An estimate of the relative muscularity of the obese adolescents may be obtained from limb circumference, when thickness of the subcutaneous fat is measured at the same level, the limb being regarded as a cylinder for such calculations. These were the results: it appears that obese adolescents display a greater estimated upper arm musculature than the nonobese of the same age, and the calf musculature of the obese adolescents is somewhat greater than that of the nonobese girls of the same approximate age level.

With arm and calf "muscle masses" larger in the obese than in the nonobese girls, the obese adolescent females would appear to be more muscled generally. But note should be taken that the somewhat greater degree of muscularity in the obese girls does not necessarily imply greater muscular tonicity. In fact, the somewhat greater muscle bulk of the obese was observed to be, for the most part, associated with relatively poor muscle tonus, a condition which is consistent with the observation among obese adolescents of decreased activity and poorer physical performance.

It is unlikely that the mesomorphic characteristics of our obese subjects are simply the result of self-selective factors in the camp portion of the group, since it was found that the fattest element in the general population sample also displayed greater robusticity of skeletal dimensions than the rest of the controls. All the available evidence thus supports a somewhat greater mesomorphic tendency in obese adolescent girls than among girls of similar age in the population at large.

The distribution of ectomorphy was just about what one would expect if the obese were endomorphs with moderate or strongly secondary mesomorphy. The absence of high ectomorphy indicates that in the obese there must be a tendency toward a restricted somatotype configuration. For, if the endomorphy observed was in fact just fat, then one would expect to find strength in the ectomorphic component in a predictable number of cases. The low ectomorphic ratings observed strengthen the argument that the obese are more than just a random sample of physical types with a marked excess of fatty tissue.

Not only are obese subjects less ectomorphic than the general population or even the highly endomorphic elements of the general population, they also reflect the total absence of a wide variety of ectomorphic physical types. The extent of this void may be judged from the fact that 63 per cent of 15-year-old public school girls, 64 per cent of a series of college girls and 78 per cent of Sheldon's series of 2,000 women have ratings of 3 and higher in the ectomorphic component—whereas the obese averaged 1.21. It would seem, therefore, that the great majority of the ectomorphic physical types usually present in the general female population are seldom, if at all, subject to obesity under ordinary nutritional conditions. Apparently nature is intolerant of obesity in ectomorphic types.

Since we know that fatter girls grow faster and mature earlier, it may be thought that the greater dimensions of our obese adolescent girls are more directly a function of an advanced stage of growth and development rather than a reflection of inherent differences in bodily structure. Are these greater dimensions simply nutritional, with the higher caloric surplus in obese girls acting to increase body size and maturation status over that of nonobese of comparable age?

From all the data obtained by my laboratory, the answer is clearly in the negative. This was strikingly illustrated in another study by a comparison of the anthropometric dimensions and proportions of 12-year-old obese girls with those of nonobese at age 15. The obese girls, while three years younger in chronological age and shorter in stature, showed larger average lateral bodily dimensions and greater relative proportions of these dimensions to stature. While we would anticipate these obese adolescents to be a few months in advance in growth status over nonobese of comparable age, they would not be expected to be advanced by as much as three years. Besides, the adolescent spurt, whether early or late, causes no radical change in body build. Accordingly, the greater skeletal dimensions of our obese adolescent girls seem to reflect inherent differences in body structure over and above what might be attributed to the effects of accelerated development or of long-term overnourishment.

These findings permit us to answer the pertinent questions posed earlier in this chapter. Obese adolescent girls do indeed differ from nonobese in body features beyond the differences of fatty tissue. Obesity does not occur in all varieties of physical types. It occurs with greater frequency in some physical types than in others.

The obese adolescent girls appear to be more endomorphic, somewhat more mesomorphic, and considerably less ectomorphic than nonobese girls of comparable age drawn from the general population. Presumably, then, the prime prerequisite for the development of obesity is a physique with at least a moderate amount of endomorphy under normal nutritional conditions. Endomorphy, which is neither a disease nor a sin, is an inherited predisposition to the laying on of fat unless insufficient diet, great activity, disease, or voluntary weight control supervenes. It should be understood, of course, that, even among endomorphs, there must be a considerable number of individual differences in the tendency to accumulate adipose tissue. Not all endomorphs become obese. But the tendency is there. It is highly probable that mesomorphy in its higher ranges manifests some special affinity for the accretion of fatty tissue. On the other hand, nature seems to be intolerant of obesity in ectomorphic types. Peoples so blessed may apparently follow the dictates of their appetite without fear of growing fat.

I must emphasize that the above findings refer to obese adolescent females. Until further studies are available, caution must be exercised in applying these conclusions to adult obese men and women, or perhaps even to obese adolescent males. In adults particularly, the problem of obesity is much more complex, because among them are physical types which are prone in middle age to a sudden blossoming into obesity. Any study of adults, therefore, must distinguish between those whose obesity is long-standing, going back to childhood and adolescence, and those for whom it is a singular characteristic of midlife. Actually, our preliminary studies in adult women suggest that in middle age, as in adolescence, not all physical types are equally prone to become obese. There, too, very ectomorphic types with long, narrow hands and feet just do not become obese.

Interestingly enough, the existence of a relationship between body build and obesity has parallels in studies of experimental obesities in animals. Genetic transmission of obesity is associated with other modifications of organ size and body composition. In the mouse, "yellow obesity" is accompanied, particularly in males, by a longer and larger body. And the obese hyperglycemic syndrome of mice, a genetically determined obesity accompanied by diabetes which has been extensively studied in my laboratory, is leagued with larger viscera, but a smaller muscle mass.

Clearly there are constitutional factors operating in the predisposition to obesity. While this in no way detracts from the concept that caloric intake in excess of caloric expenditure is the immediate cause of obesity, a recognition of the constitutional individuality of the person may well give a greater understanding of the familiar phenomenon that, under similar circumstances, some of us become obese and others do not.

Finally, if one wants to obtain figures for the number of obese individuals in our population at a given time, one must realize that this prevalence of obesity varies according to the standards used. The limitation of height-weight tables to determine the presence or absence of obesity in a given individual has been discussed above. However, such tables can be used to obtain some approximation of the prevalence of obesity in a population. The United States Public Health Service has used these tables in its study (1950–52) of the prevalence of overweight in adults. The percentage of persons overweight was found to vary from one area of the United States to another and to range from the rate of 40 per cent in Boston, Massachusetts, down to 10 per cent in Atlanta, Georgia, and 9 per cent in Indianapolis, Indiana. The numbers examined, however, were not very great except in Atlanta (140,000) and in Richmond (36,-000, 12 per cent overweight). In whites, the prevalence of overweight in males was nearly twice that in females. Negro groups showed a higher incidence of female obesity than male obesity.

Another interesting question as regards adults is whether the prevalence of obesity has been increasing. Comparison of 1943 draftees with 1917 draftees shows that the World War II draftees were heavier for their height than World War I draftees, a finding not necessarily synonymous with an increase in the prevalence of obesity. The data available to the United States Public Health Service do suggest, however, a tendency to increase prevalence of overweight in males during the course of the century in this country.

In children, my studies of middle class suburbs in the Boston area indicate that the prevalence of extreme overweight, as defined by a weight-height ratio greater than that corresponding to the "heaviest" channel in the Wetzel Grid, the commonly used height-weight diagram, is over 12 per cent, probably as high as 15 or 16 per cent by the time they graduate from high school. Comparable data obtained in the Berkeley, California area suggest that the prevalence of obesity there is only half as high as in Newton and Brookline, Massachusetts, reflecting either differences in the genetic and social background of the population (see Chapter 6) or, more likely, the fact that the climate is more conducive to the year-round practice of exercise.

chapter 3
Genes
and Obesity

Animal husbandry has always been a favorite source of illustrative material for "health education" and "nutrition education" programs. The fact that, in order to insure good growth in fur-bearing or meat-producing animals, or to increase the yield in milk or eggs of milch cows or hens, it is necessary to provide the animals with generous supplies of calories, proteins, vitamins, and minerals has always been held as a legitimate example to be followed in human nutrition. Children, too, will require these nutrients to grow well and, in rural communities, the extrapolation from farm animals to children has often been relied on to "push" school-feeding schemes or "better breakfast" propaganda, increase the consumption of vegetables, whole wheat bread or dairy products, or decrease intake of candy and soft drinks. Teaching future mothers to feed themselves well during pregnancy and nursing has similarly been enlivened by stories of poorly fed sows giving birth to piglets with cleft palates or missing eyeballs, and by reports of the rapid exhaustion of the milk of starved Holsteins or Guernseys.

The similarity of genetics in animals and man is readily conceded when such harmless facts as the color of the eyes or the fuzziness of the hair, fur, or wool is considered. Even height is regarded, to a certain extent, as a proper object of comparative study: Pygmies are smaller than Zulus, as ponies are smaller than horses. The recognition of the fact that man is subjected to genetic vicissitudes not unlike those experienced by other mammalians ends abruptly, however, as soon as obesity is mentioned.

Animal breeders have long known that extreme adiposity could be induced readily in certain varieties and not in others. For example, the Aberdeen-Angus stock of cattle becomes very fat much more commonly and easily than does the Jersey. The Berkshire hog is a very portly creature, while Razorback swine are leaner and more suited to the production of ham and pork chops than to the development of lard and fat bacon. Chows and bulldogs "run more easily to fat" than do grey-hounds or fox terriers. All this, of course, is due to genes. But we are told daily by health educators and women's page writers—as well as by a few "medical" columnists—that "genes have nothing to do with obesity" and "obesity is not due to heredity, but simply to overeating." The great fear implicit in this denial is that, if it is once admitted that genetic background may condition the development of obesity (or of an increased appetite leading to obesity), obese patients will blame their grandparents for their condition and adopt a fatalistic attitude. The failure of their efforts at self-denial will be anticipated as a matter of course. Impending obesity will be regarded as inevitable, like Fate in Greek tragedies, and the resultant resignation will lead to abandonment of the diet. Worse still, the sternly censorious attitude of the therapists will have to be mitigated. At least in democratic societies, it is considered poor form to blame a man for the genetic pattern inflicted upon him by his ancestors.

If we come to obesity proper, gross, unmistakable obesity, can we show that it is ever "determined" by genes? The answer to that question once again comes from the laboratory. A number of scientists have devoted their lives (or at least important parts thereof) to the study of hereditary processes in mice. Lest this appear to stern utilitarians a somewhat futile pastime, let it be pointed out that it is difficult for man to study the genetics of his own species, because by the time he has seen two or three generations appear, the observer is dead. Biblical observers who, according to the Scriptures, very much outlived the commonly allotted three-score-and-ten, and who did pay close attention to genealogy, do not seem to have made use of their fine opportunity to study human genetics.

Mice, helpfully enough, present much more extensive opportunities for gathering useful genetic information than do men. Mice become of marriageable age seven or eight weeks after birth. Pregnancy lasts three weeks and mice nurse their young for about four weeks, but they can become pregnant again while they are nursing. The total life span is of the order of two years, so that a mouse can see a considerable number of generations (in the Biblical sense) before it dies. Observations of hereditary processes in these little creatures have taught us more in a few years than we could have learned if the ancient Egyptians had trained us to count blue and brown eyes instead of stars.

Furthermore, there are no limitations, among experimental mice, about who can be bred to whom. Among human beings, even in societies which do not leave the choice of a mate to chance and romantic love, such practices as brother-sister or mother-son marriages are discouraged. It may be that one of the reasons for the strong taboos which universally forbid choosing a parent, a brother, or a sister for a spouse is precisely the reason why this type of mating is such a useful tool in genetics; it brings to light and allows one to recognize and study hitherto hidden characteristics which, in the case of the human race, might profitably remain in a discreet shadow.

In the hands of "mouse" geneticists, the use of incest as the basis for producing new generations, or perhaps "half generations" in some cases, has taught us much about the heredity of disease. In particular, we have learned something about the heredity of skeletal malformations and other "congenital" abnormalities, of susceptibility to infection and of the so-called degenerative conditions, often characteristic of old age, like kidney diseases. Above all, the mice have taught us a great deal about the hereditary factors in cancer and about the way in which environmental influences interplay with constitutional traits to cause or prevent the appearance of tumors.

The genetic transmission of a number of forms of obesity in mice has been studied by these same techniques. The earliest observations of "hereditary" obesity were concerned with the so-called "yellow" mouse, a variety of the common house mouse, with a yellowish tinge to its coat and a strong propensity toward extreme adiposity. Although these animals have the same birth weight as their nonyellow brothers and sisters, they may weigh two to three times as much when mature. In the mid-1920's Danforth made a particularly careful study of these animals. He mated yellow males to females of various colors. A large proportion of the offspring in the succeeding generation were yellow. These and the descendants of other colors were kept in similar cages and fed the same diet. All animals showed similar weight curves until they became sexually mature. From then on the yellow mice, and more particularly the females among them, accumulated weight much in excess of normal, until they weighed twice the normal weight or more. Mating two yellow mice to each other did not produce any young. Apparently the yellow-obese gene is "lethal" when homozygous (i.e. the egg does not develop into an organism capable of living when both the ovum and the spermatozoa carry the gene). The gene is dominant, so that geneticists will describe the obesity it determines as "invariably found in mice which are heterozygous for the dominant gene producing the yellow coat." (Heterozygous means, of course, that either the spermatozoa or the ovum, but not both, carry the gene.)

I have studied extensively another form of genetic obesity, this one a Mendelian "recessive" type. (The reader no doubt remembers the meaning of the terms "dominant" and "recessive" from his or her elementary biology. When yellow and blue flowers of a given species are crossed, the first-generation seeds yield flowers of the "dominant" color, say yellow. In the next generation, one fourth are pure "dominant" yellow flowers, which, in turn, would have nothing but yellow offspring; one fourth are pure "recessive" blue; one half are yellow, but carrying blue genes which can manifest themselves in future generations.) I have called this form of obesity the "hereditary obese hyperglycemic syndrome." A *syndrome* is a group of signs and symptoms which appear together and are to be regarded as the various facets of a single disease entity. In this case, the animals which are obese also show, or can easily be made to develop, a high blood sugar, or, in Greek, *hyperglycemia*. It was first observed by Margaret Dickie, a worker at the world-famous Jackson Laboratory at Bar Harbor, Maine, the mecca of mouse genetics, where more than a million mice have been bred since its foundation. This unique institution was destroyed in the great Bar Harbor fire of the late 1940's. But almost immediately the undaunted Jackson scientists set out to reconstitute the colony from a few escapees rescued from the flames, as well as from the progeny of native Bar Harbor mice which had been sent to outside institutions. As is often the case with matings in times of great upheaval, some of the unplanned unions were followed by unexpected results. For example, when Doctor Dickie crossed a "V" male with a "Black 57" female, animals appeared in the descendants of the mating in a proportion which conformed to the rules for a Mendelian "recessive" gene (one fourth), which, as they developed, became grossly obese, weighing two, three, sometimes four times as much as their normal-weight brothers and sisters; they were round, soft, placid little balls of mouse fat, somewhat more susceptible to fatal diseases than the normal, but seemingly contented.

Although these animals dutifully conformed to the laws of genetics, there was a practical difficulty in obtaining enough of them for study: as mentioned earlier, they did not reproduce. Still they *could* be obtained, though slowly at first, by finding out through trial marriages which ones among the thin male and female mice carried the recessive "obese" gene and then mating males and females who were both carriers. When two dozen or so of these animals had been produced in 1950, they were sent to me for study in my laboratory where they joined my collection of different types of experimental obesity. Since then, I have studied more than a thousand of the little creatures in an attempt to find out the exact nature of the abnormality leading to the obesity.

By their very existence, of course, these obese mice contradict all the "authoritative" teaching about heredity and obesity still found in too many textbooks of medicine, nutrition, and psychiatry. After all, here are these animals, being served the same food as the thin ones, moving about in the same socio-economic environment as the thin ones, and triumphantly Mendelian in their obesity. Another distressing trait of the obese mice is their attitude toward exercise. Orthodox teaching holds that exercise is no way to reduce. (In Chapter 5, I shall list evidence demonstrating the fallacy of this contention.) The obese mice, who have not heard—or have heard and have not believed—this proposition, are extraordinarily inert as compared to their nonobese brothers and sisters; yet they can be reduced by exercising them on a treadmill or by "breeding in" the so-called "waltzing" gene which impels them to run around in their cages. The genetically obese mice deal to the classical concepts of obesity other low blows, the extreme offensiveness of which may not be apparent to the layman. For example, textbooks say that obese subjects should display a normal "basal metabolic rate." This type of fat mice does no such thing. Their basal metabolism is low and may be half the normal (in human parlance, minus fifty). Their endocrine glands misbehave. (Yet, we hear, "obesity has nothing to do with hormones and glands. . . .") For example, they develop a form of diabetes, more resistant to insulin than the ordinary variety, which as a matter of fact, is not unlike that frequently seen in obese human patients of middle age. Their blood glucose levels, already high, can be stepped up further under the influence of very small amounts of certain hormones, like growth hormones or the glucose-elevating hormone of the pancreas which we have encountered earlier, glucagon (and also, incidentally, by caffeine). Their blood cholesterol is about twice as high as that of their nonobese littermates.

If these mice are placed in the cold (42° F.) they will die within a few hours despite their enormous paddings of fat, while nonobese mice will survive indefinitely. More vexing, if you fast them, they will lose weight, but much of this weight will be protein, not fat. In fact, if they are starved for a long period so that they eventually weigh quite a bit less than normal animals, they still contain more fat than the normal ones, while their muscles have melted away. It can be shown, using foodstuffs and chemical constituents of the body marked with radioactive isotopes (which enable us to trace their metabolism), that these mice will make fat out of their food under the most unlikely circumstances, even when half starved.

In the genetic sense, then, these animals are really "obese" from birth; if obesity is defined as the presence of an excessive amount of fat in the body rather than excessive weight, they can be "obese" even when reduced to a normal weight. It will be seen that other forms of experimental obesity, such as those that can be produced as a result of chemical or surgical intervention in the previously thin brothers and sisters of genetically obese mice are infinitely more orthodox in their behavior. Actually, after about fifteen years of research, I believe that I have elucidated the nature of the particular biochemical error which is transmitted genetically in this syndrome. To make it intelligible a little bit of biochemistry is necessary.

Chemical reactions within the body proceed well at a temperature which is low as compared to the temperature needed for the same reactions in factory vats and without the use of other extraordinary conditions (such as very high pressures), because of the presence of *catalysts* —the *enzymes* which activate molecules and make them more reactive. In turn, the formation of these enzymes is determined by the genes characteristic of the species. Other genes may determine the existence of *repressors,* which mask the action of genes in certain tissues. Now, in adipose tissue, the synthesis of fat proceeds when three molecules of fatty acid react with a molecule of glycerophosphate, which, in turn, has to be formed from glucose. When fats are utilized, the first phase of the operation releases glycerol from its combination with the fatty acids. The glycerol thus liberated cannot be reutilized by *normal* adipose tissue: the enzyme glycerokinase, which catalyzes the formation of glycerophosphate, is inactivated by a repressor in this normal adipose tissue. The adipose tissue of obese-hyperglycemic mice appears, however, to lack such a repressor. As a result of this hereditary abnormality, the adipose tissue of these animals can reutilize the glycerol it has just produced, and thus its synthetic processes are not as dependent upon the metabolism of glucose (and less subject to the controls of this metabolism) as those of normal animals (or of animals made obese by other means). The accumulation of glycerophosphate in the fat tissue of these animals may be responsible for the backing up of glucose—hence, the diabetic-like blood sugar levels. In an effort to cope with these high blood glucose levels, the pancreatic cells which secrete insulin multiply excessively, the insulin production and release are stepped up, and the combination of high blood-glucose levels and high blood-insulin levels leads to a tremendous increase in fat production by the liver. The research leading to these results is described in more detail in Chapter 4.

Thus far, two forms of hereditary obesity have been mentioned: that of the yellow mouse and that of the hereditary obese-hyperglycemic mouse. Other forms of hereditary obesity include yet another type of mouse, one studied in South America. In this brown strain (the hereditary obese-hyperglycemic syndrome, unlike this and the yellow is not associated with a particular coat color), there occurs a spontaneous degeneration of midbrain centers concerned with the regulation of appetite, and, again, obesity (but of different characteristics) is the result. There is also a strain of rats which develop diabetes, especially among the males, and generally a certain degree of obesity. Finally, I have studied, again in collaboration with Bar Harbor geneticists, a type of recessive Mendelian (one-out-of-four) obesity in the Shetland sheepdog. The obese animals weighed, by the time they reached adulthood, three or four times as much as their normal-weight brothers and sisters. They did not, however, exhibit the diabetes characteristic of their small neighbors.

In man it is, of course, common experience that obesity, like many other physical traits, "runs in the family." In man's particular case, however, it is paradoxically claimed that only environmental influences are concerned, not genes. First, on the face of it, this elimination of genes is absurd. We—all living creatures—are the result of the interaction of our genetic determinants *and* the environment. No biological phenomenon is independent of some form of genetic direction. Genes determine whether we belong to the human species in the first place. Susceptibility to pathologic conditions, from measles on, has been shown to be influenced by the genetic background of the individual. The inheritance of mental conditions, for example, has been extensively studied.

Even Lysenko (who at one time almost eradicated genetics—and geneticists—in the U.S.S.R.) at his shrillest would not have dared emulate the categorical pronouncements of the antigenetic crusaders. The fact that the Nazis perverted the use of human genetics is no excuse for denying that the human egg, like the egg of all other animals, has chromosomes and that these play an essential role in the subsequent fate of the individual—including, presumably, his obesity. Because, as recalled above, human generations take a quarter of a century to appear and because marriages between closely related individuals are generally discouraged (an exception would be the compulsory marriages between first cousins in Madras), the science of human genetics has progressed but slowly. The study of the subject of genetic factors in human obesity may have been further discouraged by the forceful statements of many respectable clinicians to the effect that there was no such thing.

It is true that the same people who deny the existence of hereditary factors in obesity will readily recognize that the accumulation of certain abnormal fats, of ordinary fat in localized parts of the body, or even of ordinary fat all over the body as a component of certain diseases, can be strictly determined by hereditary background. For example, the forms of "familial" or hereditary illnesses which go by the intimidating names of Nieman-Pick and Tay Sachs diseases, Hand-Schuller-Christian syndrome, and Gaucher's disease, are characterized by the accumulation of large amounts of fats which, while they occur normally in certain parts of the body—the brain, for example—are not usually manufactured and retained on such massive scales. The genetically controlled assembly of normal fat in one locus is illustrated by the steatopygia of Bushman and Hottentot women. This form of obesity, localized to the derrière (and doubtless considered "ideal" and "desirable" by Bushmen and Hottentots, to borrow from the vocabulary of the life insurance statistics), seems to be biologically comparable to the fatty hump on the back of certain cattle species and to the fat tail seen in certain varieties of sheep. Such genetically determined, "sex-linked, localized lipophilia" (in plain words, unusually adipose buttocks, inherited by women and compatible with an otherwise thin body) is also characteristic of certain other intramarrying African tribes.

In addition, it is readily recognized that certain hereditary diseases may result indirectly in obesity. For instance, Von Gierke's disease, where a low blood sugar results from an impairment of the liver, and the disease described by Bauer under the formidable name of "macrosomia adipose congenita" are clearly familial diseases. Often in the case of the former, invariably in the case of the latter, they show obesity as one of the symptoms. In congenital adipose macrosomia, the obesity is present at birth and ravenous appetite is immediately observable. (Incidentally, "congenital" is usually meant to include both strictly hereditary traits—that is, *traits determined by genes*—and *traits resulting from intrauterine influences.* Lately, the second aspect of the meaning has been emphasized. In the case of adipose macrosomia, "hereditary" would appear to be the proper term.) Most infants with this condition die within the first year. In another disease, "familial monstrous infantile obesity," the excessive weight is not present at birth and overeating does not become striking until a few months later. The chances for the infant's survival are good. Other forms of hereditary human obesity are associated with the genetically determined diseases which go by the arcane names of Laurence-Moon-Biedle syndrome (usually characterized by, among other signs, an excessive number of fingers) and "hyperostosis frontalis interna" (excessive bony development of the forehead is responsible for the name of the disease).

But what about "ordinary" obesity in otherwise normal individuals? Bouchard, a French physician who investigated obesity in the seventies and eighties of the last century, and Von Noorden, who worked at the beginning of this century, observed that most obese patients had at least one obese parent. Roney in Chicago in the thirties observed that, among his large "collection" of unselected cases of obesity, over two-thirds of the patients had one obese parent; in one-fourth of the cases, both parents were obese. Dunlop in Edinburgh found almost identical proportions among his patients. So did Bauer in Vienna. Gurney, Angel, Iversen, and others, working in different cities of different countries, all contributed similar results, as did our own recent studies in the Boston area.

It is generally argued, however, that the demonstration of familial associations in obesity supports the view that faulty familial food habits cause obesity and indeed cannot be construed as an indication of the intervention of genetic determinants in the development of the condition. Two types of studies, however,—those dealing with body weight of identical twins and those dealing with the number, sex, and weight of the progeny of marriages classified according to the body type of the spouses—have yielded results which would be difficult to explain solely on the basis of familial habits or, indeed, by any combination of purely environmental factors.

Identical twins are, genetically speaking, the same individual. They start life with the same genes in identical chromosomes. Any differences which develop between them are due to environmental (prenatal or postnatal) influences. The inherited mechanisms determining body weight are therefore the same and the differences which arise illustrate the influence of environmental factors.

Studies conducted on large numbers of such identical twins neatly demonstrate that the evolution of body weight is determined both by environmental and genetic factors. Von Vershuer, working in Germany in the early twenties studied 57 pairs of identical twins, aged three to fifty-one years. He measured their weight, height, length of each arm, width of mouth, circumference of neck, waist, and head, along with many other anthropometric characteristics and calculated the variability of these measurements. Weight differed more from one twin to the other than did any of the other anthropological measurements. Similar results were reported by others, such as Newman, and indicated that, while weight is to a large extent genetically determined, it is more susceptible to environmental influences than are other measurements.

This effect of environment is even more definitely emphasized by the results of the comparison between identical twins raised in "identical" and in different environments. Von Vershuer considered that the environment was identical if the twins had the same weight at birth, obtained the same nursing in infancy, lived in the same house, not only in childhood but in adolescence and adulthood as well, and had the same occupation. If one or more of these conditions differed, the environment was considered different. As might be expected, the variability of all measurements was greater for twins living in dissimilar environments. Again, of all anthropometric characteristics, body weight could be shown to be most influenced by environment. The "average percentual variation" was almost three times as great with the twins raised in dissimilar environments as with the twins raised in identical surroundings.

Does this sensitivity of body weight to environment mean that genetic factors are of no importance? Not at all. And to show this, let us turn to the comparison published in 1937 by Newman, of the University of Chicago, between the variability of body weights of identical twins and that of body weights of "fraternal twins" (nonidentical twins of the same sex) and of "nontwin" brothers and sisters grouped according to sex. Such comparisons are founded on the idea that nonidentical twins of like sex live in the same family environment (same socio-economic milieu, same family surroundings, same parents, same place in the order of children). Identical twins have all these in common and, besides, have the same genetic "composition." Any similarity or degree of resemblance exhibited by identical twins and *not* by fraternal twins is, therefore, probably due to genetic rather than to environmental similarities.

The subjects studied by Newman were mostly adults. Fraternal twins and "nontwin" brothers and sisters of like sex were found to be considerably more variable in body weight than were identical twins. Actually, the fact of being fraternal twins did not seem to reduce the variability of body weight as compared to nontwin brothers and sisters. Results were very clear-cut—both these groups were two and a half times more variable than identical twins. Only two per cent of the identical twins differed by more than twelve pounds in weight as opposed to slightly more than fifty per cent for the fraternal twins and the "nontwins." The fact that genetic factors are of paramount importance is clearly demonstrated by the finding that fraternal twins and nontwins were much more similar to each other than were the two types of twins. If environmental factors were of overriding importance, one would expect identical and fraternal twins to resemble each other more closely, as opposed to non-twin brothers and sisters.

The additional observations of Newman and his collaborators on 19 pairs of identical twins who had been separated since early childhood clearly showed that both environmental and genetic factors played a role in the determination of body weight. In five pairs of twins, considerable differences of body weight were found; in each case, extreme environmental differences had been encountered. In three pairs, tuberculosis or chronic ill health had been responsible for greatly different modes of life, muscular development, and body weight. In a fourth pair, one of the sisters had had five pregnancies and had become more obese with each one, while the other sister had had only one pregnancy and had been in poor health since that time.

The history of the fifth pair is of particular interest and has been cited many times. These "identical" sisters, Ada and Ida, separated at three, lived as different lives as could be imagined, Ada in cities, Ida on farms. Ida contracted goiter while Ada was protected by eating iodized salt. Ada married at seventeen, had a stormy married life, and was divorced at twenty-seven. Ida married at thirty-four and led a placid married life. At fifty-nine, Ada weighed 208, Ida 221 pounds, a difference of 13 pounds.

The other separated pairs showed much smaller differences in weight, mostly less than five pounds. Thus, it appears that when environment is not greatly different, genetic factors are paramount. Even when extremes in environment occur, genetic traits, if powerful enough, will override them as in the cases of Ada and Ida. Generally speaking, where the histories reported in the medical literature of the various pairs of obese identical twins separated from infancy are analyzed and compared to pairs of lean identical twins, the former show greater variability in weight, but are (unfortunately) sufficiently similar to indicate the persistence of genetic influence.

If there are genes concerned with predisposing subjects to obesity, the next question is: how are these genes passed from one generation to the succeeding ones? Earlier in this chapter I have given examples of dominant and recessive genes in experimental obesity; there are also sex-linked or sex-limited genes involved, such as in steatopygia, the enormously fat or obese derrière in certain African ladies. Considering the extreme complexity of the physical and psychological mechanisms regulating appetite which we have already discussed, it is to be expected that a great many genes may intervene, in different fashions, to set the stage for leanness or for obesity. Liebendoerfer studied the family trees of 25 extremely obese subjects. He found that in almost all cases at least one of the parents was obese, and concluded that obesity is probably inherited by Mendelian transmission of a number of dominant factors. Davenport, the most famous early American student of the problem of body build, ho worked at the Carnegie Institution, extended these studies in 1923 to a large number of individuals. He tried to put some order into the classification of "obese" and "lean" individuals. He derived a coefficient the ratio of the weight by the square of the height) which, if these quantities are expressed in grams and in centimeters, varies from 1.5 to 4 and upward. Very slender (VS) individuals are in the 1.5 to 1.75 range; slender people (S) in the 1.8 to 2.1 range; medium persons (M) from 2.2 to 2.5; "fleshy" persons (F) from 2.6 to 3.0; and "very fleshy" (VF) persons from 3.1 to 4.1 and more. The "index of body build" can thus be de-

Table 2

DAVENPORT'S GENETIC OBSERVATIONS

PARENT		CHILDREN
"SLENDER" X "SLENDER"	⟶	"SLENDER" (VERY FEW "FLESHY")
"FLESHY" X "FLESHY"	⟶	"FLESHY" (A FEW MEDIUM OR "SLENDER")
"SLENDER" X "FLESHY"	⟶	MAJORITY "FLESHY"

ermined for parents and offspring and the offspring can be divided according to the various combinations: one parent very slender, one slender VS x S); both parents slender (S x S); and so on, (S x F, M x M, M x F, etc.). He found that the matings of slender parents (S x S, VS x S, etc.) gave rise to slender offspring, with only exceptionally any fat offspring. The offspring of "fleshy" parents were "fleshy" themselves, but showed greater variability in that they not infrequently had medium or even slender offspring. In more genetic terms, the results showed "segregation" i.e. the offspring showed a well-defined pattern), and showed "regression toward mediocrity" (i.e. a shift toward average) to a greater degree in the progeny of the obese than of the lean individuals. Obese individuals thus presumably carry "gametes" for both obesity and leanness, while lean people carry gametes for obesity only very rarely. The fact that the S x F matings produced an excess of F over S would suggest that stoutness is dominant over leanness. Actually, Davenport believed that his results supported the view that there were at least three independent genes at play, at least one of them dominant.

More recently, (in 1936), Gurney, studying in Buffalo a large group of obese women and a group of thin women with otherwise similar medical histories, concluded that pregnancy or a major operative procedure acting on the proper genetic background was the most common factor associated with the onset of obesity. Granted, obesity did not develop in the thin woman with approximately the same incidence of pregnancies and operations. But when the weights of the parents of the two groups were compared, it was found that the incidence of stoutness was twice

as high for mothers, several (nine) times as high for fathers, and fiv
times as high for both parents in the "stout" group as in the "thin"
group. The data on "segregation" thus strikingly confirmed Davenport
The percentages were quite similar (e.g. only nine per cent of nonstout
nonstout matings produced fat offspring, etc.).

In 1949, Angel, working in Philadelphia, investigated the correlatio
between weight of parents and not only fatness of offspring, but als
the number of offspring, their sex, and the incidence of obesity in eac
of the subgroups. His parents were selected on the basis of having a
least one obese child. His conclusions are therefore valid within thi
limitation—probably tantamount to saying that they are valid when a
least one parent carries obese genes. He found, as had others before him
that "segregation" took place with half of the offspring of fat x average
and two thirds of the offspring of fat x fat matings. But he furthe
found that there were fewer males, and larger families, among the
progeny of average x average matings and fat females x average male
matings than among the offspring of fat x fat and average female x fa
male unions. Angel concludes that this is not inconsistent with a
hypothesis that one of the genes which in some cases helps to determine
obesity is a sex-linked recessive lethal gene. Such a gene might be ex
pected to be more frequent among the females of the average x average
matings with at least one obese daughter (the basis of selection), where
presumably the interacting nonrecessive genes mainly responsible for
obesity would be less frequent than in matings involving one or more
fat parents (especially a fat father). On the other hand, he recognizes
that the "relatively larger family size of the average x average and fa
female x average male marriages may have purely psychological or 'social
biological' and not genetic determinants." Likewise, the relative excess
of fat females over fat males among the parents and siblings of the
obese (about 60 per cent of females are fat as opposed to 40 per cent o
males) may express as strongly the effects of genetic sex limitations and
social sex differences in activity as the effects of a hypothetical sex-linked
recessive lethal factor which present data are inadequate to test. One
of the difficulties in this type of study is the fact that the well-controlled
potentially obese are difficult to detect. It is similarly difficult to be sure
whether observable obesity in an adult female is genetically determined
or whether exaggerated intakes resulted from a physiologic accident, say,
in pregnancy. Incidentally, Angel's work suggests a method for solving
the latter question more reliably than interrogation: he noticed that the
distribution of fat is somewhat different in women who become obese
following a pregnancy than in the "all-over fleshiness" of endomorphic
obesity in women obese since childhood. Recent work, based on skinfold
measurements in the "old" and "recent" obese, confirms this observation.

Angel, being an anthropologist, lays particular stress on the anthropometric characteristics of the obese. After allowing for excess fat covering

it, he finds the obese physique, in his Philadelphia sample, to be endomorphic, short, with a long and deep trunk compared to rather short extremities, round head and face, small blunt nose, relatively good teeth, and frequent greenish eye pigmentation. He associated these characteristics with the predominance of Alpine and other paleolithic-derived physical types, and considers that they agree with the idea that ice-age selection favored massiveness and obesity.

It has already been seen in Chapter 2 that the body types of obese, such as the size and shape of the skeleton and the muscle mass, and even such traits as the relation of length to width of the hand—girls with long, narrow hands never seem to be obese—argue strongly for the genetic determination of obesity: we know that body type is an essentially hereditary characteristic. Similarly, the studies of Withers on the high degree of correlation between weight of parents and weight of natural offspring along with the lack of correlation between weight of parents and weight of adopted children, even if these were adopted at birth, demonstrate the importance of genetic factors.

It can be agreed then, that, while the evidence is neither as complete nor even as conclusive as would be desired, indications are that in man, as in experimental animals, genetic traits largely determine, if not obesity, at least potentialities for overeating (or underexercising) and obesity. In a society such as ours, where for most people food is abundant and physical work unnecessary, we have the ideal conditions for genetic potentialities to express themselves, or as biologists say, for the phenotype (the organism as it appears) to be an expression of the genotype (the organism as his genes alone would determine it to be). Does this mean that we must be fatalistic and abandon any further attempt at control? Not necessarily. While genes may make one susceptible to obesity, the actual overeating, underexercising, or both, leading to a positive energy balance still has to take place before obesity develops. Not only that, but recognizing (instead of denying) that genetic factors are involved in the development of obesity may give us a much more solid basis for preventive treatment. In diabetes, recognition of genetic determination has led to systematic testing of relatives of diabetic subjects and the detection of a great many likely diabetics who would otherwise have remained untreated. Preventive work has been made easier. Similarly, if it is once recognized that children with one obese parent are *likely* candidates for obesity and that children with two overweight parents are *probable* candidates for obesity, there is a chance to develop early those food habits and tastes for exercise which will minimize the development of the condition. Facts, after all, are our best allies if we want to dominate and modify nature.

chapter 4

Physiological Factors in Obesity

The mechanism of regulation of food intake is, as the reader must now be convinced, an extremely complicated one. It is therefore not astonishing that a great many unrelated factors may lead to overeating or undereating, with resulting obesities or emaciation. I am very much aware of the fact that the exposition which follows is not going to be an easy one for a reader who does not have a strong background in biology. I was tempted to simplify it in the extreme, at the cost of losing much of the significant information. I resisted this temptation because I believe that the public has been subjected to too much oversimplification and, in particular, to many unfounded easy pseudo-psychiatric "explanations." It seems to me indispensable to give an exposition of the complexity of the physiology of obesity so that there will be an appreciation of the numerous disorders or disturbances which may lead to an appetite greater than normal, a rate of fat synthesis greater than normal, or a rate of fat mobilization smaller than normal. We now have experimental models of various types of obesity; we understand how some of them—and in particular genetically determined obesities—develop; we know, at least in one case, how a disorder of fat metabolism can lead both to obesity and to diabetes. These experimental advances are harbingers of coming advances in medicine. They give hope that if we do not content ourselves with facile generalizations about oral gratification, the cultural function of food or its rewarding role, we may be able to cure rather than simply to *control* obesity.

But first, let us look at the obesities. I use this term in the plural because from the beginning of my studies I became convinced that I was looking not at one but at a number of different syndromes. (This concept is universally accepted now, but I remember that, in the early fifties, when I was beginning to accumulate the experiments proving this diversity, I met with considerable intellectual opposition.) Because it is easier to think of a number of objects if they can be arranged in some order, let us look at classifications of obesities.

Obesities can be classified according to their causes or according to the mechanisms of their development. The former approach—the etiologic—

MULTIPLE FACTORS IN HYPERPHAGIA

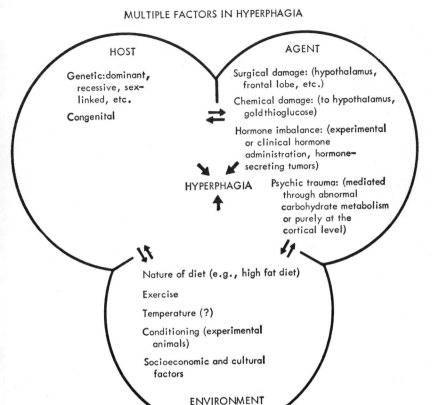

Figure 7

A schematic view of constitutional (genetic and congenital), traumatic, and environmental factors in the etiology of obesity. A great many different types of factors, acting singly or together, may cause hyperphagia (overeating).

distinguishes among genetic, traumatic, and environmental factors. Obviously, such a classification (which I introduced in an article in *Physiological Review* in 1953), although useful, is somewhat too arbitrary. For obesity to develop, there have to be permissive interactions of the right genetic and environmental factors, or of traumatic factors with a favorable genetic and environmental background. However, this classification is helpful in singling out the characteristic element in the evolution of a particular obesity. Table 3 gives an inventory of known obesities, classified for each species, including man, along this etiological approach.

As our knowledge of the intimate mechanism increased, I developed another method of classification and grouped obesities into two categories, "regulatory" and "metabolic." I found through studies in experimental animals that a general distinction could be made between regulatory obesities, in which the primary impairment is of the central mechanism regulating food intake, and metabolic obesities, in which the primary

Table 3 TYPES OF OBESITY

In Mice

Genetic: "Yellow obesity," associated with coat color: heterozygous, dominant character; normal mating.

"Hereditary obese hyperglycemia syndrome": homozygous, recessive character, associated with absence of mating.

"NZO" obesity: homozygous, recessive character, normal mating.

Of hypothalamic origin: Spontaneous; in one form genetically determined; surgically induced; induced by goldthioglucose.

Of endocrine origin: Caused by grafting of pituitary tumors secreting adrenocorticotropic hormones (for genetic determination of endocrine obesities, see above).

Otherwise induced: By high-fat diet; by certain chemical agents.

In Rats

Genetic: Associated with diabetes.

Of hypothalamic origin: Induced by bilateral or unilateral lesions.

Of other central nervous system origin: From frontal lobe damage.

Of endocrine origin: From hypertrophy of adrenal cortical tissue; from prolonged treatment with protamine zinc insulin, or insulin with forced feeding; after thyroidectomy with hypothalamic lesions or with forced feeding.

Otherwise induced: By immobilization; by high-fat diet; by conditioning.

In Dogs

Genetic: In the Shetland sheepdog; recessive character.

Of hypothalamic origin: Spontaneous; surgically induced; due to paraventricular degeneration (caused by adrenocorticotropic hormone or cortisone).

Of other central nervous origin: Bilateral destruction of amygdalian cortex.

Otherwise induced: By immobilization.

In Monkeys

Of hypothalamic origin: Surgically induced.

Of other central nervous system origin: Surgically induced by lesions of the thalamus; surgical destruction of orbitoinsulo temporal region.

In Farm Animals

Genetic: In strains selectively bred for fat, in particular, pigs bred for lard.

Of hypothalamic origin: Surgically induced in goats.

Of endocrine origin: Induced by castration and by estrogens in the fowl; by castration and implants of estrogens in male cattle.

Otherwise induced: By immobilization in pigs, cattle, and geese; by forced feeding in geese for production of *foie gras*.

In Man

Genetic: A multiplicity of genes have been studied by Newman, Von Verschuer, Bauer, Gurney, Rony, Angel, and others; in congenital adipose macrosomia; in monstrous infantile obesity; associated with Laurence-Moon-Biedl syndrome; associated with hyperostosis frontalis interna; associated with Von Gierke's disease; in familial hypoglycemosis (congenital lack of alpha cells).

Of hypothalamic origin: In dystrophia adiposogenitalis, with discrete or diffuse hypothalamic injury; occasionally with panhypopituitarism and narcolepsy; Kleine-Levin syndrome.

Of other central nervous system origin: After frontal lobotomy; in association with cortical lesions, in particular bilateral frontal lesions.

Of endocrine origin: With insulin-producing adenoma of the islets of Langerhans, with diffuse hyperplasia of the islets, and in association with diabetes; with chromophobe adenoma of the pituitary without hypothalamic injury; in Cushing's syndrome (hyperglycocorticoidism); from treatment with cortisone or adrenocorticotropic hormone; in the Bongiovanni-Eisenmenger syndrome. In disorders of the reproductive system: gynandrism and gynism, aspermatogenetic gynecomastia without aleydigism; male hypogonadism (sometimes with bulimia), post-pubertal castration, menopause, ovarian disorder, paradoxical (Gilbert-Dreyfus) disorder.

Otherwise induced: By immobilization in adults and children; by psychic disturbance; by social and cultural pressure;

---

lesion is an inborn or acquired error in the metabolism of tissues per se. In the first case, habitual overeating may lead to secondary metabolic abnormalities. In the second case, peripheral metabolic dysfunction may, in turn, interfere with the proper operation of the central nervous system. This distinction was demonstrated in my laboratory primarily by comparisons between different types of obesity in mice and was extended later to other animals. I believe that it is valid in man as well.

Regulatory obesities are exemplified by the hypothalamic obesities induced either by surgery or by goldthioglucose administration. Animals with these syndromes eat ravenously and may gain up to four times their normal weights. The rate at which their bodies manufacture fat and cholesterol increases in proportion to the amount they are allowed to overeat. Prolonged fasting brings their fat production rate down to normal fasted levels. Their rate of absorption of glucose by the intestine increases, but again this is a result of habitual overeating. When such obese animals are reduced by fasting, their body composition returns to normal. To put it simply, what is wrong with these animals is that because of their brain lesions, they eat too much.

The situation in metabolic obesities, such as the hereditary obese hyperglycemic syndrome, the "New Zealand obesity," and the obesity caused by grafting of ACTH-secreting pituitary tumors is in striking contrast to that in regulatory obesities. In animals with metabolic obesities, there is something wrong in the tissues, and this is in turn what causes the animals to overeat.

We have already encountered the obese-hyperglycemic syndrome, a genetically determined condition which manifests itself in mice of various sizes and colors—black, grey, brown, etc.—and of either sex, both parents of which carry the (recessive) gene.

The obesity of mice with the hereditary obese hyperglycemic syndrome (which has been under intensive study in my laboratory since its discovery in the early fifties) is as extreme as that observed in mice of the hypothalamic types. However, their hyperphagia is usually less pronounced than the latter's since their caloric surplus is partially caused by relative inactivity. The blood sugar is elevated in varying degrees. Further elevation is readily brought forth by the administration of growth hormone. This hormone has little or no effect on the levels of blood glucose in normal littermates or in littermates made obese by hypothalamic lesions induced by surgery or administration of goldthioglucose. Obese hyperglycemic mice also show marked high blood cholesterol. They evince a variety of abnormal responses to the administration of hormones such as insulin, glucagon, corticosteroids, growth hormone, ACTH, and thyroid hormone. Although their means of "physical" defense against cold (such as hair-raising and blanching of the skin due to peripheral contractions of arterioles, which decrease heat loss) are intact, the animals are incapable of increasing their metabolism, and hence their heat production, when exposed to low temperatures and, therefore, die rapidly.

Mice with the obese hyperglycemic syndrome show considerably enlarged islets of Langerhans with increased numbers of both "alpha" and "beta" cells, increased pancreatic insulin and glucagon content, and increased circulating insulin. The reader may like to be reminded that the pancreas is an important organ because of its role in both digestion and the regulation of the metabolism of sugar. As a digestive gland it fulfills an *exocrine* role. By exocrine is meant that secretory ("acinar") cells secrete pancreatic juice into a canal or canals leading to the intestine. As a gland involved in glucose metabolism, it is an *endocrine* gland. This means that the secretory cells secrete their chemical messengers ("Hormones") into the blood, rather than into a canal. There are two important types of cells: "beta cells," secreting insulin, the blood glucose-lowering hormone, secreted in insufficient amounts by the pancreas of all young and many older diabetics; and "alpha cells," which secrete glucagon, a recently discovered hormone which releases glucose from the liver and which may, according to some of the work done in my laboratory, be involved in the mechanism of satiety. These cells are grouped in little islands known as "islets of Langerhans."

The pancreas, normally characterized by the proliferation of large, degranulated islets of Langerhans, shows a very abnormal response to injections of alloxan, a compound which normally causes destruction of the beta cells and permanent diabetes.

In obese hyperglycemic mice, alloxan administration causes the islets to become massively regranulated while the blood glucose goes down to nearly normal values. (The granules are apparently storage forms of insulin.) The adipose tissue of these mice has many abnormal characteristics: a high coenzyme A activity (that is, a great excess of a special enzyme involved in the production of fat); even under fasting conditions, tremendously increased fat production from acetate (a precursor of fat made up of only two carbon atoms plus hydrogens, which is the building block from which the fourteen, sixteen, or eighteen carbon chains of fatty acids are made); and decreased uptake of glucose. There are other peculiarities: absence on effect of the nature of dietary fat (normally, "hard" fat in food leads to "harder"—less saturated—fat in depots); of epinephrine on fatty acid release from adipose tissue (epinephrine—adrenaline—normally releases "free" fatty acids from fat; these, in turn, are available for muscle activity, heat, etc.); and the presence of "glycerokinase activity" (an enzymatic abnormality which will be explained below).

Of particular critical importance in the definition of metabolic obesities is the fact that they are characterized by rates of fat production increased over normal rates, even when the obese animals are not allowed to eat more than normal animals. This is true even in fasts, a state when fat is normally not produced. Also, in this class of obesities, fasting does not cause higher blood ketones. Ketones, partially oxygenated products of the incomplete combustion of fats are produced in quantity whenever the breakdown of fat (triglycerides) into fatty acids and glycerol proceeds faster than the oxidation of fatty acids. This is a phenomenon seen whenever a normal animal (or person) is fasted for a long enough time. It does not occur in metabolic obesities. Reducing animals with metabolic obesities to normal weight by underfeeding them does not bring body composition back to normal, but leaves them with a fat content still considerably greater than the normal fat content at the expense of nonfat tissue. The obese-hyperglycemic syndrome was found to be a prototype of metabolic obesity with all these phenomena strikingly demonstrated.

I believe that after years of search, (after having had to discard a number of alternative hypotheses), I have elucidated the mechanism of development of this syndrome. It appears to be due to a hereditary metabolic error in the adipose tissue. Of particular interest is the fact that the diabetic component of the syndrome is secondary to this error in the adipose tissue. I have mentioned this genetic lesion in Chapter 3. Let me try to be more detailed now.

My research indicates that the adipose ("fat") tissue of these mice has an extra enzyme—one of those highly necessary protein molecules which make chemical reactions happen in tissues at rates hundreds of times greater than if they were absent and on which, consequently, the whole chemistry of living matter rests. The particular enzyme which is manifest in the fat tissue of these mice, glycerokinase, is one which is present normally in many tissues, but which is repressed in fat tissue by a repressor which is apparently genetically absent in these animals. As a result of this extra enzyme, the adipose tissue of the mice can reconstitute fat inside fat cells without having to receive activated glucose from the outside. A fat molecule is made of a triple alcohol, glycerol, with each alcoholic function being "esterified"—coupled—with a molecule of fatty acid. The nature of the fatty acids gives the fat its characteristic—saturated fatty acids leading to hard fat, "unsaturated" fatty acids (characterized by missing hydrogen atoms in the carbon chain) leading to oils. As the fat is hydrolyzed, that is, as the fat is split into glycerol and fatty acids (a process normally very slow at body temperature, but enormously accelerated by enzymes), it is irreversibly split. Only the availability of an activated glycerophosphate compound which is produced as glucose is broken down permits the resynthesis. In the obese-hyperglycemic mice, however, there is a "glycerokinase" which reincorporates the glycerol just released by hydrolysis into fat. The net effect of the presence of considerable glycerokinase activity is that less fatty acids are released from fat cells, particularly when the need is increased. For example, less fatty acids are released in the cold (hence the death of these mice in the cold), or during fasting (hence the fact that these animals have to burn some of their protein to stay alive when fasted, instead of easily consuming their fat).

I believe that it is this abnormality which is "primary"—that is, comes first. It appears that the high content of glycerophosphate in the fat cells keeps the glucose out; it is not so needed for fat synthesis. The resultant high blood glucose, in turn, causes the pancreas to secrete a lot of insulin. The combination of a high concentration of glucose and a high concentration of insulin in the blood causes the liver and other organs to make much more fat from sugar than normal, hence a number of "secondary" enzymatic adjustments. That fat, of course, is carried to the adipose tissue both in free form and piggy-back on certain blood proteins, the "lipo-proteins."

The syndrome may thus be the first example of a diabetes which is not primarily a disease of the pancreas. It may be a model for the so-called "maturity-onset diabetes," the diabetes seen in obese, middle-aged humans. This type of diabetes is not usually characterized by a lack of insulin, as is the diabetes characteristic of (thin) youngsters.

It is interesting to note that another type of genetic obesity in mice, also associated with high blood sugar, has been described recently by investigators in New Zealand. They have observed certain "NZO" mice which exhibit a syndrome that, in spite of certain resemblances, is different from the hereditary obese hyperglycemic syndrome. The "NZO" (New Zealand obese) mice are fat and diabetic like the obese hyperglycemic mice, but show different idiosyncrasies. First of all, NZO mice mate and produce offspring, in contrast to the mice my associates and I have used, which do not mate and have to be obtained by mating nonobese carriers of the obese gene or by artificial insemination of ovum transplantation. Extensive metabolic studies have not yet been published by the discoverers of this syndrome, but reaction of the levels of blood glucose to fasting appears quite different in these animals. The usually high blood sugar levels in NZO mice may go even higher during fasting, instead of going down rapidly when food is withdrawn, as they do in mice with the hereditary obese-hyperglycemic syndrome. In the NZO mice, low glucose values are observed during pregnancy, and very low values at delivery. Like the hereditarily obese-hyperglycemic mice, the NZO mice show insulin resistance, that is it takes a great deal of insulin to bring their blood glucose down. We found that mice made obese by grafting ACTH-secreting tumors reveal still different metabolic abnormalities. ACTH is the adrenocorticotropic hormone which is secreted by the pituitary and stimulates the production of cortisone-like steroids by the adrenals. The tumors which we grafted had developed in mice exposed to the first atomic bomb at Alamogordo and been passed on from mouse to mouse during the next twenty years. In these animals, levels of blood glucose are again high but they show a remarkable stability under fasting conditions. Levels of liver glycogen, the storage form of blood sugar, also remain higher than normal under fasting conditions, doubtless reflecting more active glycogen production because of increase in circulating corticosteroids, the adrenal hormones involved in the conversion of protein into sugar. Liver glucose-6-phosphatase (the hormone responsible for the final step in the release of glucose from liver glycogen) activity is high, unlike the finding in the obese hyperglycemic syndrome where the activity of this enzyme is normal, but where that of phosphorylase, the enzyme involved in the *first* step of the release of glucose is elevated.

As in other forms of metabolic obesity, the rate of fat production in these ACTH obese mice during fasting is greater than that in normal animals during fasting. When they are reduced to normal weight by fasting, their fat content remains much higher than normal. They lose a great deal of protein tissue to make up for the fact that their fat is less available than normal. This is characteristic of metabolic obesities. Another difference between regulatory and metabolic obesities is that in all metabolic obesities tested thus far, the animals fail to show the normal rise in blood ketones which accompanies starvation. We have seen that ketone bodies, the product of incomplete oxidation of fat, appear whenever fat is mobilized and hydrolyzed into fatty acids and glycerol faster than the fatty acids can be oxidized. Animals with metabolic obesity, such as the mice with the obese-hyperglycemic syndrome, are characterized by partial blocks in breakdown of fat or by rapid resynthesis of fat. This causes a massive mobilization of fat so great as to exceed the need for final oxidation which is seen in "normal" mammalians fasted completely for a long period. (It is seen also in diabetics lacking insulin where, again, fat is mobilized and partly oxidized to ketones more rapidly than the organism can dispose of these ketones. The result is an elevation of the blood ketones, the patient smells of acetone—one of the blood ketones—and is said to be ketotic.)

Behavioral studies also emphasize the difference between regulatory and metabolic obesities in mice. Regulatory and metabolic types react differently to different diets. Similarly, the association with pathologic conditions differs between the two classes. To give but one example, obese-hyperglycemic mice are more resistant to ascites tumors, a form of liver tumor which can be injected into mice, than normal animals, and goldthioglucose-hypothalamic mice are more sensitive to spontaneous mammary tumors.

It should be immediately recognized that the prevalence of the different forms of obesity discussed in this chapter, and of those listed in Table 3 is extremely varied. Some forms—like the Laurence-Moon-Biedl syndrome—are extremely rare. Some—like the obesity due to inactivity— are extremely common. It is worth enumerating the rare forms of obesity for at least two reasons.

First, we see the great variety of factors which may cause an increase of body fat. Second, this suggests the possibility that, while we may know how to diagnose certain well characterized syndromes causing rapid development of obesity, we do not know how to recognize less advanced states which lead to a more progressive development of this condition. Two examples of the former are "mild" hyperinsulism (a disease in which too much insulin is secreted by the islets of Langerhans either constantly or as a response to carbohydrates, causing blood glucose to drop, and hunger to appear), and "mild" glycogen disease (where liver glycogen is not released as glucose, blood glucose drops, and if the disease is extreme, the individual becomes thin and stops growing. If it is mild, however, he gets very fat). By contrast, we do not know yet how to identify that lower part of the "normal" range of blood glucose—not characteristic of an identified disease—which will cause a tendency for frequent hunger, a somewhat increased level of circulating insulin (the normal range is quite broad), and a somewhat decreased capacity to release glucose from liver glycogen.

The ability to measure precisely the level of circulating insulin in the blood is only a few years old and has not been done systematically in various types of obesity, at various ages, and at various stages (such as the state of "dynamic" obesity, when fat is actively accumulated, as contrasted with the stage of "static" obesity, when fat has been stored and is simply retained without further accumulation).

Similarly, my laboratory has been working on a method permitting the determination of the level of circulating adrenalin—a hormone which, as first shown by Walter Cannon, drastically stops the contractions and sensations of hunger. It is quite possible that different concentrations of these two hormones, one of which elevates blood glucose (adrenalin), one of which lowers it (insulin), may result in the same blood glucose. Yet in the long run, the various concentrations of these two hormones, one of which favors fat mobilization and oxydation or the consumption of existing fat (adrenalin), one of which favors fat synthesis (insulin), may have different effects on the fat content of the body. It is probable that different concentrations of these hormones in blood are characteristic of different body types and fat contents, even though, again, the blood glucose levels are similar in the different body types.

Finally, although I have chosen to discuss these two hormones because they affect with particular vigor hunger, on the one hand, and fat mobilization, on the other, there are many other hormones involved in the overall endocrine balance of the body—thyroid hormones, glucagon, the hormones of the adrenal cortex, growth hormone, sex hormones, etc. Even the gastrointestinal hormones may be implicated. Different body types may correspond to different balances between these hormones. We don't know at all what, in the long run, a balance obtained with various sets of concentrations of these factors means in terms of hunger and fat deposition.

We have spoken so far of constitutional, static differences in endocrine constitution. Our ignorance is even more acutely felt when we remember that we are not dealing with a static situation, but that all sorts of reactions to stress and to changes of various sorts are involved. After all, a difference of intake of a few per cent—or even of less than one per cent—may make quite a difference in weight over the years. To give an example, it was shown by investigators at Yale that the mere fact of exposing rats to food once a day instead of all day increased their capacity to make fat (though not their overall food intake). Similarly, chickens fed only once a day become a little fatter. Presumably, the concentrations of hormones and enzymes are modified slightly to accommodate to the new regimen. What does such a change of regimen do, in man, to the endocrine and enzymatic balance, and, over the long run, in predisposing to obesity? (Incidentally we do know that in some individuals, replacing a few large meals by more numerous snacks is useful in controlling weight; it may also have a favorable effect on the cholesterol level of patients with very high serum cholesterols.)

At the beginning of this century, when hormones were first discovered, it was commonly believed that obesity would be found to be due to the absolute excess or deficiency of a single hormone. When this was found to be almost never true, the popular medical position swung to the other extreme: "obesity is almost never due to hormonal disturbances; it is almost always due to overeating." Actually, the reasonable position ought to be: "in order to be obese, you always have to eat more than you expend for a certain period. How often this is due to a slight shift of relative or absolute hormone concentrations, each one of which is in the 'normal' range, we don't know."

The analysis I have just given, suggesting that mild predisposition to metabolic obesity can be due to a slight abnormality in enzymatic activity or in hormone circulation which we cannot yet diagnose, can be repeated for regulatory obesities. Gross lesions of the hypothalamus due to brain or pituitary tumors can be diagnosed and the development of massive bulimia (an enormous increase in food intake) and obesity can be clearly ascribed to them. Already more subtle is the syndrome which my associates and I have studied recently in man and reproduced in experimental animals, where an elevation of cerebrospinal fluid pressure causes hypothalamic malfunction and obesity. But what of the slight error in the "setting" of the hypothalamic control mechanism which meal after meal causes the subject to be satisfied only if he or she has a little too much food?

Again, the psychiatric patient with obvious "oral compulsion," who will stuff his mouth with food or even with undigestible material, and is obese, is a rare but easily diagnosed subject. But what of the person who has not been taught (or taught himself) to act on normal satiety signals and waits until he feels stuffed or full to stop eating? The extra calories ingested may be few, but we must remember that an extra 100 calories a day—33 per meal—representing less than 5 per cent of the intake of an adult—are enough to cause deposition of ten pounds of fat a year.

The significance of the experimental models studied in the laboratory is thus manifold. They may be models for various obesities in man. They may give us clues for the understanding and the treatment of dangerous conditions often associated with obesity, such as maturity-onset diabetes, hypertension, and hypercholesterolemia. And they suggest that many of the less dramatic, progressive forms of obesity may be due to only slightly "abnormal" constitutional traits or very mild physiologic or psychologic impairments which, while they would not cause obesity in individuals working hard physically to obtain a bare subsistence, allow adiposity to develop in an environment where physical work is unnecessary and food is abundant.

chapter 5

Activity
and Weight Control

The view that exercise expends relatively little energy is completely erroneous. The fact that it is erroneous is known today by all nutritionists and all physicians. It should be similarly known by most alert laymen, because of the wide public exposure I and several of my colleagues have given it, particularly over the last decade in popular periodicals, the press, and on both television and radio. It is vital that it be recognized as truth by every otherwise healthy person who aspires to combat obesity.

But old myths, especially harmful myths, seem to have incredible staying power. And for too long, it appears, too many people were told too often, frequently by misled "authorities," that exercise is of no value as a reducing agent. The notion is still widely held by obese patients in hospitals, clinics, and the offices of physicians.

If the view that exercise is a negligible factor in the output of energy and, accordingly, in the loss of weight were true, physical activity, particularly moderate physical activity, could be of only small importance in maintaining the balance between calorie intake and calorie outgo. It is this balance, of course, which determines the extent of overweight. Another false idea which continues to have broad and pernicious acceptance is that, at any level of calorie intake, an increase of physical activity is automatically followed by an increase in appetite and is, therefore, self-defeating as a weight-control measure. The facts overwhelmingly demonstrate that exercise *is* the great variable in energy expenditure and that exercise does *not* necessarily increase food intake. It is vital that sufferers from obesity be convincingly assured that an increase in food intake follows an increase in exercise only under limited conditions.

The first misconception, the minimizing of the cost of physical activity, could be avoided by anyone who had occasion to look thoughtfully at a table of "Recommended Dietary Allowances" such as has been elaborated by the United States National Research Council, and other national and international agencies. For example, the daily allowances for men given by the National Research Council vary from 2,400 calories for "sedentary" men to 4,500 calories for "very active" men. Laborers, soldiers in the field, and athletes are advised by the NRC that they may require up to (and occasionally more than) 6,000 calories. The range of 2,400 to 6,000 calories should weaken the belief that physical activity plays but a negligible role in the daily energy balance.

One of the most striking illustrations of what happens if you don't compensate for the increased energy expenditure caused by physical activity is provided in the systematic studies made by the peculiarly devoted nutritionists of the Third Reich. These "scientists" had been given the problem of finding out the degree of undernutrition compatible with continued production of coal by foreign miners pressed into service in the mines of the Ruhr. The Nazis discovered that it did not pay to try to reduce the intake of these prisoners to a level corresponding to that suitable for sedentary activities. The health of the victims disintegrated and their production fell to nothing—proof, if one were needed, that steady physical activity consumes a perceptible quantity of calories.

Actually, the cost of physical activity has been carefully determined, for many activities. It has been measured directly (by having the subjects perform various tasks in a calorimetric chamber—a room specially constructed to permit the trapping and determination of the heat produced by a man and his physical work. This can be done, for example, by having the walls full of slowly circulating water which enters the system at a constant temperature and which leaves it at a temperature dependent on the amount of heat given off. Another method calls for thousands of thermocouples in the floor, the ceiling, and the walls). It has been measured indirectly (by having the subjects breathe in and out of tanks of compressed air and measuring the amount of oxygen used). We have by these techniques obtained figures for the energy cost of a multitude of exercises and occupations. A summary obtained for 150-pound men and 120-pound women gives the energy cost of a number of sports and other activities (Appendix III).

And yet how frequently, even in this time when such facts as nutritionists possess have been so extensively and emphatically circulated, we are exposed to assertions such as "A pound of fat can be worked off only by walking thirty-six hours, or splitting wood for seven hours, or playing volley ball for eleven hours." The enemies of exercise visualize any given wearying performance as being accomplished in a single uninterrupted stretch. The energy expenditure accompanying physical activity takes place, however, whether the activity is performed in a day or a decade. Splitting wood for seven consecutive hours would be difficult for anyone other than Paul Bunyan, but splitting wood for half an hour a day—in no way an impossible assignment for a healthy man—will add up to the desired seven hours in a fortnight. If this thirty-minute lumbering operation represents a regular practice, it would be, according to the very reasoning of the foes of physical activity, calorically equivalent in one year to 26 pounds of body fat (since a pound of fat is calorically equivalent to 3,500 calories).

Energy expenditure in most types of activity, where only parts of the body are moved, is directly proportional to body weight. A tennis player who weighs 150 pounds expends about one per cent of the cost of playing tennis in moving his racket, about 99 per cent in moving his body. In the case of a heavier man, expenditure would be proportionately greater. A 200-pound player going through the same movements would expend in work one-third more than his 150-pound opponent. He would either lose more weight or need more food to cover the expense of his three sets than would the thinner man. For the "mean" man, then, examples of energy expenditure per hour over that of sitting are: walking (not running), 100 to 550 calories, depending on the speed; cycling, up to 585; swimming and skating, up to 685 calories; skiing, up to 950; climbing, the same.

These hourly expenditures above the resting level are still lower, incidentally, than the peaks reached in athletic competition. For a sport like rowing, such peaks may approach 1,300 calories per hour. A caloric expenditure of 500 to 600 calories per hour above the resting level represents a degree of physical activity which can be endured by the average out-of-condition adult for half an hour without undue discomfort. A trained man should feel all the better after a full hour or more of such exercise. For those for whom translation into foods is more meaningful than caloric counts, the expenditure corresponding to thirty minutes of this kind of exercise is equivalent for our "mean" man to an average piece of pie decorated by a standard scoop of ice cream. Regular exercise, it becomes clear, can be a substitute for—or a mitigating companion to—regular deprivation.

Moreover, if excess body weight is such that it impairs body movements, the cost of exercise will actually increase faster than body weight. It follows that an overweight person will require more energy (and, hence, unless fed more, burn a greater amount of body fat) for the same amount of exercise than will a person of normal weight. Twenty per cent overweight will increase the cost by more if the overweight makes the exerciser more clumsy and less efficient.

The dependence of the cost of physical activity on body weight has another important consequence. Any increase of calorie intake above the balance level will cause only a modest increase in weight in a physically active individual, because of the energy cost in moving the extra poundage. By contrast, in a sedentary individual, less energy will be expended moving the extra weight; weight gain, therefore, will be more rapid and more pronounced. If a Swiss mountaineer suddenly increases his food intake by a moderate amount, he will quickly stabilize his weight. He will use up the increase to carry uphill the two or three pounds which he at first accumulates. His streetcar or auto-riding Zurich brother lacks such an automatic self-correcting mechanism. The latter may add five or ten pounds before the slow increase of heat loss which follows the expansion of his waistline eventually starts matching the daily addition to his caloric consumption of, say, a dessert at supper. The active man has two brakes on weight gain: increased cost of exercise (a very potent one) and increased basal metabolism. (Basal metabolism is the minimum rate of energy expenditure, measured at rest, at a comfortable temperature, after an overnight fast.) The sedentary brother has only the less effective increased basal on which to rely, and he will curb his progressive fattening much more slowly.

The second widespread misconception, somewhat more difficult to dispel, is regrettably embodied in a proposition which not only sounds plausible, but is also in part true. It is the oft-repeated allegation that exercise is of no value in weight reduction because an increase in physical activity always causes an increase in appetite and food intake which is at least as great in energy value as the energy expended in exercise.

That an increase in appetite follows an increase in activity in a normal animal or person is true enough. It explans why the weight of most adults is relatively constant. A fine adjustment of appetite prevents the body from burning away its substance when the individual is called upon to perform at a higher level of exertion than has been his custom. This adjustment of caloric intake to caloric expenditure admits of definite limitations even in a normal person. Energy expenditure must not be raised above a certain upper limit; it must not be lowered below a certain minimal limit. These statements can be substantiated by observing laboratory animals as well as human beings. In the Nutrition Department at Harvard, my collaborators and I have studied the way the food intake of white rats varies when their exercise is varied. We used a motor-driven treadmill and accustomed a large group of rats to running on it. Then we divided the large group into a number of smaller groups, which were exercised, respectively, for one, two, three, up to ten hours daily; we measured their food intake during a few weeks of this regimen and their weights after it. Finally, we compared them with rats which had been left unexercised in their cages.

We learned that rats exercised one or two hours daily did not eat more than did the unexercised rats; indeed, they ate somewhat less. From two hours onward, increasing duration of exercise was accompanied by increasing food intake, up to a duration of exercise which represented the peak that rats could endure. Higher durations could not be maintained. The animals became exhausted, ate less, and lost weight. Swimming the rats, instead of running them, gave the same results. Figure 8 is a summary of our experiment with the running rats.

The range of inactivity, in which decrease of food intake no longer responds to decrease in activity, can be truly termed the sedentary range.

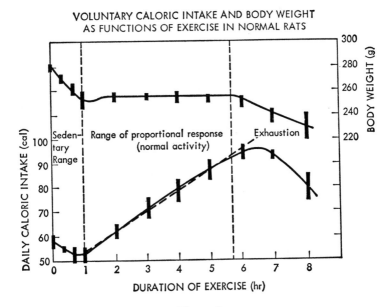

VOLUNTARY CALORIC INTAKE AND BODY WEIGHT
AS FUNCTIONS OF EXERCISE IN NORMAL RATS

Figure 8

The regulation of food intake generally operates with precision only in the area of "normal activity." With low levels of exercise, an increase in exercise is not accompanied by an increase in food intake. At extremely low levels of activity, voluntary food intake is greater than at moderate levels. In the range of "normal activity," the regulation of food intake is functioning: as activity increases, food intake increases correspondingly and weight is maintained. At excessively high levels of activity, both food intake and weight decrease.

Above this comes the range of normal activity where appetite and exercise are attuned. Above the normal range is the exhaustion range, where an increase in activity is no longer followed by an increase in appetite, but by a decrease. This last is obviously an unstable situation which cannot be endured indefinitely. Neither the sedentary nor the exhaustion range represents a normal mode of life. Animals are not meant to be caged. They are not designed to be pushed beyond the limits of what the body can stand. In the central zone, that of normal activity, appetite reveals itself as a sensitive and reliable mechanism for equating energy intake to energy expenditure.

Such conclusions, gathered from these helpful rats, also apply to man. The sedentary range is presented in its extreme form by studies of Dr. James H. Greene of Iowa City, who "collected" 200 patients in whom the beginning of obesity could be traced directly to a sudden decrease in

BODY WEIGHT AND CALORIC INTAKE AS A FUNCTION OF PHYSICAL ACTIVITY IN MAN

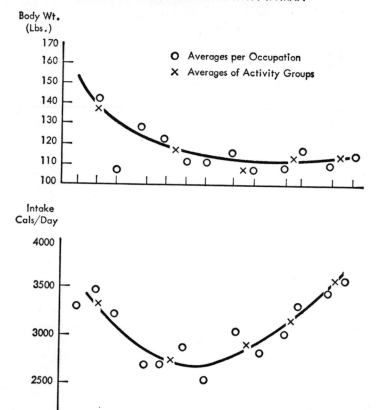

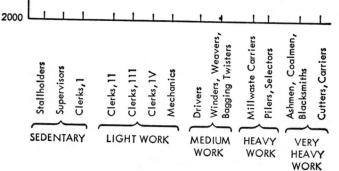

Figure 9

activity resulting from a change in occupation, blindness, fractures, and the like. A massive "experiment" conducted after World War II on millions of young men discharged from the active life of fighting units and "rehabilitated" in class rooms and offices, has perhaps not received enough attention. Returning veterans had a tendency to put on weight rapidly. This was not due exclusively to a return to home cooking and a peaceful atmosphere, but to a very sedentary life as well.

In the summer of 1954 I had an opportunity to conduct a study on an industrial population of West Bengal (India) which has a particularly wide range of physical activity, from bazaar tailors and clerks to coolies carrying enormous loads on their heads or backs for nine hours a day. The determination of food intake was facilitated by the fact that most of the workers surveyed lived away from their families and thus bought their food and cooked for themselves. The diet was extraordinarily uniform, in both quantity and content, for each person, and showed little variety within groups and from group to group. Individual one-day dietary recalls, checked by buying records, and studies on amounts spent per week on food gave results generally identical with exhaustive dietary histories and appeared more representative of long-range intakes than did corresponding data obtained in a Western society.

Activity was measured by detailed schedules and industrial ratings of physical effort. Clerks were further subdivided into four classes, according to the mileage walked daily to and from work. The various occupations or subgroups were each represented by at least ten persons and were grouped according to a broad classification of activity. One extreme included the merchants, supervisors, and "non-walking" clerks. At the other extreme were the selectors and "pilers," two occupations where heavy weights of jute mattings were borne; carriers, whose loads were up to 190 pounds of unprocessed jute each; coalmen and ashmen, who were burdened by equally heavy bags of coal and ashes and unloaded them in an awkward manner; and cutters, who spent their whole day swinging heavy cutting knives with practically no pause. For men of the same height (5 feet, 2 inches, to 5 feet, 4 inches), individual weights varied from 67 to 198 pounds at the extremes of the range, with most weights between 100 and 130 pounds.

Economic differences, cultural, religious, and ethnic factors could be accounted for and ruled out in the analysis of the results. Figure 9,

---

Figure 9

In a study done in West Bengal by the author, the voluntary food intake of 300 workers was studied. Note that the lowest voluntary food intake is seen in workers who engage in light regular activity. Sedentary workers eat more and are much fatter. Workers performing heavy work eat more but their weight is still light.

which summarizes the experiment, shows that the curves obtained for the food intake and the body weight of our working men are very similar to the curves obtained for the "sedentary" range and the range of "normal activity" in the rats. Again there was a sedentary range which corresponded to no further decrease in food intake (in fact, to an increase), where increasing degrees of overweight followed decreasing exercise. Incidentally, the physiological cause of the actual increase in food intake seen in men and in the various kinds of animals in which the phenomenon has been studied, is not understood. It may indicate decreased availability of body reserves, possibly as a result of the circulatory sluggishness due to lack of body motion, or, as some recent results suggest, hormonal changes due to inactivity. Whatever the reason, the finding in the Indian study shows that in men as in rats, the subjects with regular moderate activity ate somewhat less (and were considerably thinner) than the inactive subjects.

This finding, as it happens, fits into the secular lore of farmers and breeders. Readers who are familiar with the conditioning of race horses and boxers know that exercise, as much as or more than rationing, is relied upon to avoid overweight. By contrast, an old and universal practice in fattening young hogs, geese, or steers consists in restricting their activity by cooping them up in pens or tethering them. Whatever misguided downgraders of the value of exercise in a weight-reduction program may preach, farmers all over the world agree that the first step in the production of lard or of paté de foie gras is to prevent the producing animals from increasing their energy output by unhampered wandering.

The role of decreased activity seems of particular importance, as I shall point out later, in childhood obesity. Numerous articles and books have been written on why obese children eat more than nonobese—as an escape from tensions at home, as a substitute for the affection of one parent or of both, as a result of parental neglect or oversolicitousness, because of desire for importance, or as a compensation for excessive shyness. Although a few psychiatrists, such as Hilde Bruch, have observed that obese children are often inactive, it is only recently that the basic assumption has really been questioned. Do obese children really overeat or do they get their surplus calories from underexercising?

The studies I conducted with Mary Louise Johnson, using as subjects high-school girls from Newton and Brookline, Massachusetts, as far back as 1953 suggested that relative inactivity was a more important factor than relative overeating in the development of obesity in most youngsters. A very careful examination of the dietary intake of equal groups of overweight and normal-weight girls, matched for age and height, showed that the obese students fell into two groups. One, by far the larger, consisted of girls who ate a little less than the normal-weight girls, but exercised considerably less. All the "sitting" activities were emphasized at the expense of walking and active sports. Watching television consumed four times as many hours in this group as it did in the normal-weight group. There was also a small group of active obese girls, who ate more than, and exercised as much as, the normal. This latter group, incidentally, was of the red-cheeked, cheerful variety. Dr. Johnson found that this group appeared more muscular, so that, while "overweight," they were probably less "overfat" than the inactive group.

A recent study which I conducted (described in more detail in the chapter about adolescents) demonstrated that during the periods which are characterized by the obese youngsters as "exercise," they do in fact spend far less time in motion than nonobese youngsters of the same age and social background. Motion pictures of obese and nonobese children swimming or playing volley ball or tennis revealed that the obese were in motion only a fraction of the time during which the nonobese moved. Even when the actual amount of calories expended by both groups is calculated, taking into account the larger mass of the obese, these youngsters were still using up less energy than the nonobese.

A similar study with obese and nonobese boys yielded similar results. Conversely, increasing the physical activity of obese youngsters does not increase their food intake to the same extent as it does in nonobese children and adolescents. When the food intake of obese boys and of nonobese boys matched for age, height, and socio-economic background was determined before and after joining a summer camp where a higher level of physical activity was enforced, it was found that the food intake of the nonobese boys increased considerably more than that of the obese boys, who lost weight (or at least lost fat, as measured by skinfold thickness), while the nonobese gained during the summer.

The association between moderate appetite, inactivity, and fatness may start early in life. In a study on babies completed in 1967, Dr. Hedwig Rose and I studied the food intake, the physical activity (through the use of tiny pedometers strapped to the limbs), and the fatness of infants from four to six months old. We found no correlation between fatness and food intake, none between growth and intake, but a very marked correlation between physical activity and intake. Fat babies had small to moderate intakes but were very inactive. Very thin babies were very active and a number of them (often quite linear in shape) had large food intakes. Perpetuation of inactivity may well mean perpetuation of a physique fatter than average and, in many cases, obesity.

All these findings inevitably bring us to the conclusion that, with respect to physical activity, obesity is in many instances clearly "a disease of civilization." Mechanization and the development of modern means of transportation combine to decrease physical exercise. For many individuals, physical activity is depressed to such an extent that the sedentary state is reached, and excessive calories accordingly accumulate fat.

We eat less, probably, than our grandfathers did. The sight of an old-time wedding menu is enough to demonstrate this point. But, in order to get to the wedding, grandpa had to walk or ride horseback for long distances even in the dead of winter. Old-fashioned dancing, too, was generally more strenuous than the modern variety. By the time our grandparents were home, they had expended a large part of the surplus calories they had accumulated.

On a primitive farm, both the husband and the wife worked in the fields, plowing, hoeing, harvesting. The use of oxen for many of the farming operations imposed a slow rhythm on the farmer. As better plows and other improved implements became available and as tractors were introduced, the productivity of the farmer soared. Today he no longer requires the help of his wife for the heavy work of the fields; she has become a housewife, with perhaps only the relatively minor chores of a vegetable garden or the milking of cows and the care of rabbits or chickens. Meanwhile, the physical expenditure of the farmer has hardly decreased; the new implements are heavy and continue to involve a lot of vigorous manual activity; driving a big tractor requires considerable muscular effort, and gone are the pauses at the end of the furrow. Now the farmer's work is only slightly less arduous and it is much more continuous. It is only when the degree of farm mechanization symbolized by, say, milking machines is reached that the energy expenditure of the farmer really drops. Meanwhile, if the appetite of the farm woman has declined too slowly, either because her activity has dropped into the nonresponsive sedentary zone or because customs and the necessity of still providing big meals for her men-folk have influenced her unduly, she has become fat.

It is always a dangerous operation to tell modern suburbanized or urbanized women, young mothers or career girls, that in the physiologic sense of the term they don't perform a great deal of work. It is prudent to add quickly that what is meant is that hard physical work and tiring activity are not necessarily synonymous. Most of the occupations of the modern "active" woman may be tiring, but they don't involve a great deal of pushing, or of carrying considerable loads for long distances, or of picking up heavy objects several times a minute. Ironing and climbing stairs are perhaps typical of today's common heavier expenditures. These involve, respectively, elevating repeatedly a ten-pound object, and elevating continuously (for a short period) the weight of the body. Although the care of several small children, or driving downtown, or the strain of working for an exacting executive may be nerve-racking, it still does not compare with a day spent hoeing potatoes, as far as calories expended are concerned.

The result of all this is that, by and large, overestimates of the energy needs of women have traditionally been tremendous. In addition, caloric requirements of women were overestimated because they were not *measured on* women, but *calculated for* women. Several recent surveys in England, in Scotland, and in the American Middle West, in which the caloric intake of normal-weight housewives and career women was determined, have shown that these women consumed only 1,500 to 1,900 calories, instead of the 2,000 to 2,200 calories which had been postulated for them. In our experience in Boston, most of the women who ate what past textbooks and official tables prescribed for either sedentary or light activity were overweight women who were getting rapidly more obese. Any woman who was conscientious enough to eat what used to be widely represented by nutritionists to be the ideal diet for the modern American woman would quickly find herself in the obese category.

There is one serious situation, as a matter of fact, where this dilemma still often arises; it is during pregnancy. To the normal diet, already overestimated calorically, are added, at least for the second half of the pregnancy, 300 or 400 calories for the growth of the baby. No second thought is given to the fact that, in Western societies at any rate, the mother's physical activity is so far decreased during the latter period by rests and the slowness of her movements as to have already compensated, in large part, for her increased requirement.

The poor girl is nevertheless often given a model diet, rich in milk, meat, eggs, butter, and warned of the terrible consequences of skimpy intakes for herself and for her child. Further, she is weighed twice a month and threatened with even more terrible consequences, again for herself and for her child, if she puts on too much weight. In all this, the caloric intake of women is badly estimated, again fundamentally because of deficient appreciation for the influence of exercise.

For all this, in our society the woman is physically more active than her husband: she does housework, walks with the children, pushes little carts in supermarkets, window shops. Her husband, on the other hand, the modern American man, is incredibly inactive. He gets up, and, after briefly standing in front of his mirror using his electric toothbrush and his electric razor, sits down at the breakfast table, goes on to sit in his car, in his office, at coffee break, at lunch, in his office, in his car, at dinner, and in front of the television set; and, after lying in a warm bath for a while, goes on to lie in bed. Should he (or his wife) be briefly disturbed during the evening meal or when he is already in bed by the ring of the telephone, extensions have been placed in his house to prevent his having to stir himself. (The claims of the American Telephone and Telegraph Company that an extension cord avoids walking 70 miles a year means, by the same token, that the 150-pound person will not expend another 5,000 calories a year—the equivalent of 15 pounds of fat in ten years.) It is amusing, in view of this, that few men consider themselves truly sedentary. They feel—and are—busy and, through the same confusion between work and physical exercise noted in the case of their wives, consider themselves "moderately active." If they played a lot of games when they were young and were on the golf course last week, particularly if they did not use a golf-mobile, they feel that they are physically

Table 4 Energy Equivalents of Food Calories Expressed in Minutes of Activity*

Food	Calories	Walking[1]	Riding bicycle[2]	Swimming[3]	Running[4]	Reclining[5]
Apple, large	101	19	12	9	5	78
Bacon, 2 strips	96	18	12	9	5	74
Banana, small	88	17	11	8	4	68
Beans, green, 1 c.	27	5	3	2	1	21
Beer, 1 glass	114	22	14	10	6	88
Bread and butter	78	15	10	7	4	60
Cake, 2-layer, 1/12	356	68	43	32	18	274
Carbonated beverage, 1 glass	106	20	13	9	5	82
Carrot, raw	42	8	5	4	2	32
Cereal, dry, 1/2 c. with milk, sugar	200	38	24	18	10	154
Cheese, cottage, 1 tbsp.	27	5	3	2	1	21
Cheese, Cheddar, 1 oz.	111	21	14	10	6	85
Chicken, fried, 1/2 breast	232	45	28	21	12	178
Chicken, TV dinner	542	104	66	48	28	417
Cookie, plain	15	3	2	1	1	12
Cookie, chocolate chip	51	10	6	5	3	39
Doughnut	151	29	18	13	8	116
Egg, fried	110	21	13	10	6	85
Egg, boiled	77	15	9	7	4	59
French dressing, 1 tbsp.	59	11	7	5	3	45
Halibut steak, 1/4 lb.	205	39	25	18	11	158
Ham, 2 slices	167	32	20	15	9	128
Ice cream, 1/6 qt.	193	37	24	17	10	148
Ice cream soda	255	49	31	23	13	196
Ice milk, 1/6 qt.	144	28	18	13	7	111
Gelatin, with cream	117	23	14	10	6	90
Malted milk shake	502	97	61	45	26	386
Mayonnaise, 1 tbsp.	92	18	11	8	5	71
Milk, 1 glass	166	32	20	15	9	128
Milk, skim, 1 glass	81	16	10	7	4	62
Milk shake	421	81	51	38	22	324
Orange, medium	68	13	8	6	4	52
Orange juice, 1 glass	120	23	15	11	6	92
Pancake with syrup	124	24	15	11	6	95

Table 4   (cont.)

| | | Minutes of Activity | | | | |
Food	Calories	Walking[1]	Riding bicycle[2]	Swim-ming[3]	Running[4]	Reclining[5]
Peach, medium	46	9	6	4	2	35
Peas, green, 1/2 c.	56	11	7	5	3	43
Pie, apple, 1/6	377	73	46	34	19	290
Pie, raisin, 1/6	437	84	53	39	23	336
Pizza, cheese, 1/8	180	35	22	16	9	138
Pork chop, loin	314	60	38	28	16	242
Potato chips, 1 serving	108	21	13	10	6	83
Sandwiches:						
Club	590	113	72	53	30	454
Hamburger	350	67	43	31	18	269
Roast beef with gravy	430	83	52	38	22	331
Tuna fish salad	278	53	34	25	14	214
Sherbet, 1/6 qt.	177	34	22	16	9	136
Shrimp, French fried	180	35	22	16	9	138
Spaghetti, 1 serving	396	76	48	35	20	305
Steak, T-bone	235	45	29	21	12	181
Strawberry shortcake	400	77	49	36	21	308

[1] Energy cost of walking for 150-lb. individual = 5.2 calories per minute at 3.5 m.p.h.
[2] Energy cost of riding bicycle = 8.2 calories per minute.
[3] Energy cost of swimming = 11.2 calories per minute.
[4] Energy cost of running = 19.4 calories per minute.
[5] Energy cost of reclining = 1.3 calories per minute.

* From: Konishi, F. "Food energy equivalents of various activities," *J. Amer. Dietetic Assoc.*, 46 (1965), 186. Used by permission.

active. (A man who exercises an hour every day is an "exercise nut.") When I studied the schedule of Swiss mountain farmers to see if constant exercise permitted persons on a high milk fat diet to keep a low cholesterol (it did), I realized that, in our society, we have forgotten what really hard physical labor is.

In fact, I am more and more convinced that men are victimized by their complete lack of awareness of the increasingly sedentary quality of contemporary living in the Western world. Passmore, an excellent British physiologist, has declared: "It is not generally realized how sedentary is the life led by most urban people. Even young military cadets spend 17¾ hours a day either lying, sitting, or standing; the corresponding figure for coal miners is 18¾ hours a day and for colliery clerks, 20 hours a day. Military cadets and miners have two of the most physically active occupations, and yet about three-quarters of their life is sedentary. The daily physical activity of many thousands of light work ers may be below the threshold needed for appetite to function normally For this reason they may overeat and become obese."

We twentieth-century human beings—and nature will not permit us to forget it—are the sons and daughters of the cave man. For hundreds of thousands of years, natural selection succeeded in producing a group of tough, resourceful mammalians, who could roam the vast, empty stretches of wilderness, spend days pursuing herds of game, migrate from Central Asia to the shores of the Atlantic, cross deserts and climb moun tains in search of a better environment, run for their lives before their enemies, and remain on the go all day—sometimes all night as well.

We, their children, modern Westerners, sleep all night in comfortable beds, ride to work, sit all day in front of our desks, or stand before our work benches. We ride back home, sit before the dinner table, sit to read our papers and magazines, sit at a motion picture or in front of our television set—and so to bed. We are using our bodies and their mar-velous regulatory mechanisms in a way for which they were never de-signed. Small wonder that, living thus on the fat of the land, so many of us become fat. The wonder is that, for many others, appetite does adjust to this extraordinary set of circumstances.

I am convinced that inactivity is the most important factor explain-ing the frequency of "creeping" overweight in modern societies. Our bodies' regulation of food intake was just not designed for the highly mechanized sedentary conditions of modern life. This appears to be par-ticularly true for individuals with large mesomorphic and endomorphic components in their physique, as noted earlier in Chapter 2. Adapting to these conditions without developing obesity means either that the in-dividual will have to step up his activity or that he will be mildly or acutely hungry all his life. The first solution is difficult, especially as present conditions in the United States—particularly in cities—offer little inducement to walking and often only poorly organized facilities for adult exercise. Even among the young, highly competitive sports for the few are emphasized at the expense of individual sports which all could learn and continue to enjoy after the high school and college years are over. But, if stepping up activity is difficult, it is well to remem-ber that the alternative (lifetime hunger) is so much more difficult that relying on it exclusively for weight-control programs will only continue to lead to the fiascoes of the past. Strenuous exercise on an irregular basis is obviously not advocated for untrained obese persons. However, a reorganization of one's life to include regular exercise adapted to one's physical potentialities is a justified return to the wisdom of the ages.

In many ways what is happening to our bodies might be a warning of what our civilization may do to us generally. Our mode of life is chang-ing in ways which very often we do not really want, but into which we are pushed by our technology. We adapt to this new life in the sense that we continue to produce children and contribute to the Gross National Product, but very often this adaptation is obtained at the cost of certain elements of happiness. We sacrifice fitness, looks, and often our health to the "need" for automobiles, and the beauty of our landscapes to roads and pollution, again for the sake of quicker transportation or mass availability of cheap goods. As a society, we have been generally blind to the long-term cost of progress, when the exercise of some foresight would have given us its advantages without its cost. This is a theme to which we shall return, as I believe that it needs to be emphasized over and over again if we are to avoid the mistakes of the past. Suffice it to conclude here that the development of obesity (and of heart disease as well as a number of other pathologic conditions) is to a large extent the result of the lack of foresight of a civilization which spends tens of billions annually on cars, but is unwilling to include a swimming pool and tennis courts in the plans of every high school.

chapter 6
Social Attitudes
and the Obese

Wherever fat people have existed and whenever a literature has reflected aspects of the lives and values of the period, a record has been left of the low regard usually held for the obese by the thinner and clearly more virtuous observer.

Saint Jerome contended that "a fat paunch never breeds fine thoughts." Chesterfield declared that "obesity and stupidity are such companions that they are considered synonymous." In one of his journals Arnold Bennet referred to an acquaintance, Jimmy Glover, as a "fat man." It was as if he, having said that, need say no more.

There is a most respectable precedent for the terseness of Bennet's comment. The Old Testament (Judges 4:17) informs us that "Eglon, King of Moab, was a very fat man." It is as if the peculiar and unattractive qualities of fat people legitimize their employment as scapegoats, as licensed figures of fun, and as fit objects of contempt, abuse, and moral instruction.

Back in the days of the two-line joke, audiences were permitted to be delighted by such wheezes as these: "You should be ashamed, laughing at that fat man." "I'm just having fun at his expanse." or "Why is it you fat fellows are always good-natured?" "Because we can't either fight or run." A very thin man met a very fat man in a hotel lobby. "From the looks of you," said the fat man, "there might have been a famine." "From the looks of you," replied the thin man, "you might have caused it." Obesity has been laboriously defined as a "surplus gone to waist." And we've been told of the woman who was so fat that when she fell down, she rocked herself to sleep trying to get up.

There has always been something so fascinating about the mere fact of fatness that men of all nations and of many degrees of wisdom or lack of it have formulated opinions ·on the state, its origins, and its correction. Shakespeare's characters are at their most eloquent when the topic is obesity. "Make less thy body hence and more thy grace. Leave gormandizing. Know the grave doth gape for thee thrice wider than for other men." And, of course, to Julius Caesar, the Bard attributed the notion of the harmlessness of fat companions in warning against "the lean and hungry look" of "Yon Cassius."

In *Coming Up for Air*, George Orwell has the narrator, himself a fat man, sum it up: "They all think a fat man doesn't have any feelings. A man who's been fat from birth isn't quite like other men. He goes through life on a light-comedy plane . . . as low farce." Sometimes the situation is just as sad and much less tolerable. When W. D. Howells was consul at Venice, he was told by a tall lanky man, "If I were as fat as you, I would hang myself." And Osborn in his otherwise lightly satirical picture-essay, *The Vulgarians*, pontificates, "The fat and the fatuous are interchangeable."

There are, most certainly, rationalizations galore to supply seeming justification for the frequent rudeness and the occasional brutality which fat people encounter in person and in print. Obesity, as we have already noted, is usually taken to be a self-induced condition which can be easily remedied by a modest exercise of will. It is attributed to one of the easiest forms of self-indulgence in a prosperous culture. Further, overeating where food is in abundance requires neither courage nor skill, neither learning nor guile. Gluttony demands less energy than lust, less industry than avarice. The fat human being, accordingly, is taken to be both physically and morally absurd, and to constitute a living testimony to the reality and the vapidity of his sins.

In his first popular success, *The Bridge of San Luis Rey*, Thornton Wilder says this of the obese Archbishop of Lima: "Some days he regarded his bulk ruefully; but the distress of remorse was less poignant than the distress of fasting, and he was presently found deliberating over the secret messages that a certain roast sends to a certain salad that will follow it."

Occasionally an author permits himself to be distressed at the presence of obesity and to be kindly toward its victims, to the degree of suggesting that they have little choice. Giuseppe di Lampedusa in *The Leopard* has Prince Fabrizio express his distaste for the plump young ladies of Palermo: "Incredibly short, improbably dark, unbearably giggly." He charges their condition to, among other factors, the dearth of proteins and the overabundance of starch in their food. But William Barrett, writing in *Partisan Review* of American tourists in Europe, labels them: "Eaters of soft white doughy bread, ice cream, pie and doughnuts." And Maugham reminds us: "Tolstoi made the plump Pierre Bezukjov in *War and Peace* a moral weakling."

One Michael Argyle, described as a lecturer in social psychology, informed an Oxford audience a few years ago (and the *New York Times* duly reported it) that "thin people have higher moral standards than fat people." (*New York Times*, August 2, 1961) Graham Greene, in describing the glib journalist Parkinson in the novel, *The Burned-out Case* said, "Virtue had died long ago within that mountain of flesh for lack of air."

Alberto Moravia went so far as to give one of his stories the title "Appetite." In it, Faustina denounces Carlo, who weighs 210 pounds, "I'm angry at you for what you are—a great fat glutton." And in *Lord of the Flies,* a book which threatened for a while to be confused with revelation, the character Piggy loomed as a flabby symbol of moral debility and ethical ineffectiveness.

All this business of devouring more food than one needs takes place and is noted in a world where for most of mankind getting enough food has always been and continues to be the difficult, even the impossible thing. On successive days in 1962, two significant stories were in the news. From Jakarta it was said that residents, described as foreigners and wealthy Indonesians, were driving 72 miles to get a loaf of bread at almost 50 cents. Then from Erzerum came word of

> a small bowl containing a little flour meal and a lot of boiled water. Its contents will serve as breakfast, lunch and dinner for several of the victims of the severe famine that grips Turkey's eastern provinces. (*New York Times,* January 19, 1962; January 20, 1962)

All wealth has been impolitely defined as theft. Is it possible that among those who are openly hostile to fat people there are some who equate the overnourishment of one particular individual with the undernourishment, even the starvation of another?

Is there a case for such a contention, or is a cause-and-effect relationship completely absent? It would be well for the obese to know. In January of 1966 Dr. Albert Szent-Gyorgyi, Nobel Laureate in Physiology and Medicine, predicted that if the world's present rate of population growth continues, "human beings ultimately will have to kill and eat one another." It is not difficult to guess which group, the obese or the nonobese, would be likely to be the first candidates for the kitchens. In any event, fat people are fortunate that their enemies in civilized countries usually employ against them only the weapon of verbal aggression. For in certain institutions built around the command-obedience syndrome fat people have often had a painful time.

A Providence, Rhode Island judge (July 27, 1953) once ordered a woman to reduce from 225 pounds to 190 in ten weeks. A Cincinnati patrolman was fired (*New York Herald Tribune,* January 12, 1960) because he had gained 13 pounds. A Connecticut State Police commissioner embarked on a program intended to "trim his troopers." They were warned if they wanted promotions they'd better start tightening their belts. (*Boston Globe,* July 16, 1959) Much attention (*Boston Globe,* February 9, 1963) was given to the plight of an airman first class. He was five feet nine, and weighed 225 pounds, an amount held by his superiors to be 37 pounds too much. It was said that he was told to "reduce or be discharged without pension rights." In the *Saturday Evening Post* (September 25, 1965) James Phelan stated, "There are no fat FBI agents." About eight years before, all agents had been instructed to bring themselves within the limits set by an insurance chart. And from Denmark there came in September 1965 (*Boston Globe,* September 19, 1965) a new political group, the "Reform Party," which included in its program a plan to tax fat people. "For every two pounds of overweight, citizens would hand over one hour's pay every month."

Fat people do reduce. At least, some of them do. Some of these even remain reduced. When a newsmaking person embarks on or completes a weight-losing program, either the man himself or the press gives us the word. Alfred Hitchcock (*Saturday Evening Post,* August 1957) revealed that when younger he'd weighed 365 pounds, but he'd brought his weight down to 200 by eating only steak and cutting out liquor. The *New York Times* disclosed that rigid dieting had lowered the weight of Maria Callas from 215 to 135 (October 30, 1956). The *Herald Tribune* (August 25, 1958) announced that Jackie Gleason had cut down from 280 to 220. From the *Boston Globe* we learned (November 5, 1961) that Bernard Goldfine had lost 40 pounds after six months in jail. Walter Winchell (December 19, 1957) proclaimed that "Count Basie took off 50 pounds 'Off liquor, on steaks' " and that Joe Louis shed 45 pounds on the same regimen. Leonard Lyons was our source of information (*Boston Herald,* January 11, 1961) that the then Vice-President Lyndon Baines Johnson had "dieted away 31 pounds" in less than ten weeks since being elected to that post. Clearly the press believes the reducing prowess of the notable to be a matter of public interest.

The potential for this interest must have existed for a long time. And it extended to the eating habits of the celebrated, their attitudes toward their own obesity and to that of others, and their programs, if any, for defeating it. For much information of this character is available to us.

We're told that Abbot Mendel was too fat to travel comfortably, that Gibbon was so obese he could not rise, that Emperor Charles V of the Holy Roman Empire ate himself to death. Frank Harris, who had so much to say about his own behavior, said also this: "I've bought myself a stomach pump and one half hour after dinner I pump myself out." Accounts have reached us of the extreme obesity of Swift, Gautier, Balzac, Dryden (Swift's cousin), and Boccaccio, and of Lord Byron's invention of a reducing diet . . . cold boiled potatoes and wine. Axel Munthe, however, happily recalled that Maupassant "did not fancy thin women and that his Yvonne drank bottles of cod liver oil by the dozen in an unsuccessful effort to get fat."

A. T. Banker tells us that Dylan Thomas said of himself, "I am fat and slothful." O. Henry sounds almost personal in his "The Skylight Room" when he writes of "the tragedy of tallow, the bane of bulk, the calamity of corpulence." Samuel Chotzinoff has said (*Holiday,* June 1963) that Gian-Carlo Menotti "shuns fat people like the plague." And Norman

Douglas cautioned, "Beware of the fat Neapolitan." Back in the 1920's there was an American popular song called "O Katerina" one of the lines of which maintained that "to win my love you must be leaner." It is rare that a writer of fiction thinks of a fat person as conceivably lovable. In *Some Came Running* James Jones has his hero Dave Hirsch say to Gwen French, "Is the truth, the reason you won't go out with me, won't have an affair with me, is it because I'm fat?" In his earlier novel, *From Here to Eternity,* Jones devised a character of pathologic brutality, whose associates gave him a nickname that he deeply hated, "Fatso." In *Summertime Ends* a half-tract, half-novel, its author John Hargrave tells of "Trimnal the parson, a tub of lard." In a James Michener story, a character states that "the warden was fat, cowardly." And John Osborne's self-pitying Jimmy Porter in *Look Back in Anger* declaims "I'm not a pig. I just like food. That's all."

Whole novels have been written on one or another aspect of getting fat, being fat, or attempting to become less fat. Gerda Rhoads (Ballantine, 1957) wrote one called *The Lonely Women,* held to be "a frank and biting novel about the slimming industry." Another novel, *The Man Who Ate the World* (Ballantine, 1960), by Frederick Pohl dealt with Sonnie Trumie, a compulsive eater who "ate until eating was pain and then he sat there sobbing until he could eat no more." James M. Cain in *The Butterfly* wrote largely about a woman's heroic efforts to reduce. And back in 1922 Henri Beraud won the Prix Goncourt with his *The Martyrdom of the Obese.*

The obese, let it be noted, are not completely without friends. The *New York Times* (December 9, 1962) in its 1962 appeal for help for the "One Hundred Neediest Cases" included two fat girls. Case 2 was Etta, nine years old and "seriously overweight—may require extensive therapy, since doctors can find no physical cause for her obesity." Case 8 was Fanny. She was "fifteen, weighs 180 pounds and is so ridiculed by her schoolmates she often refuses to go to school." Aldous Huxley (*Ends and Means*) asserts that "people have a right to be plump." The 230-pound president of the Club Sympathique des Femmes Fortes (*Boston Traveler,* March 14, 1957) exulted, "The fat woman is a Rubens who doesn't know it." Edward Weeks (*Atlantic Monthly,* October 1965) confided: "There is something about a fat man that invites confidence." And the New York columnist Jimmy Breslin (*Boston Globe,* September 24, 1963) found in Queens (or in his heart) a six-foot-five saloon-keeper named Gibby. Gibby, Breslin alleged, weighed 611½ pounds and his wife, Eileen, was said to insist there were "acres and acres of him and they're all mine."

These are a few shining exceptions in a world that looks at fat people and likes them not and sometimes seems to wish them ill. Even those servants moving toward mastery, the machines, may have received and welcomed the message. For the *New York Times* of January 26, 1962 had an ominous Associated Press account from London. In busy Victoria Station there was an "I-speak-your-weight machine." "One night recently . . . an unusually obese man stepped on the scales." The machine's voice reported the man's weight as 18-stone-7 (259 pounds). And then, "it went on chanting '18-stone-7, 18-stone-7, 18-stone-7' for the next ten minutes until a repair man finally muzzled it."

The anthropologist, Dr. Ashley Montagu, supplies an explanation for the occurrence of instances of public approval of obesity. "Obesity in some cultures," he says, "constitutes a validation of both success of the male and of his obese female. In some African, Polynesian and Middle Eastern cultures, women and sometimes men (particularly those of high caste) were especially fattened as a form of both conspicuous consumption and social desirability." Montagu continues,

> . . . being well-padded came to stand not only for affluence but also for the ability to survive. Thus, to this day in regions where food is abundant, many mothers in the Western world do not consider that their young children are prospering unless they approximate a globe. Such a globular view of the ability to survive probably harks back to the time when food was less abundant and the focus of attention was on keeping children adequately nourished.

The time "when food was less abundant" for millions of people in the United States was not so long ago. In his book, *Eat, Drink, and Be Wary*, published in 1935, I. G. Schlink declared that "only about 10 per cent of the population received an income which permits them to eat good, well-selected foods in adequate amounts." A year later Paul de Kruif, in *Why Keep Them Alive*, stated, "Malnourished wretchedness among children is widespread, notorious, too terrible for any luckier, well-fed human being to face and go on living." In the *Atlantic Monthly* of January 1937, Maxine Davis in an article called "Hungry Children" wrote that the Children's Bureau, examining households in Atlanta, Memphis, Racine, Terre Haute, . . . found "one-fifth of the families' diet consisted of bread, beans, and potatoes." And David Shannon in his *The Great Depression* refers to a speech made by Congressman George Huddleston of Alabama on January 5, 1932 before a subcommittee on manufacturing, in which the Representative insisted that "men are actually starving by the thousands today, children are being stunted by lack of food, old people are having their lives cut short." It is surely not strange that attitudes formed during days when starvation was for some a fact and for others a threat should lead many in the abundant today to eat too much, and many to become obese.

It is useful to remember that these days are not altogether over, even in overfed, prosperous America. In 1967 we still have some ill-fed and actually underfed groups in the United States: Negro cotton farm workers displaced by mechanization of cotton-picking and replacement of cotton by corn crops in Alabama and Mississippi; migrant farm workers—on the Eastern stream, mostly Negroes, and on the West Coast stream, mostly Mexicans; Indian denizens of certain reservations; groups of Alaskan Eskimos and Indians; and some of the poorest inhabitants of our big-city slums.

That social attitudes may in turn affect the prevalence of obesity in a particular community is strongly indicated by some of the results of the Midtown Manhattan Study. This study was originally designed to be a comprehensive survey of the epidemiology of mental illness. One hundred and ten thousand individuals—all the adults between 20 and 59 years of age who occupied a certain residential area in New York City—were the group investigated. A major focus of the survey was the relationship between social class and mental illness, and an important discovery was the striking relationship between socio-economic status and obesity. Moore, Stunkard, and Srole examined the correlation between weight-to-height relationship and socio-economic status and found that it was high, particularly in women. The prevalence of obesity was seven times higher among women reared in the lowest social-class category as compared with those raised in the highest category.

This finding was later independently confirmed by Ernest Abramson who stated, "In an investigation of body weight in Swedish women, we found that women from the highest income group did not increase in weight after the age of 35, while women from lower income groups increased in weight up to over 60 years of age."

Moore, Stunkard, and Srole were understandably elated over the finding in regard to the class-conditioned character of obesity presented by the Midtown Manhattan Study data. It, they believe,

> has profound implications for theory and therapy. For it means that whatever its genetic and biochemical determinants, obesity in man is susceptible to an extraordinary degree of control by social factors. It suggests that a broad-scale assault on the problem need not await further understanding of the physiological determinants of obesity.

What they look to is "a program of education and control designed to reproduce certain critical influences to which society has already exposed its upper-class members."

I must confess to being a little less sanguine than my Philadelphia friends. For one thing, I am not as sure of the interpretation of their study as they are. This is in part because my own results, among an admittedly much smaller group of adolescents, in a more homogeneous community (Newton, Massachusetts), did not show much correlation between obesity and social class (in spite of their demonstrating once again the familial character of obesity). This may mean—and the Swedish results tend to suggest it—that social pressures are most useful as regards the control of "creeping" middle-age obesity in hitherto nonobese subjects, while they exert little influence on obesity among the young.

Another variable may be that in New York the different ethnic groups are characterized at the same time by different tendencies to obesity and by different socio-economic background. Few people would deny that white Protestants in New York City belong to a higher social class on the average than the Puerto Ricans. Their body types are anthropologically different and it is not unreasonable to think that there may be differences in susceptibility to obesity. Within the white group, Anglo-Saxon Episcopalians are at the same time richer and more ectomorphic than Germanic Lutherans, and hence a comparison between two subgroups does—in part for genetic reasons—appear to confirm the primacy of the environment.

Finally, my study showing a strong bias in college admissions against obese boys and even more against obese girls makes me wonder whether a cause-and-effect-relationship is not also involved: to stay with the ladies (who show by far the strongest correlation between overweight and social class in the Manhattan study), an obese girl has only one-third as much chance to get into a "prestige" college, the college of her choice, or indeed any college, as a nonobese girl. She is thus likely to go down in socio-economic status. Decreased likelihood of advancing socially through marriage is also an obvious penalty which the obese girl—the ugly duckling of our age—has to pay. She may thus be lower-class because she is obese, as much as or rather than, be obese because she is lower-class.

This is not to say that I would not welcome a large-scale program based on education, on the creation of recreational facilities, and on the recognition of existing social pressures to try to control our mounting prevalence of obesity. Understanding of existing attitudes is essential if such a mass program is to succeed. (We shall see that it is equally essential if one is going to deal intelligently with a single individual.) People who are not fat have attitudes, mostly hostile, toward those who are. People who are fat have attitudes, mostly self-deprecatory, toward themselves. And when an entire segment of society—the most prosperous citizens, in this instance, of a large urban community—give obesity a strong negative value, its members, within the limits of their genetic possibilities and latitude of choosing their mode of life, control their obesity better than people who despise it less.

chapter 7
The Psychology of Obesity

Millions of Americans become fat, and to their great disadvantage remain fat. Most extremely fat people live less zestfully than their less corpulent cousins, are ill more frequently and more seriously, and die much earlier. Not only are their lives less fulfilling than they well might be in both quality and length, but for all their days they are scolded, heckled, and blamed for their condition. All this does occur with a surface plausibility. For was not their fat and are not its consequences self-inflicted? Why did they let themselves become fat in the first place and then compound the error by staying that way?

The obese individual is usually as curious about the answers to these questions as is his smug contemner. For rarely is he pleased with his condition or with its by-products and their apparent implication of moral weakness and lack of general worth. Has he not tried again and again to rid himself of his grotesque burden and failed again and again, if not to get his fat off, to keep it off?

For some of the obese, there is as I have emphasized earlier, the cold-comfort assurance that the load they carry is not of their own making. I have shown that genetic, traumatic, and environmental factors all could contribute in experimental animals to a positive energy balance leading to obesity. From the standpoint of mechanism, we have seen that these "guilt-free" obesities could be classified under two general headings: the *metabolic*, where a structural error in metabolism causes increased fat to be formed even when no overeating takes place; and the *regulatory*, where a lesion in the central nervous mechanism regulating food intake directly leads to overeating. Among examples of the latter type is conditioned obesity, which can be induced in experimental animals by punishing them unless they overeat. This particular situation may seem unlikely to have any parallel in human experience, unless we remind ourselves that there are at any given moment thousands of children busily earning their parents' approval by eating "everything that's put before them" even when it's both more than they need and more than they want.

We whose lives are devoted to the understanding of nutrition are not in a position at present to point to a strict correspondence between models studied in rats, mice, etc., and types of obesities in men, but we are in a position to assume that the diversity of origins of overeating and obesity found in animals is also present in man. However, because the central nervous system, the intellectual and emotional activities, and the socio-cultural environment are so much more complex in man than in lower animals, it is reasonable to assume that obesity rooted in psychology is much more widespread in the human species.

In fact, the latter assumption has received such overwhelming acceptance, both professional and lay, that it has tended to obscure the fact that there are probably a number of cases of obesity which are not due to psychological causes alone or at all. A striking example of such cases, the obesity due to inactivity, has been discussed in some detail earlier. While in some instances, inactivity may be due to psychological disturbances from the moderate to the acute, inactivity in general is the result of social and economic conditions which have eliminated the need for physical work, without creating the leisure, the means, or the incentive for voluntary physical exercise. And, in addition to emotionally rooted obesity, the fact of being obese, for whatever cause, particularly in a society such as ours which has been trained to view obesity as a sign of gluttony, self-indulgence, and lack of will-power, does in itself bring about important psychological consequences. What's more, cutting down food intake to bring about weight loss has also important psychological implications, both because of the resulting hunger and because of the weight loss itself. Failure to reduce, in spite of repeated—sometimes heroic—efforts, has also psychological connotations, not the least of which is injury to the failer's self-esteem.

Not enough is yet known of all the psychological aspects of obesity to permit unqualified statements about them to be made in such a manner as to provide universal application in the particular. Even a sympathetic and learned physician may be unable to analyze how a given patient became and continues to be obese. But enough information and insights are beginning to be available to make it possible for us to speak in the general direction of enlightenment on the psychological elements of reducing. For such comfort as it may provide, we can say with complete confidence to the fat man and woman whose obesity has considerable psychological involvement, "You are not alone," and add with only a trifle less assurance, "Help, to some degree at least, seems to be on the way."

One of the ablest psychiatrists in the field of obesity, Dr. Hilde Bruch, has classified possibilities of association of body weight and emotional adjustment in the following fashion:

(1) slenderness with good adjustment;
(2) slenderness with poor adjustment;

(3) continued obesity, usually of moderate degree, with good adjustment, and
(4) continued obesity with maladjustment.

In her thinking, type (3), continued obesity with good adjustment, represents a "constitutional" obesity compatible with an otherwise normal personality.

She assumes the obesity in this case to be due essentially to physiological factors. People of this type, who might be described as "naturally somewhat fat" are usually obese from childhood, and they remain obese as they mature. They get along all right with both their world and with themselves. Dr. Bruch feels that for them psychological difficulties related to their overweight are likely to arise or become serious only if pressure is put on them to reduce.

The situation is quite different in what Dr. Bruch terms "reactive obesity," where overeating is a response to and a compensation for tension and frustration. In many individuals, as Dr. Albert J. Stunkard, the excellent Philadelphia psychiatrist, has also emphasized, the situations leading to overeating also provoke a drastic decrease in activity. Both of these factors, of course, work together in causing markedly positive caloric balance: that is, the individuals consume more than they expend. Episodes of grief or of severe depression thus coincide with drastic increases of weight. Dr. Bruch considers this reactive obesity the characteristic form of psychological obesity in adulthood and middle age. She has observed but few instances of reactive obesity in childhood.

Among such potentially depressed reactive obese patients, Dr. Stunkard has emphasized the frequency of a distinctive eating pattern which he has called the "night-eating" syndrome. The existence of this pattern had been hinted at by a study which I conducted several years ago with Dr. Rachel Beaudoin. We had observed that an unselected group of obese women tended to distribute their calories so that they consumed more in proportion during the later hours of the day. Dr. Stunkard has shown that this effect was particularly marked in obesity associated with frequent bouts of depression. In many such patients the actual bulk of the daily calories may be consumed in the evening hours or at night. These periods are well known to be the periods of the day when depression is most severe.

Stunkard and H. B. Wolff have shown that, besides this characteristic eating pattern and the decreased activity during periods of intense depression, this type of obese patient exhibits in many instances drastic changes in carbohydrate metabolism which coincide with the episodes of drastic weight gain. It is thus possible that physiological changes in many of these patients mediate the psychological trauma which indirectly leads to overeating—from gloom, as it were, to gluttony. Interaction between psychological and endocrine factors may explain why certain patients will tend to accumulate considerable excess weight during a period of grief, while others faced with the same trauma may lose weight during that time.

"Developmental obesity" is described by Dr. Bruch as a common form of obesity during childhood. She feels that in many obese children in whom the obesity is not due to purely physiological factors, the emotional development centers around eating as much as they want, avoiding physical activity and social contacts, and being fat. Usually, such children are growing in a family setting in which they are used by one or the other parent (sometimes by both) as objects fulfilling their needs and compensating for failure and frustration in their own lives. The child is fussed over excessively, overprotected and overfed. Generally, the mother plays the dominant role in the emotional life of such families, indulges the obese child, and keeps him or her close to herself by constant and excessive demands. But sometimes it is the father who keeps a child too close or makes unrealistic demands on him. Ironically, as the child grows older, the obesity which results from parental pressures becomes an object of attack and condemnation from the parents who made it probable if not inevitable.

Overeating and obesity, either due to physiological lesions or to psychological factors of various types, have in themselves physiological and psychological consequences. I have shown that among the former are enlargement of certain organs such as the liver and the kidney, an increased rate of absorption of sugar from the inside of the intestine by the blood, and generally some degree of decrease in spontaneous activity, even in the case where inactivity was not a factor in the origin of the obesity.

The manner in which the psychological consequences manifest themselves depends on the cultural environment of the obese individuals. In certain societies and at certain periods in other societies, fat men and women have been described as jovial, cheerful, and easy-going. In this country there has been a tendency to refer to obese individuals as lethargic, lazy, and weak-willed, so that obesity becomes an object of ridicule and humiliation. Obese individuals not only feel excluded, but, in a number of social situations and job competitions are discriminated against. This hostile attitude is likely to have a profound influence on the obese person, particularly, as our studies of obese adolescent girls demonstrate, on the young. The fact that brothers and sisters, parents, teachers, physicians, all tend to reproach the obese child for his bulk and for his appetite may have a destructive effect on his personality. This constant reproaching often makes the obesity self-perpetuating: obese young people may be so embarrassed by the persons in their immediate environment that they become more and more withdrawn (witness the obese campers in Chapter 9), avoid sports and physical activities performed in public, and thus place themselves in the very conditions most likely to perpetuate a constant imbalance between food intake and energy expenditure.

There is an all-too-widespread belief that a patient will not suffer hunger while on a reducing diet. It is my contention, based on years of observation, that this belief is at the root of many failures in therapy. Actually, when an obese patient is placed on a reducing diet, we add, to the physiological or psychological difficulties he had to start with, the additional torment of being hungry a large fraction of the time. The findings of Ancel Keys and his co-workers previously referred to have illustrated the psychological reactions of normal-weight individuals placed on a prolonged negative caloric balance—that is, given less to eat than they are expected to expend in energy. Their volunteers in this enterprise became less and less interested in matters previously of some concern to them, such as the opposite sex. They became continuously preoccupied with food. In fact, in several cases the experiment had to be discontinued because of increasingly serious emotional disturbances.

Now, it is true that obese individuals do have large stores of fat which can be drawn on for nourishment during a reducing diet. This should and does decrease the physiological difficulties of losing weight. It must be pointed out, however, that certain types of animals with experimental obesities, the metabolic types, suffer protein loss as well as fat loss when fasted. Animals with these forms of obesity can be brought down to normal weight or even to underweight levels by prolonged undernutrition. Yet even at the resulting lower weight levels, they are obese in terms of composition; their normal or subnormal weight still contains a much larger proportion of fat than that of normal animals. It may well be that there is a substantial proportion of human subjects with metabolic obesity in whom the effect of underfeeding is similar. Dr. Ohlson and her co-workers in Iowa have shown that even when large amounts of protein are included in reducing diets, some subjects constantly consume part of their body protein. It is, therefore, not surprising that these individuals are among those who experience the greatest discomfort during reduction and most quickly regain the lost weight at the end of the experimental reduction period.

Even in those individuals for whom metabolic factors are not primary causes of obesity, burning of body fat does not fulfill satiety requirements to the same extent as food. This may explain why a few fat patients react to dieting as though they were starving. They show an acute craving for all sorts of food, even some which they do not usually like. They are constantly in a state of extreme tension, they feel dizzy and sleepless at night, and in some severe cases, they may show an almost complete disintegration of personality. A number of psychiatrists have warned against the danger of precipitating acute nervous disorders and even psychoses in emotionally unstable patients who are reduced too vigorously.

In a study at a New York hospital, Stunkard encountered unwelcome emotional reactions to a weight-reduction program among an alarming proportion, a full half, of a group of unselected obese female patients. In 25 patients who were studied in detail, nine cases of severe emotional disorders were connected with dieting. Stunkard found also that the incidence of severe illness was statistically higher during the period of reducing than in other periods in the patients' lives. Clearly the excessive food intake and underactivity may be a protective factor in the emotional health of such obese patients as these.

In another study—this at the general medical clinic of the Hospital of the University of Pennsylvania—Stunkard observed 17 obese and 18 nonobese women who were, after fasting, tested for the existence of hunger contractions. He discovered that the nonobese usually "reported hunger" during contractions of the empty stomach, while the obese usually "failed to report hunger" under the same circumstances. He suggests that the "denial of hunger occurs in persons with a conflict over eating who are simultaneously subjected to strong social pressures in this regard." The function of the act of denial, he believes, is to "exclude from awareness any stimuli that signal an approaching caloric deficit with its concomitant conflict over eating." Another student of emotions and their relation to the development and persistence of obesity, Stanley Shackter, has proposed that obesity may sometimes result "from a failure to differentiate between hunger feelings and feelings of anxiety created by emotional states." He also thinks it probable that this confusion "of emotion with hunger is most likely in the first-born." My own studies on a very large number of children fail incidentally to confirm that the rank order of birth is of particular significance.

The effect of weight reduction on mental health has been evaluated by Robert Olson and Marvin Plessett, then at Pittsburgh. They note that dieting has been thought by some to be "fraught with serious emotional consequences; e.g. conversion symptoms, depression, suicide, or psychosis." They quote Stunkard to the effect that "for a large number of overweight persons, the mechanical prescription of reducing diets has had unfortunate consequences, for a smaller number it has been disastrous." They note Hamburger's statement that overeating appears "to be a specific defense against depression" and Brosin's declaration that reducing regimens "are often accompanied by anxiety, depressive and other reactive states, sometimes with suicidal attempts."

At the same time Olson and Plessett call attention to the fact that not all investigators agree that dieting is responsible for severe emotional upsets. They mention a clinician's suspicion that the obese have "an automatic safety valve which causes them to abandon the diet before they get into serious trouble" and another's statement that "I think the incidence of depression in patients who are dieting is no greater than the incidence in the general population." Olson and Plessett assert that the obese tend more than the general population to be poor, single, divorced, separated or widowed, and suggest that the "advancing weight of the middle-aged sedentary person may present quite a different problem than the 'truly' obese." "The former," they say, "may lose more weight more easily and with less distress, since the overweight is less meaningful; i.e. less integrated and therefore less tenaciously held." They regard obesity as a "kind of steady state, albeit a pathologic one, at least from the point of view of general health and longevity," and see dieting as "an attack on this equilibrium which will be resisted unconsciously (and sometimes consciously) even in the presence of ego pressures for weight-reduction." Actually, this controversy cannot be resolved without statistical studies. In order to know whether dieting causes depression, one would need to define a yardstick of depression and study a sufficient number of obese who are dieting (with or without success) and obese who are not and see whether there is a difference between the groups and whether increased incidence of depression is more frequent as caloric restriction is more severe. In the absence of such data, many of the statements quoted above, like much of psychiatry, remain conjectural or, at best, anecdotal.

Living, as man keeps finding out and platitudinously announcing, is a difficult business for most people. For some people, such studies as the above strongly suggest becoming and remaining fat is a solution of sorts. To attempt with many such people to remove that solution in the interest of greater physical well-being is to leave them with the problems which, partially at least, brought about their obesity, or with the problems they have produced since becoming obese, and to add to either of these conditions, or both, new problems born of their efforts, in so many cases doomed to be unsuccessful, to reduce. The goal of any treatment is the improvement of the patient's condition, not the aggravation of it to the peril of his emotional health. And it must be recognized that the obese population of a nutrition outpatient department or of a psychotherapy clinic is probably not a cross section of the obese population at large. There are many individuals who, with such guidance as they obtain from a book like this, can successfully cope with their own weight problems without professional help. For others, treatment of obesity is more difficult, but still possible with the help of the physician, the dietitian, or the resources of a specialized clinic. But for still others, as I have here attempted to show, the consideration of weight reduction is a more delicate, even more desperate matter. These are the people who know themselves or are known by professionals to be more than a little emotionally disturbed, or to have been emotionally disturbed, or who find the prospect of attempting weight reduction emotionally threatening. Such people need and should have access to the counsel and guidance of a psychiatrist, a clinical psychologist, or a psychiatric social worker wise in the emotional characteristics and potentials of the obese. Dr. Bruch has warned against the encouragement of romantic notions about the likely by-products of a triumphant effort at weight reduction. "Even physicians," she insists, "will promise success and resolution of life's difficulties as reward for becoming slim." She emphasizes that losing weight is the single intelligible purpose of a reducing program and that great danger awaits the obese person who looks forward to slimness as if it were going to be a combination of Aladdin's Lamp, the Magic Carpet, and the Holy Grail.

chapter 8
Obesity
and Disease

Obesity has been associated with four different types of hazards to health: changes in various normal functions of the body; an increased risk of developing certain diseases; detrimental effects on established diseases; adverse psychological reactions. Each of the first three hazards will be discussed separately, because they differ in prevalence, in severity, and in the specificity of their relationship to obesity. The fourth, adverse psychological effects of obesity, has already been discussed at length in Chapters 6 and 7, and will also be discussed in Chapter 9. Cardiovascular diseases will be emphasized because, particularly in the United States, and increasingly in other "developed" countries, they have become the great pandemic of the twentieth century. We now have in America over a million cardiovascular deaths per year (of which 60 per cent are coronary deaths). The increase in cardiovascular mortality has held our life expectancy essentially at the 1950 level despite the tripling of our medical bill per person since then. It has also caused United States life expectancy for men to go down in international rank since 1950 from approximately tenth place in the world to fortieth.

There have been reports of at least transitory abnormalities of almost every body function in obese persons. Yet some extraordinarily obese persons may escape these abnormalities, while others, who are only mildly overweight, may develop major derangements. For many of these derangements, to be sure, obesity may be a *co-existing,* rather than a *causal* feature—a distinction important to keep in mind throughout this chapter. Nevertheless, certain disorders have so often been noted in obese patients that a direct (or causal) relationship may exist. And, in general, the greater the amount of obesity, the more likely are the abnormalities to occur and to be severe.

Important and frequent among these abnormalities are respiratory difficulties. Fat people have regularly been noted to have less exercise tolerance, more difficulty in normal breathing, and a higher frequency of respiratory infections than people of normal weight. Marked obesity may produce two particular sets of respiratory complications. The first is lethargy or somnolence, which is due to accumulation of carbon dioxide in the blood because of the decreased ventilation. A second complication, also attributable to reduced ventilation, is lowered oxygenation of arterial blood. It may possibly lead to blood clotting and hemorrhages in the skin. In addition, cardiac enlargement and congestive failure may be an indirect consequence of these respiratory difficulties.

There are really two main conditions which underlie most cases of heart disease:

(1) hypertension (high blood pressure) and

(2) atherosclerosis (hardening of the arteries), generally closely related to hypercholesterolemia (high blood cholesterol).

Both of these conditions bear a relation to obesity. Hypercholesterolemia is associated with the consumption of a diet high in saturated fats—those of butter, meat, eggs, and hard margarine. "Hard" margarine is characterized, as are hard fats generally, by the fact that the fatty acids which esterify the glycerol are long-chain *saturated* fatty acids, where the full complement of hydrogen atoms is attached to a chain comprising 14, 16, 18, or more carbon atoms. By contrast, in "soft" margarines, as in oils, unsaturated and polyunsaturated fatty acids predominate. In *unsaturated* fatty acids, two hydrogen atoms are missing in adjacent carbon atoms, leading these to be attached by a "double bond." In *polyunsaturated* fatty acids, several pairs of hydrogen atoms are missing, leading to the presence of several double bonds in the molecule. Blood cholesterol (and presumably atherogenesis, the deposition of this fat-like material on the walls of such vessels as the coronary arteries and the aorta) increases during periods of active weight gain. We shall see later in this chapter that inactivity also favors high blood cholesterol. Thus, it is not surprising that obesity and a high blood cholesterol are often associated in our population (among males in particular).

The resistance of transit of blood in the capillaries, particularly in the subcutaneous area, seems to be increased when the adipose tissue is filled with fat. Conversely, it will be seen in this chapter that high blood pressure in obese patients is frequently lowered by weight reduction of sufficient magnitude. Again, inactivity, and the consumption of a large amount of food high in salt (a characteristic of American food habits) and high in saturated fat favor the development of high blood pressure.

The risk to health is compounded by the fact, uncovered in the large-scale study conducted on the population of Framingham, Massachusetts, that mortality from heart disease is much higher than normal among individuals with hypertension, and higher than normal among individuals with hypercholesterolemia. Initial observation suggested that obesity, if accompanied neither by hypertension nor by hypercholesterolemia, did not increase the risk of heart disease unless it was very extreme, but that it did considerably magnify the risk of a fatal coronary attack, if it was present at the same time as hypertension or hypercholesterolemia, or both. More recent results, covering a longer period (12 years by now) show that, in men, antecedent relative weight and weight gain after the age of 25 are strongly correlated with the risk of angina pectoris and sudden death, but are unrelated to the development of myocardial infarction. In other words, an increased risk of angina pectoris and sudden death appears to exist in obese men, whether or not they show elevation of blood pressure and serum cholesterol, indicating that obesity by itself contributes to the rate of development of these manifestations of heart disease. Thus, the Framingham data show once again that obesity is dangerous for cardiovascular function when it imposes an increased workload on a heart with an already compromised coronary circulation.

Inasmuch as this latest study could get lost, in the mind of the reader, in the growing accumulation of published reports on the relation of obesity to heart disease, let us review the facts as they have been uncovered so far in this field. Facts not only are still too few in this *all-important* field, but also are not necessarily in agreement with widespread opinions.

According to many textbooks and to many recent press releases, the association between obesity and coronary heart disease is so striking that it has always been observed by good physicians. It has been said that (making allowance for the fact that coronary heart disease as such is of recent diagnosis) Hippocrates himself recognized the relationship between something like coronary disease and obesity.

When you look into this, as Keys has done, you find extremely little on the subject of obesity in Hippocrates. Actually, there are only three remarks on this subject in those of his treatises which have survived: one on the infertility of fat women among the Scythians and two sentences about obesity in "Aphorisms." Aphorism number 35 says: "In all maladies, those who are fat about the belly do best. It is bad to be very thin and wasted there." This remark is never quoted in lectures on obesity. Instead, there is very frequent quotation of aphorism number 44, which says, "Sudden death is more common in those who are naturally fat than in those who are lean." So much for the ancient writers.

The evidence of a strong correlation between obesity—or rather, overweight—and heart disease, first noticed by Rogers in 1901, and so well presented by Dublin and Marks and their collaborators, in the insurance field, does not need to be recalled here. One may recall that mortality in overweight men from all causes is 150 per cent of the normal. In overweight women, it is 147 per cent, and the difference is particularly striking for heart disease—142 per cent for men, 175 per cent for women (see Table 5).

The implication usually drawn from these data is that obesity *causes* heart disease. This is a type of reasoning which is dangerous. If one looks at the same table, one finds that the mortality from tuberculosis

Table 5 PRINCIPAL CAUSES OF DEATH AMONG MEN AND WOMEN RATED FOR OVERWEIGHT. ATTAINED AGES 25–74 YEARS

Ratio of Actual to Expected Deaths According to Estimates
of Contemporaneous Mortality Experience on Standard Risks

Metropolitan Life Insurance Company, Ordinary Department
Issues of 1925 to 1934, Traced to Policy Anniversary, 1950

| | *Men* | | *Women* | |
| | Deaths | Per Cent Actual of Expected Deaths | Deaths | Per Cent Actual of Expected Deaths |
Cause of Death				
Principal cardiovascular-renal diseases	1,867	149	1,103	177
Organic heart disease, diseases of the coronary arteries and angina pectoris	1,377	142	697	175
Organic heart disease	748	*	515	*
Coronary disease and angina pectoris	629	*	182	*
Cerebral hemorrhage	247	159	226	162
Chronic nephritis	243	191	180	212
Cancer, all forms	385	97	476	100
Stomach	62	85	34	86
Liver and gall bladder	33	168	46	211
Peritoneum, intestines and rectum	103	115	93	104
Pancreas	19	93	21	149
Respiratory organs	39	78 **	—	—
Breast	—	—	81	69
Genital organs	—	—	132	107
Uterus	—	—	103	121
Leukemia and Hodgkins disease	26	100	23	110
Diabetes	205	383	235	372
Tuberculosis, all forms	24	21	20	35
Pneumonia, all forms	98	102	78	129
Cirrhosis of the liver	96	249	32	147
Appendicitis	76	2¯3	41	195
Hernia and intestinal obstruction	39	154 **	31	141 **
Biliary calculi and other gall bladder diseases	32	152 **	30	188 **
Biliary calculi	19	206	50	284
Ulcer of stomach and duodenum	30	67	—	—
Puerperal conditions	—	—	43	162
Suicide	63	78	23	73
Accidents, total	177	111	74	135
Auto	76	131	27	120
Falls	32	131	—	—

* Satisfactory basis for comparison not available.
** Based on mortality rates on Standard risks for 1935–39.
NOTE: Percentages which have been underlined indicate statistically significant deviations from experience on Standard risks.

among overweight insured men and women is very low—21 and 35 per cent, respectively, and that suicide is also very significantly lowered—70 per cent, as compared to the normal mortality. Yet nobody has suggested that overweight as such protects against, say, the infection by tubercle bacillus. It has been shown by a careful long-term study in England that the association between overweight and decreased mortality from tuberculosis is not an artifact due to the effect of a wasting disease, but the result of a decreased tuberculosis morbidity among obese individuals.

Similarly, the decreased incidence of suicide among the overweight has never been ascribed seriously to obesity as a causal factor. If such a relationship existed, we would have to blame suicide on inability to drag yourself to the window or get through it, or the impossibility of getting a strong enough rope with which to hang yourself.

It is obviously more reasonable to assume that there is an association there, that is, some of the factors that make for obesity also make for a decreased tendency to suicide rather than their causing decreased suicide. So I think we should be wary of interpreting too literally such correlation through *causation,* even though the fact is incontrovertible that the *association* is striking in any statistics which involve a large enough number of cases.

Now, by contrast, when one looks at reports of smaller and supposedly more careful studies, one finds almost every opinion as regards the possible association of obesity, overweight, and heart disease. For example, in a study of 5- and 10-year survival rates at the Mayo Clinic, conducted on about 6,000 angina patients, it was found that, by and large, the obese patients did better than the normal—70 per cent obese versus 59 per cent nonobese surviving after five years, 44 versus 35 per cent after ten years.

Again, this does not necessarily mean that obesity protects against the consequences of angina pectoris; in fact, it could suggest almost the reverse—that obese individuals may be more likely than nonobese subjects to have mild cases (which they then survive). Again, considerable difficulty is encountered in interpreting results.

Results of autopsies are by no means clear either. To give some examples: a study by Rosenthal showed no correlation between atherosclerosis and obesity; a study by Wilens showed a strong correlation between obesity and overweight, and, furthermore, included the interesting suggestion that a wasting disease or exhaustion from lack of nourishment actually decreased the degree of atherosclerosis, even when this was already established.

Some of the studies done during World War II, particularly in Finland and in the Netherlands, showed a correlation between decreased caloric intake and decreased atherosclerosis. Actually, there were many variables other than caloric intake even among nutritional factors (qualitative, as well as quantitative, changes took place as a result of dietary restriction).

In a study which Wright conducted on about a thousand patients, there was very little correlation. between weight and myocardial infarction. The study which Keys conducted in his laboratory on a group of about a hundred coronary patients showed no difference in weight distribution from that observed in a hundred otherwise similar non-diseased patients.

It has been suggested recently that the correlation between fatness and heart disease is better than that between weight and heart disease. In other words, obesity is more dangerous than overweight. Recent findings on small groups of patients have indeed tended to show that, even though there was no difference between the weight of coronary patients and that of normal individuals of the same age, the coronary patients were fatter as detected by calipers. Such studies are, however, difficult to interpret because one of the effects of coronary disease is probably decreased physical activity and this could account for increased shift from muscle to fat. Considerations of body composition may be also involved in the findings of Breslow on the relatively superior health record of overweight longshoremen.

In a study reported by Wilkins, Roberts, and their collaborators in 1959, there was a strong correlation between weight and atherosclerosis as seen at autopsies. The study done in Framingham by Dawber, Moore, and Mann suggests a definite degree of correlation between overweight and heart disease. Initial results indicate that very overweight individuals are more prone to have heart disease than very underweight individuals, with a wide zone in between where it is difficult to observe a correlation. It also appears that the correlation may be more directly one between overweight and hypertension, with the effect on heart disease secondary to the occurrence of hypertension.

Generally speaking, I think that it is fair to conclude from these and from many other studies that there is a correlation between overweight and heart disease, but that there are a number of qualifications which must be kept in mind. First of all, overweight appears to be only one of the many contributory factors involved. If the sample is too small or the selection of the experimental group is slanted one way or the other, the correlation may disappear. The correlation is good when one looks at population groups made up largely of very thin people, such as the Bantus or the population of southern Italy—and particularly in populations which have, like these two, very low serum cholesterol.

The correlation is also good if one compares extremely obese with normal individuals. However, between these extremes in weight, unless there is a very large group, the effect of obesity is not that definite and may be lost. Therefore, I believe it is fair to conclude that in very large groups obesity is a factor in heart disease which justifies weight reduction as a preventive measure, at least for most individuals.

Now, if we try to go a little deeper into the problem and think of possible mechanisms, we encounter the possibility that obesity has a differential effect on atherogenesis and on coronary disaster. For that matter there appears to be a definite difference between the effect of obesity on the coronary artery and the effect of obesity on the aorta. The correlation between obesity and atherogenesis and arteriosclerosis is much stronger for the coronary artery than it is for the aorta.

We also have the possibility that obesity and heart disease are linked by association rather than by causation. One possible link is the role of exercise and physical activity. We have outlined—and this book contains no more important point—that, contrary to general thought, while an increase in physical activity for an already active individual is accompanied by an increase in food intake, a decrease in physical activity below a certain point is *not* accompanied by a decrease in food intake, and the individual becomes fat instead.

Now, inasmuch as Morris (whose work is discussed below) in particular has shown that there may be a strong correlation between lack of physical activity and incidence of heart disease, and inasmuch as there is a strong correlation between lack of physical activity and overweight, we have to acknowledge a possibility that both overweight and heart disease may be in part due to the same factors, rather than one "causing" the other.

Early experiments on the relationship of exercise and cardiovascular disease were conducted in animals. Some of the conclusions were equivocal. This writer could not find that one hour a day of treadmill exercise for 30 days had any effect on the cholesterol levels of two types of obese mice—one with genetically determined hypercholesteremia, the other with nearly normal cholesterol levels—or on their nonobese littermates. Other investigators, using even shorter daily exercise periods (10 to 20 minutes), could not demonstrate any effect on serum cholesterol or occurrence of atherosclerosis in the aortas of New Zealand rabbits fed a cholesterol-containing diet. It is doubtful that the duration of exercise, in terms of both days and hours per day, was sufficient in either type of experiment to have permitted the demonstration of an effect. This conclusion is bolstered retrospectively by some of the observations on human populations reported in this chapter which suggest that an appreciable level of activity has to be maintained for a long period for an influence on cholesterol to be manifest, and also by recent Swedish studies which show that somewhat more vigorous and prolonged exercise does lower the serum cholesterol of rats.

That a more direct relationship than that dependent on obesity may exist between exercise and heart disease was first suggested by the studies of Morris and his co-workers, who found that London bus drivers exhibited a higher incidence and a greater severity of coronary heart disease than did bus conductors. The dietary habits of the two groups of men

/ere similar, and it appeared that the two variables differentiating the
wo groups were

1) the possibly greater stress associated with driving in city traffic than with
   selling and checking tickets; and

2) the definitely greater physical activity of conductors, who were on their feet
   and climbing the steps all day in the two-story buses.

Three studies conducted in different parts of the world have recently
brought additional and, to this writer, fairly convincing evidence that
inactivity is associated with a higher incidence of coronary heart disease.

First, a study of Finnish lumberjacks yielded some highly suggestive
data. Karvonen and his co-workers studied the food consumption of
lumberjacks in five camps in eastern Finland and found a mean energy
intake of 4,763 calories, 45 per cent of which was derived from fat. This
is an unusually large proportion of a large intake. Only 35 per cent of
the calories consumed by the local population were derived from fat.
In absolute figures, the lumberjacks consumed 237 grams of fat, 60 per
cent being derived from milk and butter and 30 per cent from meat. In
spite of these intakes, the serum cholesterol levels were similar to those
of other males in the local population, rising from 246 to 274 milligrams
per 100 milliliters between 20 and 59 years of age. The authors concluded: "That the serum cholesterol was no higher was probably due
to a depression of the serum cholesterol content by heavy work." Incidentally, while the authors pointed out that not all the lumberjacks
were actually timber cutters (some drove trucks or teams of horses), no
attempt appears to have been made to differentiate between various
degrees of physical activity.

Additional evidence comes from a study of mountaineers in a Swiss
Alpine village. A very comprehensive survey conducted under the direction of Fritz Verzar and Daniella Gsell of Basel indicated that populations living in the higher valleys are characterized by a high intake of
dairy fats and a low mortality from cardiovascular disease. Physical activity appeared general and intense. Dr. Gsell and I decided to study one
such village in more detail and selected Blattendorf, a village located in
a remote valley in the southern Swiss Alps. All the inhabitants are farmers. The farms and pastures are spread over steep slopes varying in
altitude from 4,000 to 8,000 feet. The village is several miles away from
the nearest road usable by automobiles, trucks, or carts. All distances,
therefore, have to be walked. The people carry hay, wood, milk, and
building materials on their backs. Men frequently carry loads of one
hundred pounds or more, and elderly women carry loads of 50 to 60
pounds up and down the mountain paths. Each day during the summer
the villagers walk to the "higher Alps," which in local parlance desig-

nates the pastures situated 1,500 to 2,000 feet above the village, for cheese-making. It is thus apparent that, although quantitative determinations of physical work were not obtained—except indirectly through determinations of caloric intakes—the levels of activity of this population are extremely high and are maintained in this manner almost indefinitely.

The serum cholesterol levels of this village population were extremely interesting. (In general, the lower the cholesterol level, the lower the chances of atherosclerosis and of coronary attacks. In the United States most middle-aged adults have serum cholesterol levels well in excess of 200 milligrams per 100 milliliters.) We found that the serum cholesterol levels of the men in the village ranged from 164 mg. per 100 ml. for the 30- to 39-year-old group, to 200 mg. per 100 ml. for those 50 to 59 years old. The women showed cholesterol levels ranging from 160 to 190 respectively, in the same age groups. Of interest is the fact that the mean serum cholesterol of men started dropping at age 42 in Blattendorf, compared with 12 to 15 years later in Basel or the United States. In general, the levels of serum cholesterol in the villagers were found to be considerably lower than those seen in a group of working-class men and women of a similar ancestry who were studied in the city of Basel. These men and women were of essentially the same height and weight as the group in Blattendorf.

A two-week dietary survey conducted by the inventory method among the Alpine families indicated a per capita consumption of 3,643 calories, of which 34 per cent came from fat. Animal fats made up 27 per cent of the total caloric intake. Dairy products made up a large fraction of their diet. This Alpine group also consumed large amounts of potatoes and bread. By contrast, the urban (Basel) group consumed only 2,643 calories, of which a similar fraction (37 per cent) came from fat, with the proportion of animal fats and saturated and unsaturated fatty acids essentially similar to that in the diet of the villagers. This, of course, means that the absolute intake of fat, animal fat and saturated fat, was about 30 per cent greater among the Alpine people.

Yet, in spite of the qualitative similarity between the two diets and the villagers' much greater absolute consumption of calories and fat, the latter showed a much *lower* cholesterol level. In fact, while the average level of the Basel group was similar to values reported for inhabitants of the United States, the levels of serum cholesterol observed among the villagers were of the same order as those seen among Costa Rican Indians or Bantus, who have much less fat in their diets.

It is unlikely that the differences in altitude and climate between Basel and Blattendorf are of particular relevance to explain the observed differences in serum cholesterol. South African Europeans living in Johannesburg at an altitude greater than 6,000 feet show serum cholesterol levels similar to those seen in the United States. Climate was not ound to influence serum cholesterol in a comparison of Maine and 'lorida populations. A low environmental temperature has been shown o elevate the serum cholesterol level but, since the mean annual temperature was lower in Blattendorf than in Basel (42 versus 50 degrees F.), his effect would increase rather than decrease the significance of the bserved difference.

Smoking habits and serum magnesium levels, two variables correlated vith serum cholesterol levels in other studies, were the same in the 3asel and the Blattendorf groups. It thus appears that the one major lifference between the two groups was the much greater physical activity f the mountain villagers. While the Basel group was probably less sedenary than a comparable group would be in the United States (as few had ars, which meant some degree of walking, and half the men never sat for ong periods of time during their work), they obviously did not perform he daily intense physical work done by the Alpine group. I concluded hat, while such dietary factors as fat content of the diet and proportion f saturated and unsaturated fat are probably important in determining erum cholesterol levels, they appear to be *less* important than the activity factor; alternately, they may manifest their importance only in physically inactive populations.

The third example is the study of Taylor and his co-workers who, attacking the problem of exercise and heart disease from another angle, reached similar conclusions. They examined three groups of United States railroad workers: clerks, switchmen, and section-hands. They found that mortality from arteriosclerotic heart disease was inversely correlated with the physical activity characteristic of each type of job. Mortality from arteriosclerotic heart disease was 5.7 per 1,000 for the clerks, 3.9 for the switchmen, and 2.8 for the section-hands.

This study covered white men 40 to 64 years old who had worked at their respective jobs for 9½ years by December 1951 and who were still working in 1954. Data were obtained from the records of the Railroad Retirement Board. The men in this study showed a greater fixity of occupation than is usual in American industry. Different occupations are covered by different union contracts, which specify that an individual who changes his postion loses his seniority. Job changes accordingly tend to occur at the beginning of a man's working life.

Clerks in all age groups from 40 to 64 showed a higher incidence of arteriosclerotic heart disease rates than did switchmen and section-hands. The differences between groups increased with age. In the 60-to-64-year-old group, clerks showed a death rate of 10.4 per 1,000, switchmen 6.7, and section men 4.2. The authors do recognize that their data, as is true of ours on the mountain population, are limited in some important ways. The higher death rate from violence among section men may have exerted some influence on the results; some of the accidental deaths may have been precipitated by coronary attacks, although they were not reported as such. A larger proportion of section-hands than of clerks and switchmen live in small communities; railroad offices and switchyards are generally in metropolitan areas. Despite these possible limitations, the evidence remains impressive.

It must be noted that exercise and the prevention of heart disease may be interrelated in several ways, which the studies cited here only partially differentiate. There appears to be a beneficial effect on body weight; the combination of a lowering of serum cholesterol and of body weight may represent more than the sum of its parts if, as the Framingham heart study shows, overweight is of special significance if accompanied by hypercholesteremia or hypertension, and of even greater significance if accompanied by both. In addition, intensity of exercise is also a factor. Kraus and Raab have summarized the evidence showing that regular exercise of sufficient intensity may retard loss of elasticity and contractility of the heart muscle. Regular exercise of sufficient intensity may also help to maintain the elasticity of blood vessels. It thus appears that the entire mode of life, not nutrition alone, may be of importance in retarding or accelerating the occurrence of what has become in this century the number-one killer in the United States.

Clearly, both overweight and heart disease may be due to the same factors, one of them underactivity. Another possibility is the following: As indicated in Chapter 4, we know about eight or ten different forms of obesity that are present in experimental animals. These, as we noted, have been divided into two classes. One we called regulatory obesities, which are essentially due to a dysfunction in the regulating mechanism—to give two examples, hypothalamic obesity and the obesity one can produce by punishing an animal unless it overeats. Such forms of obesity in experimental animals are not accompanied by hypercholesteremia. By contrast, the metabolic obesities occur where a primary metabolic lesion causes the overeating. Examples are the obese-hyperglycemic syndrome, the so-called yellow obesity, and the obesity due to ACTH-secreting pituitary tumors. Such obesities show hypercholesteremia or disorders of cholesterol metabolism as part of the syndrome. Thus, it is quite possible that in speaking of "obesity" and "heart disease" and implying that there is one obesity and one heart disease, we are using a primitive type of thinking. Instead, there are a number of forms of obesity which have various relationships to the many aspects of the disease process.

To give but one example: in hypothalamic obesity, although there is no effect on cholesterol, prolonged overeating affects the kidneys, and a long-term hypertension without any concomitant effect on cholesterol metabolism may thus be the result of overeating.

Finally, there is the possible interrelationship between genetics and the effect of fat diets in animals. Different types or strains of animals react quite differently to a high-fat diet.

The relationship of atherosclerosis and heart disease to nutritional factors other than calories has been studied in at least three different ways. The first is the possible direct linking of coronary disease to nutrition and particularly to fat intake. The second is the possible linking of nutrition to cholesterol metabolism, leading to a possible relation of cholesterol levels to coronary disease. The third possibility is that of a relationship of fat intake either to atheroma or thrombosis as components of coronary disease, with emphasis on clotting time; this is supported by claims of increased and more prolonged rise in blood lipids following ingestion of fat in coronary patients.

The first hypothesis is largely based on surveys. These have been widely discussed, so that we shall not spend much time on them except to recall that Keys found (or thought he had found) a relationship between heart disease and total fat intake. But Yudkin, working on the same data in London, found no correlation. Yerushalmy and Hilleboe, two of our most distinguished epidemiologists, found that the apparent association decreased if additional countries were considered. Hollingsworth, a well-known English nutritionist, could find no correlation between the increase in incidence of heart disease in Britain between the pre- and post-war period and changes in fat consumption. Among others, one of the most recent comparisons—that of Jolliffe and Archer of New York—is particularly interesting in that it is more sophisticated and tries to relate death from heart disease not to one component, but to the interaction of various components (such as proportion of saturated fat in the diet and prevalence of telephones in the population).

Even if we limit ourselves to experimental studies on human subjects (as distinct from either epidemiological studies or experimental studies in animals), we find ourselves faced with the following collection of conclusions:

Keys suggests that the cholesterol-lowering ability of certain fats is related to the amount and ratio of the saturated and polyunsaturated fatty acids they contain. The saturated acids raise the serum cholesterol level, and are twice as active per gram in raising it as the polyunsaturated acids (which have the opposite effect) are in lowering it. Unsaturated acids have very little effect.

Ahrens appears to believe that the lowering of serum level is related to the total degree of unsaturation and to the iodine number, presumably with the mono- and polyunsaturated acids all being effective in proportion to their degree of unsaturation.

Kinsell concludes that the polyunsaturated acid (linoleic) is the primary factor.

Bronte-Stewart of South Africa states that the addition of a saturated oil to a highly unsaturated oil does not necessarily elevate the serum cholesterol level produced by the unsaturated oil.

Beveridge of Canada claims that hydrogenation of corn oil, which decreases the unsaturation of this fat, has very little influence on the ability of corn oil to lower the serum cholesterol.

Hegsted at Harvard thinks he can demonstrate that the product obtained by multiplying the concentration of saturated acids by that of linoleic acid has a high negative correlation with the serum cholesterol levels.

In other words, there is some diversity of views, but an almost general acceptance of the idea that, by and large, saturated acids tend to elevate and polyunsaturated to lower the level of cholesterol.

That there are other dietary factors involved in the determination of serum cholesterol is likely. The amount of cholesterol in the diet is more important than was thought for a time. In other words, the cholesterol you eat and absorb is added in part to the cholesterol you synthesize. Egg yolks, for example, contain not only saturated fats, but appreciable amounts of cholesterol and ought to be avoided by coronary-prone individuals (and probably by most middle-aged American males). Fiber and pectins, if absorbed in sufficient amounts, drain some of the cholesterol down the gastrointestinal tract and prevent the cholesterol secreted in bile from being reabsorbed—a mechanism not unlike the mode of action of some of the new drugs containing polystyramine, a resin which similarly "traps" cholesterol. It has been suggested that consumption of very large amounts of sucrose—ordinary sugar—leads to higher cholesterol than consumption of equivalent amounts of starch. Some of the mineral components of the diet are thought not only to influence the cholesterol level but perhaps also the incidence of coronary catastrophes. Finally, it has been said—though with very little experimental and clinical foundation so far—that some of the vitamins may also be involved in the determination of cholesterol levels.

Many observers have noted that blood pressure often increased when body weight increased, and that such elevations frequently returned to normal levels after a significant weight loss. Studies have shown that some of the previously reported hypertension has come from the increased force necessary to compress the tissues in a fat upper arm in making the blood pressure measurement. The physician can, of course, eliminate this factor by the use of a cuff of the proper size. This makes it possible to record the blood pressure accurately, even when the upper arms are fat.

In an investigation of workers in a Chicago utility company, prevalent rates of hypertension were examined in relation to weight over a period of 20 years. The small number of men who remained at or near their desirable weight throughout that time had the lowest prevalence of hypertensive disease. Among those who gained weight, more hypertension developed, with the group gaining the most weight developing the highest rates of hypertension.

Obese people frequently have an impaired carbohydrate tolerance (in other words, cannot utilize glucose properly). This may be of sufficient degree to be classified as diabetes mellitus. It has not been established that the high blood sugar, which promptly disappears with weight reduction, will lead to the same type of vascular degenerative change that often occurs in diabetics of normal weight. Even if avoidance of vascular complications is not present as an incentive for weight reduction, it is still important for people so afflicted to reduce in order to avoid complications caused by the high blood sugar, such as the need for insulin, cutaneous and other infections, and episodes of acidosis that may require hospitalization.

For pregnant women, obesity is a hazard. Toxemia, problems in delivery, and difficulties with the fetus are more common in fat women than in those of normal weight. And management of weight gain in obese pregnant women is delicate. Obese women can tolerate a smaller weight gain during pregnancy than normal-weight women if the diet is adequate in nutrients.

The possibility that in certain women a given pregnancy or successive pregnancies may predispose to obesity has been neither proved nor disproved. At any rate, the weight gain during pregnancy ought to be watched carefully: too small a weight gain, particularly in a very thin woman, is dangerous; but too great a weight gain in women of normal weight and, even more so, in obese women, is highly undesirable. In general, the consensus of modern obstetricians is that for a woman of the right weight to start with, a weight gain of two or three pounds a month during pregnancy is ideal, that is, a total gain to say, 18 to 25 pounds. (Incidentally, because women tend to decrease their physical activity as pregnancy proceeds, they may gain weight optimally without much of any increase in food intake. It becomes particularly important under these conditions to give proper attention to the *quality* of the diet.) Nursing can help to eliminate excess fat, if any, accumulated in pregnancy, but it must be remembered that it takes a great many calories to produce milk and that any drastic shortage of calories is likely to stop the flow of milk.

In men, obesity may produce the hazard of infertility if the rolls of fat in the thighs are so abundant that the scrotum is surrounded by folds of adipose tissue. This is because semen maintained at body temperature is usually unfruitful. This genital problem in obese men is, however, relatively infrequent.

The question is frequently asked: "Is the obese person otherwise in excellent health more likely to develop a major disease, or to die any sooner, than a person of equally good health and normal weight?" The generally accepted answer is that obesity does create an extra hazard for otherwise healthy people, although the data to support this conclusion were obtained by methods of less than perfect validity. We have already seen that this was so for cardiovascular diseases. The same considerations make the conclusions drawn on some other diseases similarly uncertain.

Most of the evidence comes from large-scale studies conducted by life insurance companies. These data, summarized in Table 5, show that obese people are more likely to die of a number of conditions than their thinner contemporaries.

These data and other comparable data obtained from studies of military personnel are strong evidence of the hazards of obesity for people of otherwise normal health. The lower frequency of tuberculosis, peptic ulcer, and suicide as causes of death in the obese is interesting, but the higher risk of cardiovascular-renal, diabetes, and the other cited diseases affect many more people. Moreover, associated data in the insurance company reports also suggest that the excessive mortality rate declined for overweight patients who were able to reduce sufficiently to attain a lowered insurance rating. There are limitations in the conclusions that can be drawn from the insurance company data, despite the quantity of the data and the care with which they have been treated. What the statistics show is an *association* between obesity and early mortality. They do not permit the conclusion that obesity was the *cause* of the early mortality. Once again, this distinction needs to be emphasized.

A second limitation is the question of the validity of the life insurance sample as representative of the general human population. We are compelled to ask, "What differences might have existed in the 'uninsured' population? Was there similarity in the mortality rates? Was there the same proportion of obese to nonobese persons?"

The same limitation exists in the data derived from a large-scale study conducted by the United States Army on 22,000 officers, leading to essentially the same conclusions. While these military data are more complete and accurate on both weights and causes of death than are the insurance-study data, the group of officers cannot, of course, be assumed to be representative of the general population.

A third major defect in the insurance data concerns the initial weight of the insured subject. In many instances, the weight was obtained by a verbal statement from the subject, rather than actual measurement, and there is no way for us to verify the accuracy of these reports or detect errors. Another possible source of error may have been introduced by the lack of standardization in the recording of deaths, and information subsequent to initial weight regarding weight gain or loss is usually not available. Despite these reservations, which complicate the analysis of many data, I want to repeat that the evidence is overwhelming of obesity shortening life in most individuals.

Furthermore, when we go from prevention of diseases to treatment, there are many conditions in which significant benefits are obtained with loss of co-existing excess weight. The removal of obesity can be of crucial importance in disorders of the circulatory and locomotor systems. Obesity can contribute to the further development of these disorders once they have appeared. Among such conditions are: angina pectoris, hypertension, congestive heart failure, intermittent claudication, rupture of intervertebral discs, osteoarthritis, varicose veins, and many other varieties of bone or joint disease. Obesity often adds to the immobility caused by arthritis. Loss of weight is also particularly desirable in obese patients after an acute myocardial infarction. Whether or not the relationship of obesity to maturity-onset diabetes is causal, obese diabetic patients are usually benefited by weight reduction. Such patients and others just cited often adhere to weight-reduction programs more faithfully than any other group of dieters, because the incentive to lose weight is presented to them as medically important, with adequate proof of its value in the tangible improvements experienced afterwards.

From the point of view of treatment, we are, I believe, where we were with diabetes before the discovery of insulin; and perhaps the only way open to us at present is to recommend a return to the simplest virtues: abstemiousness in diet (low calories, not too much saturated fat or fat of any kind, for that matter); enough physical activity; if possible, avoidance of unnecessary psychological stress; and I will add, although this is an area which is not covered by this book, elimination of cigarette smoking.

chapter 9

Obesity
in Adolescence

In adolescents obesity differs in several ways from the manner in which it appears in other age groups. In many cases it is more difficult to identify. Except in extreme instances, it is harder to determine how serious a matter it is. And, insofar as our current experience is concerned, it is frequently impossible to correct. At no time in life is a diagnosis based exclusively on height-weight charts more precarious. Differences in rate of vertical growth, in muscular development, in speeds of sexual maturation, introduce variables not present in younger children or in adults.

And adolescents, even the healthiest of them, bring to all their problems, including such a problem as obesity, the serious circumstance, in our culture anyway, of just being adolescents. Older people, at least in a democracy, attain some degree of autonomy at some point in their development. Younger children have less strong rebellious urges. The adolescent is neither one thing nor another, neither a child nor an adult, and he wants to be both. The adolescent who is labeled obese is fair game to such well-meant oppressions as those who surround him wish to inflict on him. And frequently, as we shall see, we train the obese adolescent to inflict similar oppressions on himself.

Before we subject an adolescent boy or girl to treatment as a victim of obesity—medical treatment or social treatment—it is vital that we first establish whether or not he or she is, in fact, obese. Commonly, just before puberty, both boys and girls have an appreciable increase of subcutaneous fat. Boys tend actually to thin out while their height increases, so that with them there is relative rather than absolute thinning. For girls the normal thinning process, if it occurs at all, takes place further along, in the late teens. Only when this deposition of "puppy" fat becomes visibly excessive or too persistent does it constitute a medical problem. This occurs in about 15 to 20 per cent of all adolescents, at least according to the findings of our studies in the Boston area.

Because of individual variations in build and relative growth and because of the normal evolution of body fat content, the most reliable method of detecting obesity, short of actual determination of body fat by soft-tissue X-ray or densimetry, is experienced clinical observation. A physician will most usually know a too-fat child when he sees one. And he can check on his judgment by the seemingly primitive, but painless and reliable technique of pinching, with or without calipers. (See Chapter 2.) Similarly, the best guide for deciding when a given obese adolescent should stop reducing is not height-weight charts, but rather a series of inspections, again by the physician, during the period of weight loss.

We must remember that obesity is not a moral issue, to be met with platitudes and punishment. It is a medical problem, complex and as yet imperfectly understood. We know, we believe, more about appetite than we did a few short years ago, but we know less than we need to know. Appetite remains, as far as our understanding goes, a confusing mechanism involving, as we have attempted to show, metabolic, gastric, hypothalamic, and cortical factors. Appetite can be disturbed by many physiological and psychological elements which may have nothing in common except the creation of a positive energy balance—a situation where the individual consumes more calories than he expends. To equate obesity with gluttony and treat the adolescent patient with an inspirational harangue and a diet sheet is, as so many physicians have unhappily discovered, a complete mistake. It often lays the groundwork for quick failure, a failure almost invariably blamed on the victim. What's more, it may seriously harm the youngster, by reinforcing feelings of guilt already induced by a censorious environment. And it may, as we have recently discovered, cause further withdrawal from the business of living into lack of social contacts, into physical inactivity, and into overeating. We must remember that no group is more uncertain about their own bodies and more easily thrown into feelings of worthlessness and depression than adolescents. And the obese adolescent, in a minority as he or she is, is too often in a sadly put-upon minority.

During the last decade, we people of the United States have been exposed to a vivid and often bitter education into the lives, the problems, and the aspirations of certain minority groups in our country. We think we know who and where our minorities are. However, some of my recent research has seemed to point to a minority in our midst which we previously did not identify as one. This minority has its troubles, serious troubles. Its members live lives of mild-to-severe anguish and selfcontempt, for which the rest of us are, much more than we are willing to admit, in differing degrees responsible. These people, our victims, come in the standard distribution of American colors, cultural levels, and economic classes. They are our obese sons and daughters, and there are hundreds of thousands of them. They look different from their slender siblings, and they behave differently as well. They are less happy, and they are less hopeful. For the improvements promised to other abused minorities are not, with any amount of conviction, presented to them.

The American Negro has a clear right to hope. He has been given some evidence that white attitudes, for whatever good or selfish reasons, are changing for the better and can and will change more. The Negro will be permitted to remain a Negro and still receive the love and respect to which he is entitled as a child of God, and such other honors as his spirit and his effort earn. The situation is not that simple for the obese adolescent and particularly for the obese young woman, white, black, yellow, or whatever. By definition she must, before being esteemed an equal of her slender sister, cease to be her plump self. She must win a basic status of acceptability that others by their supposed physical and moral excellence receive as a built-in entitlement.

If this demanded change were demonstrably possible for all fat young girls, the solution of the problem would be a simple one. But some of them, many of them, despite their best efforts and ours, are going to remain fat, as the previous discussions on body build and heredity have indicated. They are not going to change—but something that *can* change is our attitude toward them. And a happy by-product to that change would be a cheerful improvement in their attitude toward themselves. What precisely is that attitude? Is it genuinely a melancholy one? What makes us think it exists?

It came most conspicuously to our attention, as so many things come to the attention of all investigators, in the course of looking for something else. We were attempting to discover in obese adolescent girls personality traits that might help us to understand factors that made them become obese in the first place. We were interested especially in traits associated with lessened physical activity because of the existence of a body of data establishing that obese boys and girls were, indeed, less physically active than nonobese boys and girls, with the contrast particularly striking in girls. Our findings, however, lent themselves more dramatically to interpretation of these traits and attitudes as the result of social and psychological pressures on obese persons in our society.

Moreover, the striking similarities between the characteristic psychological traits of these obese adolescent girls and those of ethnic and racial minorities attributable to their status as victims of prejudice strengthened our impression that such traits were more likely the results than the cause of obesity. The girls we studied were attending two summer camps on Cape Cod, Massachusetts. One hundred obese girls came from a camp that existed for the specific purpose of helping them to reduce their weights. Each girl attending this camp was treated as an individual with a personal problem. She was put on a diet designed to maintain her health and reduce her caloric intake, and encouraged to participate in activities that would increase her caloric outgo. Sixty-five nonobese girls came from a nearby camp which had no such goals, which existed merely to fulfill the expected functions of a good summer camp for girls.

The obese girls, incidentally, ranged from 124 to 298 pounds, with a mean weight of 169 pounds; the others ranged from 84 to 170 pounds, with a mean weight of 118 pounds. The ages ran from 13 to 17. The subects came from all over the United States; and Protestants, Catholics, and Jews were among both groups.

To all the girls Miss Lenore Monello (a psychologist) and I gave three projective tests. Such tests, as is now fairly well known, have a way of showing what matters very much to those tested and how they feel about these matters. For example, a test of this nature, if a good one, given to a group of alcoholics and to one of teetotalers, with the testers not knowing which group was which, would separate the overdrinkers from the nondrinkers in the main, even if not in a particular instance. The first test was an affair of word association. The girls wrote any three words coming to mind in response to the following words: outdoors, sugar, time, boring, freedom, worry, picnic, flying, dates, and camp. The obese girls responded to the test with a larger number of words such as calories, diet, reducing, fattening, fat, heavy, and overweight, than did the nonobese. The frequent and spontaneous mention of the "weight references" even when we recognize that those giving them were obese girls in a camp which was attempting to correct their obesity, indicates a preoccupation with "overweight" similar to the heightened sensitivity and constant preoccupation with status found among members of ethnic and racial minorities. Dr. Gordon W. Allport of Harvard has called this sensitivity and preoccupation "obsessive concern." Just as the Negro rarely forgets racial discrimination, Allport reports of Jewish students "a feeling of helplessness at all times, an anxiety, a dread. . . . Anti-semitism is a constant force in the Jew's life . . . never quite free of a dim sense of some vaguely impending doom." Certainly the results of this test showed the same obsessive concern with the fact of being obese.

The girls were given also a sentence completion and a "picture story" test. The first consisted of ten sentence fragments which those tested were to complete any way they wished: The best time of day is. . . . When the baby cried, the mother. . . . When I watch TV. . . . When I am happy, I. . . . After my mother left, I. . . . When things get too hard for me, I. . . . When I saw my father coming. . . . The girl ran as fast as she could because. . . . When I am feeling bad, I. . . . The thing about camp which is most fun is. . . .

The "picture story" test consisted of nine pictures about which the subjects were asked to write stories. Four pictures were of family scenes, two were of peer groups, one was of a man and woman, and two were of single figures.

The obese adolescent girls responded to the sentence completion and "picture story" tests in a "passive" manner, the nonobese in an "active" manner. In this context, passivity has been shown to be the expression of lack of self-assertiveness and initiative, activity to be the expression of these traits. When shown a slide of a woman extending a jar to a boy, both groups saw it as the transfer of cookies from mother to son. Obese girls, however, saw the boy as a passive recipient who *received* cookies from his mother, while nonobese girls saw an assertive boy with initiative who *took* his own cookies. Both obese and nonobese girls described a slide of a woman facing a boy whose arm pointed out a doorway as a boy leaving his mother or returning to her. But the obese pictured a passive boy asking permission or being scolded, ordered, or addressed by a dominant mother, whereas the nonobese pictured an assertive boy telling his mother what he was about to do or what he had just done.

The three incomplete sentences: When things get too hard for me, I. . . . When I am feeling bad, I. . . . and When my mother left, I. . . . revealed that more obese subjects completed these sentences passively with "cry, sleep, sit and sulk, feel lonely," whereas more of the nonobese subjects wrote, "work harder, try my best, talk to someone, visit friends, do my homework, clean my room."

Previous investigators have interpreted this type of response from the obese as an expression of dependency on their families which was present prior to the onset of their obesity and continued through its development. Those of us concerned with the results of the testing which is here reported feel, however, that this passivity is perhaps better interpreted as an effect of social pressure on the obese. We believe this because the passivity of the obese is so similar to the passivity observed among victims of prejudice. Passivity with members of the "dominant group" has been noticed among Negroes who are assertive and expressive with other Negroes, but who present what Allport calls a "facade of passive acquiescence" in front of white people. Oriental people, when similarly subjected to prejudice, also often display passivity with the dominant group.

When the obese clearly associate isolation and rejection with peers they may manifest the phenomenon of "withdrawal," the behavior that recognizes or suspects that one is unwelcome and probably deservingly so. In response to a slide of a solitary boy approaching a small group of other boys, obese girls wrote that the solitary boy remained isolated from the group, whereas nonobese girls wrote of his ultimate acceptance by the group. The presence of city neighborhoods that are primarily Negro, Italian, Puerto Rican, Jewish, and Oriental exemplifies—where these neighborhoods are not the result of the forced segregation by the dominant—withdrawal from the dominant group. Similarly, the obese girls' response to this picture suggests their inclination to withdraw from their peers.

Data from a direct questionnaire given to some of the obese girls in the group tested revealed that, like other minority groups, these girls accepted in part the beliefs regarding themselves held by other members of the community. Mass media constantly reiterate that obesity is an undesirable characteristic and a handicap, that it is caused solely by "overeating" and that it can be overcome at will and should be. These views are reflected in the opinions of the obese girl's parents, brothers and isters, teachers and classmates. Ultimately, as replies to this questionnaire disclosed, these attitudes become standards by which the obese girl judges herself. The obese girls thought that their appetites were greater than those of their peers, that the total number of calories they ate was greater, or that they snacked more than their peers did. These self-destructive notions were strongly held, despite the fact that it has been demonstrated that obese girls similar to those replying to this quesionnaire differ from nonobese girls, not by their average food intake, but by their extreme inactivity.

The girls who answered the questionnaire listed eating as a "bad habit," associated with painful emotion. They reported greater parental concern with diet. They considered weight a handicap preventing participation in sports and dances. In addition, it must be remembered that these youngsters went to camp for the express purpose of losing weight, a clear indication that they or their parents, or both, considered their excess poundage undesirable. The adoption by a minority group of dominant-group values and the attempt to change distinctive traits has been observed among those Jewish people who deny their ancestry, change their names and noses, and look down on other Jewish people, and among those Negroes who straighten their hair, lighten their skin, and evolve a social status system based in part on lightness of skin color.

We found it significant that more obese girls, when examining the test pictures presented to them, failed to identify as such what were fairly obvious family scenes. They "blocked"—that is, they were repelled by the family concept, presumably because of their own conflicts within the family circle. When shown a farm slide which included a man, woman, and child, more obese girls than nonobese failed to describe the characters as constituting a family group. More obese girls labeled a woman-girl scene just that ("woman-and-girl"), or aunt-and-niece, or grandmother-and-granddaughter, while the nonobese girls called them mother-and-daughter.

Both obese and nonobese groups were similar in the extent to which they associated painful emotion with the family, and the extent to which they spontaneously mentioned the family in response to nonfamily stimuli. More obese girls who blocked in mentioning the family *also* associated painful emotion with the family, and/or spontaneously mentioned the family. In contrast, nonobese girls either blocked only, associated painful emotion with the family only, or spontaneously mentioned the family only, but did not give two or three such responses together. Our interpretation of these responses of the obese is that they indicate conflicting attitudes toward the family to a greater extent than is true of the nonobese. Presumably, girls in both groups experience tense emotions of varying violence and duration with their families, but the reaction of obese girls seems to us to be clearly more extreme. Both groups, which after all are made up of girls in the notoriously turbulent period of adolescence, have difficulties, conscious and unconscious, with their families. Both groups, it is to be believed and hoped, receive from their families some love, some protection, some companionship, some guidance. But only the obese girls are likely to live in households where they are constantly held to be guilty because they are physically what they are—fat—a condition unanimously, as far as the unfortunate girls know, held to be both contemptible and their own fault.

Members of victimized ethnic and racial minorities have certain advantages over obese adolescents. The former can often avoid people who reject them. They can employ the previously discussed techniques of passivity and withdrawal. So, the results of our tests indicate, can the fat girls. But the members of the ethnic and racial groups can frequently find people who accept them and esteem them, while there is usually no group to whom the obese girl can readily turn to find such a welcome. This often leaves her confined in a conflict with the one group of which she is so organically a part, her own family. The natural tendency of adolescents is to achieve independence of their families and to strengthen relationships with boys and girls their own age. For the obese adolescents, however, those very peers are the dominant group which rejects them and from which they tend to withdraw, thereby increasing the importance to the child of the family as a source of acceptance.

This increased importance may be reflected, in this series of tests, by the obese girl's expression of greater concern with her family. It is reasonable to suppose, however, that the obese adolescent does not find the family a wholly suitable source of acceptance. There are strong pressures on all adolescents to achieve independence from the family; in addition, the family is also part of a dominant group which rejects obesity and, accordingly, its obese child. The obese group's association of painful emotion with the family and the "blocking" performance of the group may express the other side of the conflict, the partially frustrated desire for independence. Some anecdotal evidence also suggests that this hypothesis may have validity. An administrator at the weight-reduction camp reports that, after a summer spent exclusively with obese girls, a number of campers, on returning home, for the first time in their lives have made a special effort to find obese friends.

They, thus, appear to find the companionship of obese people more satisfying, perhaps because less challenging, than that of nonobese people. It might prove interesting to study the attitudes toward their families of obese adolescents who have an obese "in-group." We might learn if these conflicts are present and to what degree, since ethnic and racial minorities who do have an "in-group" frequently do not demonstrate these conflicts at all or do so less conspicuously.

Stunkard and Mendelson have observed adult obese subjects with "distorted body images" who exhibit remarkably similar attitudes to the obsessive concern" and "identification with the dominant group" already noted in ethnic and racial minorities. They show an exaggerated preoccupation with weight. They judge people in terms of weight, feeling contempt for fat people and admiration for thin people, and consider their obesity a handicap responsible for all disappointments. Obese adults displaying such attitudes had all been obese since childhood, whereas those failing to display such attitudes had all become obese as adults. The crucial difference between these two groups may be the extent to which punitive social pressures have affected their personalities. Children and adolescents are, of course, sensitive to such pressures and would be expected to respond more strongly than adults.

Interpreting personality traits observed among obese adolescents to be *result* of their obesity, rather than a *cause,* seems even more valid when one remembers that obese young people in the United States are under constant pressure to become something they are not, and to think poorly of themselves as they are. Obesity is considered unaesthetic, undesirable, unhealthy, morally wrong, and ridiculous. Movies, television, and the periodical press idealize the thin. Magazine articles on dieting and weight reduction usually insist that obesity can and should be overcome by restricting caloric intake. High life insurance rates and disciplinary action taken by the Armed Forces are well-publicized penalties for obesity. Because obesity is equated with overeating, and eating is considered to be solely regulated by controllable sensations, derogatory attitudes are directed at the obese person's character. The expression "How can anyone let himself—or herself—get that way!" reveals contempt for the obese person's lack of self-restraint. Psychologists and psychiatrists express a more sophisticated version of this attitude when they say obesity is due to neurotic or emotional problems—again, a flaw of character.

Clearly, it is not farfetched to say that obese persons in the United States may form a minority group which suffers from prejudice and discrimination. The exact nature and extent of these prejudiced attitudes against obesity, the myriad effects they may have on the nonobese as well as on the obese, and the possible role these attitudes may play on the perpetuation of obesity, are questions that remain to be answered. At the very least, the heavy burden of inferiority and self-blame imposed by society on obese adolescent girls (and to an only slightly lesser extent, boys) is a matter to be remembered.

I have chosen to present my more recent psychological studies in obese adolescents first, rather than open this chapter with my older and well established studies in activity and food intake in these subjects, because I believe that the pressures of society on the obese, because he or she is obese, are so enormous that they have to be understood as a background before the impact of heredity, lack of exercise, and faulty food habits can be appreciated. This is, of course, not to say that the general causes of obesity which we have discussed in previous chapters are not operating in adolescents. It is rather because what separates the adolescent from the rest of the population (and what justifies having a separate chapter for them) is their peculiar physiological and psychological vulnerability at a time when awareness of the opposite sex and of one's own body is at its highest, obesity is a particularly grave misfortune, particularly in society where it is completely incompatible with attractiveness. To have genes predisposing you to obesity, to live in a society where you do not have to exercise if you don't feel like it, and where food is nevertheless freely available, is a catastrophe at the age where being "popular" is meant not only to be a pleasure but almost a duty.

We know that obesity runs in families, involving genetic as well as environmental factors. But we don't know how much of this tendency in a particular case is due to inherited factors and how much is a result of a homely tradition of piling high the festive board and clearing it. Some of these points are particularly applicable to adolescents. Studies in Massachusetts high schools have shown that less than 10 per cent of the children of parents of normal weight are obese. But the proportion rises to 40 per cent if one parent is obese, and to 80 per cent if both parents are obese. We have indicated that studies of identical and fraternal twins (see Chapter 3), some of whom were raised in different households, have shown that food habits are not the only factors involved. Instead of denying the facts of heredity, as has too long been the custom, it is more useful to employ them for locating obese youngsters and when possible, to treat them. And it seems even more important to try to prevent the development of obesity in children and adolescents whose ancestry suggests their susceptibility. For obesity is most malignant when its onset is early.

Despite the emphasis on the importance of underactivity as a contribution to obesity which my associates and I have documented in so many hundreds of youngsters in so many situations, the layman's usual explanation of the phenomenon in adolescents is overeating. Often this is only technically true. To gain in weight and bulk, the adolescent must indeed consume more food than he uses up in activity. But this is not at all what is usually meant by the allegation of overeating. Behind the charge there is, most of the time, the assumption that most adolescents the thin ones and the fat ones, are physically busy to about the same degree. The difference between the two groups is attributed to the seemingly obvious "fact" that the bulkier adolescent must just be eating more. This persisting notion is perhaps the most wrong-minded one in the whole dismal popular folklore about the adolescent obese.

Probably no single factor is more frequently responsible for the development of obesity in adolescents than lack of physical exercise. In large part, the value of exercise in adolescent weight control has been obscured by four erroneous conceptions:

) the overwhelming emphasis on caloric intake to the almost total exclusion of output;

) the general underestimation of the caloric cost of exercise;

) the mistaken belief that increase in physical activity is always followed by an increase in appetite;

) failure to realize that the kinds of participation, recognition, and success that adolescents enjoy, and the confidence which these bring, can be achieved in the main only by activities that entail physical exercise.

We should never permit ourselves to forget that energy balance is determined as much by caloric output as by caloric intake. The range of daily caloric output in adolescent boys may go from 2,800 calories for extremely inactive youngsters to over 6,000 for athletic young men engaged in strenuous sports. The caloric output per hour in many typical teen-age activities is astonishingly high.

Here are some typical values, calculated for a 150-pound subject:

Activity	Caloric Output per Hour
walking (3 mph)	270
walking (4 mph)	350
running	800–1,000
dancing	200–400
golfing	300
skiing	600–700
tennis	400–500

And, of course, we have seen that voluntary food intake does not necessarily increase with activity. To give this statement precise application, if obese adolescents spend most of their waking time sitting and loitering, then adding an hour or two of activity to their daily schedule does not increase food intake.

The accusation that obesity in adolescents is brought on solely by overindulgence in food is firmly refuted by the results of recent investigations. Repeated studies have shown that the great majority of obese adolescents eat less than the average nonobese adolescents of the same sex. The inactivity of the obese adolescent easily accounts for the calories which permit excessive fat deposition.

This extreme inactivity of the obese youngsters has been established in a number of studies, conducted with different techniques. In the first series, conducted in Brookline, Massachusetts in the early fifties, we compared as carefully as possible the schedules of activity (and the caloric intake) of 28 overweight high school girls matched for age, height, and socio-economic status with 28 girls of normal weight. The overweight girls were found to eat, on the average, several hundred calories less than the nonobese. The laws of thermodynamics were, however, not flouted by this finding, for the overweight girls spent only one-third as much time engaged in occupations which could be characterized as physicall active. A number of later studies conducted on boys as well as on gir all gave similar results.

In a very laborious piece of work which Dr. Beverly Bullen, Dr. Robe Reed, and I conducted, again in the two camps, that for obese girls an that for girls of normal weight with essentially the same background we compared the physical work performed by the two groups while the were engaged in the same activity. We used as a tool of investigation motion-picture technique, first developed for time-motion studies in in dustry, where a special camera is rigged so as to take three-second "shorts every three minutes. We ended up with about 30,000 such short motio pictures of girls playing volley ball, swimming, and playing tennis. Sinc we knew the weight of the subjects, it then became possible to analyz the motions depicted in each sequence and translate them into calori equivalents. Even coming after ten years of study of the inactivity o obese adolescents, the results were extraordinarily striking to us. Th energy expenditure due to activity in most of the obese subjects wa negligible. In fact, in 65 per cent of the "tennis sequences," in 80 pe cent of the "volley ball sequences," and in an even higher proportion o the "swimming sequences," the overweight girls were essentially motior less. Obviously, in any sport practiced for a sufficient length of time there are times when the participant does not move; for example a tennis, when your opponent collects balls, prepares to serve, or ties hi shoe-lace. This accounted for 12 to 15 per cent of the time of the non obese player, as opposed to several times as much for the overweight The inactivity in swimming was particularly unexpected, in that this i one sport where, because of greater insulation and greater buoyanc the overweight girls are at some advantage over the nonobese.

It may be added that the overweight girls are quite unaware of thei lack of participation in these activities. In a situation where a constan attempt was made to render exercising pleasant, the girls professed grea enthusiasm for sports and were, as a matter of fact, more vocal in thei praise of exercise than the nonobese girls. Participation in sports thus ap peared to present the obese girls with a conflict of which they were no aware. While they knew they were less active than their thinner peers, the failed to recognize their disinclination for active exercise—or else simpl enjoyed it as an occasion for social contact, not for its intrinsic worth

On the other hand, in a number of situations, we have been able t show that, difficult though it was to move these overweight youngsters when this was achieved, it did bring about weight reduction. In severa controlled studies taking place in summer camps, we found that activ nonobese youngsters, both boys and girls, placed in a situation wher their energy expenditure was increased through exercise, also increased their food intake and maintained their weight (or increased it only in proportion to their increase in height). By contrast, obese youngsters made to exercise tended spontaneously to keep their food intake at the same level (or sometimes decrease it slightly), so that their energy balance inclined toward the negative and they lost weight.

In a program which I directed in a large public school system, and where I supervised a team including pediatricians, psychologists, physical anthropologists, dietitians, and a large group of physical educators, several hundred obese children and adolescents were reduced and kept reduced for several years essentially through stepped-up daily physical activity. The obese youngsters (selected on the basis of high fatness by measurement of skinfold) were, to be sure, given thorough instruction in nutrition. They were taught the caloric content of foods and advised as to menu selection so as to choose a good diet from which foods high in calories and low in essential nutrients were excluded. But they were not placed on restricted diets (except in a few extreme cases). They were given psychological support, ranging from individual counseling to advice on how to dress, walk, and improve their appearance. But they were not given psychiatric treatment. They were given daily physical education in special classes and directed as to exercising on their own during weekends and holidays. The great majority of them improved steadily under this regimen, particularly if taken in hand very young (first elementary grades) or at any rate no later than junior high school. Thus, if there is any basic rule to offer to obese adolescents who wish to lose weight, it might well be to increase their physical activity.

It goes without saying that, in considering diets for adolescents, the first concern should be nutritional adequacy and balance. No other age group is more subject to fads. No other age group, with the possible exception of the very aged, is so easily victimized by quackery. The diet of adolescents is at very best often unbalanced and sometimes frankly deficient, particularly if they are trying to lose weight. No young person should be permitted to go on a reducing diet that does not meet these two standards: its source should be a physician, a dietitian, or a nutritional authority of demonstrated responsibility; and it should be planned specifically for the person who is going to use it. After all, obesity is a pathological condition and the diet is part of the treatment. At the Adolescents' Clinic of the Children's Medical Center in Boston, we have seen many adolescent girls who on their own initiative, or that of some misguided adult, went on a reducing diet so low in protein and iron that it resulted in anemia. Incidentally, this practice is a major cause of anemia in girls of this age group. Avoiding whole classes of food, some of them essential to health, because of misconceptions about their effects on skin appearance and weight, is another common dietary error of adolescents. The family physician can prevent such excesses by making sure his adolescent patient has sound basic knowledge. Without such knowledge, no reduction regimen can succeed in the long run and there is always the danger that the obese patient may make him- or herself ill.

Another major problem with the usual diets is that they tend to fail by leaving the patient hungry. A solution to this problem has been found, and it is one that works especially well for adolescents. It is to follow a regimen of smaller and more frequent meals, rather than three meals a day without snacks. The fact that most of the overeating is done at night may make it expedient to permit an after-dinner snack of stipulated size and content rather than to eliminate it altogether. Telling oneself or one's child that it's acceptable to have a glass of orange juice when out in the evening with friends is, for example, more effective than steeling oneself not to eat some specific items such as sundaes or making the difficult effort not to eat anything at all.

Diets for adolescents should be individual, adapted to the rate of growth and development of the person and to his or her energy expenditure. Weight loss, as in other age groups, should be slow to avoid excessive fatigue. This factor is especially important with adolescents, because it has been established that they have hypochondriacal concerns, that they are likely to become disturbed to an unwarranted degree about minor changes in their sensations. Ideally, if the adolescent is still growing and not too obese, he should have a caloric intake which will allow him to grow up to the ideal height for his weight at the commencement of the dietary regimen. If additional loss is needed, it should not proceed at a rate faster than a pound a week. This corresponds to a deficit of only 500 calories a day.

Not infrequently, as we have emphasized elsewhere, adolescent overeating may have psychological causes. If grief and lack of affection, success, or popularity are involved, harm may be done by superimposing the discomfort of food restrictions on a situation already difficult enough. In such cases, food deprivation may make emotional problems even more severe. A better solution may well be to induce the adolescent to increase his energy output by increasing his activities. And as the accompanying listing on page 125 shows, a daily walk of less than an hour and a half at a rate of four miles an hour, a task which should not be beyond the capacity of a healthy young person, will provide the caloric deficit of 500 per day which is our upper goal. The walk, or equivalent exercise, when taken daily by an obese adolescent with emotional problems, far from increasing anxieties or depression states as food deprivation might do, should alleviate them perceptibly in many instances.

Our society, consciously or unconsciously, is becoming more and more punitive about the obese person. A study I conducted recently yields evidence that there is even some—probably unconscious—discrimination in college admissions toward obese youngsters. At equal grades, one-third as many obese girls and two-thirds as many obese boys were admitted into the college of their choice as were nonobese girls and boys. This was true whether admission to "prestige" colleges or to colleges in general was considered. And we suspect that many obese adolescents in secondary

OBESITY IN ADOLESCENCE: A VICIOUS CIRCLE

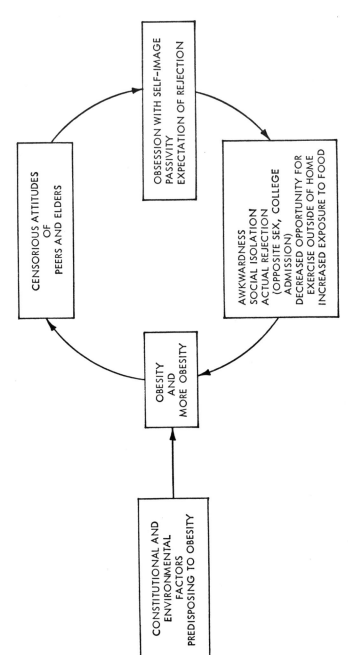

Figure 10

Schematic representation of the factors affecting obesity in adolescence.

schools fail to orient themselves to college aspirations. We would attribute this in part to the lower self-esteem which we know is felt by the obese young, and also to the matter of being intimidated by the prospect of being excluded from the fulfilling activities which are so much an ingredient of college life, particularly in the outward-going imagination of the young.

It is all too easy to encourage a sense of inadequacy in the adolescent. And we are the ones, professionally concerned with obesity, who, at the moment anyway, should feel inadequate. The fact that on a statistical basis our success in permanent weight reduction of the obese is an extremely low one should incite us to humility and further study of the problem, rather than passing the blame on to the young obese themselves. In so doing we risk making the problem worse: a sense of rejection and guilt leads to social isolation, which in turn depresses opportunities for exercise, which in turn accelerates the development of obesity. In some cases, extremely censorious attitudes will precipitate in adolescent girls with compulsive tendencies the onset of "anorexia nervosa," a condition where the subject starves herself, sometimes literally to death. My experience with a number of such subjects suggests to me that underlying the nutritional problem is a grave disturbance of body image, in which the adolescent girl or young woman continues to see herself as obese even though she has become miserably thin. She shares with the obese subjects the obsession with her body (and contempt for its fatness) and some of the expectation of rejection. The disease is fatal if 50 per cent or more of the normal weight is lost. A number of subjects stop their starving regimen at about this point of no return and in some cases go back to a near-obese status, only to starve themselves again. While such cases are rare, they constitute a warning to all of us. Liking the adolescent as a person, thin or fat, and then helping him or her to achieve a healthier, fuller, and happier life is not only kinder than blaming the patient or scaring him or her into compliance, it is also much better medicine.

chapter 10
Obesity
and the Aging

There must be few by now who doubt that the prevalence of obesity in the United States is on the increase and that it is accompanied by increased mortality from a number of diseases, particularly diabetes and diseases of the heart, liver, and kidney. While this association of obesity and degenerative disease is properly and depressingly publicized, insufficient attention has been paid to the direct effect of obesity on functional disabilities. In the aged, obesity often makes moving about and self-care difficult or impossible in hemiplegia (paralysis of one side of the body), in arthritis, and in fractures of the legs. An orthopedist notes: "It is difficult enough to train weakened muscle groups and damaged bones and joints to meet the disabilities of injury and disease without the considerable additional impediment of greater than normal extremity and total body weight." But physicians are frequently reluctant to institute a weight-reduction program in a very old patient who has done well in spite of excessive weight.

While sympathizing with the desire not to upset a time-tested physiological and psychological balance, I must point out that a slow and progressive weight reduction is usually accompanied by improved ease of movement. A decrease in weight of not more than 20 pounds may be sufficient to increase considerably the rate and extent of ability to move about and, thus, the enjoyment of life. Even in the absence of any visible improvement in muscular strength, a weight reduction also decreases the probability of further locomotor disabilities consequent to arthritis, cardiovascular disorders, or accident. Weight reduction in the aged is admittedly difficult. Where activity must be limited, decrease in food intake may be the only way to create a deficit in the energy balance.

If weight reduction is necessary in an aged patient, the diet may not only have to be severely restricted, but it may also have to be changed qualitatively so that the intake in protein, vitamins, and minerals can continue to be or begin to be adequate. Understandable resistance to changes in patterns of nutrition which have been in existence for several decades, mastication problems, and cost factors all make difficult the devising of a successful reducing diet.

Finally, the always undesirable practice of repeated crash weight reduction followed by weight gain may work an even greater stress on the elderly than it does on younger people. Follow-through with reduction programs on the part of the aged patients and follow-up by the physician are even more necessary than in other individuals.

It is both difficult and dangerous to generalize on just what foods—and how much of each of them—older people should have for optimum health and efficiency. Nevertheless, the best proof of the demand for some general guidance is the enormous volume of advertising, often of doubtful veracity, specifically directed toward our senior citizens. Contrary to such advertising claims, available facts do not support the idea that older people have *specific* nutritional needs. Any generalization about *how much* the aged should eat must be cautious.

Back in 1949, the first Committee on Calorie Requirements convened by the Food and Agriculture Organization of the United Nations (of which I was a member) recommended that after the age of 25, the caloric allowance suitable for a human being should be decreased by 7.5 per cent in each successive decade. For example, if at 25 the individual had good health, good weight, and a good fat-to-weight ratio (judgments to be professionally determined) and was consuming around 3,000 calories a day, he should start to cut that amount down so that it was 225 calories less by the time he was 35; by the time he became 45, calorie consumption should be decreased by another 225 calories per day; and so on in each succeeding decade.

During the eight years that followed the committee's original pronouncement, however, there was an impressive accumulation of facts which refuted the assumption that energy expenditures decreased steadily during the earlier stages of aging. The new data showed that the decrease was not as great as we had believed. In other words, people in the age groups concerned were, in the main, spryer and busier than had been thought; and therefore they should not be put too sternly on such short rations.

When the second Committee met in 1957, we were convinced that, provided the adult remained normally active or continued to work at an occupation which demanded physical labor, the decrease in food requirement we had recommended previously was too great during the middle years. In the intervening period, some evidence had become available that only after 45, at the earliest, did energy requirements decrease significantly. Accordingly, the Committee proposed that the caloric allowance be cut by only 3 per cent of the requirement at 25 for each of the next two decades. For the decades from 45 to 55 and 55 to 65, a 7 per cent cut of food intake was suggested, and for the decade from 65 to 75, a further decrease of 10 per cent. (These successive percentages are not applied to each new base, but are applied to the requirements obtained at 25.) It will be reassuring to the vigorous and food-fond reader of 75 that the Committee urged no further tampering with the amount of food it was willing to apportion him.

But the 1957 dicta are far from the final words on this vital subject. Still more recent information argues for both a more progressive and a more individual basis for the caloric allowances of those who are no longer young. Dr. J. V. G. A. Durnin, a Glasgow, Scotland physiologist, believes it useful to try to classify with more precision differing degrees of aging. He calls people between 65 and 75 "elderly"—that is, "getting old"—and calls people 75 and over "old." His main concern is with the elderly. His own studies, as well as those of other contemporary authorities, show that in such Western countries as Great Britain and the United States, physical activity changes little between the ages of 30 and 60 to 70. During this same long stretch, however, muscular efficiency appears to decrease with age, in part because of the slow loss of precision in muscular coordination. This decrease in strength and proficiency leads an older person to require *more* energy for a particular task than a younger person. In other words, if the older person continues to do what he did when he was younger, he will need to be nourished sufficiently to provide him with the *extra* energy required.

Finally, while there is progressive degeneration in body composition such as an increasing replacement of protein by fat, with each year after the body reaches maturity, this is not (except in really old or excessively sedentary people) always as marked as is commonly believed. Replacement of muscle tissue by fat proceeds relatively slowly in individuals who remain physically active.

The slowness in the decrease of physical activity, the changes in body composition, and the reduction of muscle efficiency thus accounts for the slight change in the total metabolism of large groups of men. This is particularly true for men whose work entails physical exertion which varies little over decades. For them, decreasing the amount of food usually becomes appropriate only when abrupt retirement brings a stop to customary physical activity. The cut in food intake, rarely an attractive program in our culture, often can be made less burdensome if a pattern of sufficiently demanding and interesting activities is substituted for the familiar ones. On the other hand, for the many Americans whose physical activity drops abruptly when they graduate from college, middle age nutrition starts at age 22 and food intake should be decreased then if they want to avoid obesity.

The limitation on food intake is applicable also to aging women, particularly housewives. For them the physical tasks of housework usually show a marked drop in later life. And for them, too, some kind of regular exercise will make it possible to have more of their customary cake by providing an outlet for its calories. We may conclude that if the caloric intake of the aged, particularly men, was not excessive in their early middle age, and if they have retained the same schedule of work and other activities, there is no reason to add the burden of eating less to the difficulties which getting old can bring.

If activity drastically diminishes because of chronic disease, change in occupation, or confinement, then, obviously, caloric intake must be decreased to prevent obesity, itself a pathological condition and, too commonly, also chronic. This, however, is true at any age. And what is good for people in general is, in most instances, good for old people too.

In view of comment and speculation in the professional and lay press concerning the effect of underfeeding on the life span of experimental animals, rats in particular, a short discussion of these experiments may be in order. Confusion seems to exist between

(1) experiments dealing with the effect on the adult life span of avoiding obesity and

(2) experiments dealing with the effect on overall longevity of retarding growth and sexual maturation.

It is a very general finding that in nonexercised animals the daily restriction of calories so as to prevent obesity causes them to live longer than nonexercised animals which are fed *ad libitum* and become obese. Frequent intermittent restriction of calories also prolongs life by reducing early mortality. Anton Carlson of Chicago showed that, by fasting animals one day in three, he could increase the life expectancy by about 15 per cent in rats receiving an omnivorous diet (that is, one containing all kinds of foods). The gain was less with a vegetarian diet. Evidence is not conclusive that avoidance of obesity through exercise in animals fed *ad libitum* provides life spans as long as or longer than those achieved by avoidance of obesity through caloric restriction in nonexercised animals, but it points in this direction.

It is the second type of experiment, dealing with the effects on over-all longevity of undernutrition and growth retardation in young animals, which has most often been misunderstood. The prevention of obesity in adult animals, effective as it is, prolongs life only for a period equivalent to a few years in man; by contrast, growth retardation and delay in sexual maturation produced by drastic caloric restriction cause a tremendous increase in the total life span of many species. This *early* restriction produces animals whose life spans are equivalent to that of the famous and perhaps mythical Shropshire farmer, Thomas Parr, who reputedly was 153 years old when he died in 1635. The life cycle of many invertebrates, insects in particular, can be lengthened in some or all of its stages by curtailing the rate of early growth and development through food restriction. Slowing down the growth of beetle larvae extends their life from one to many years. In cockroaches, the optimal protein intake for longevity is about half that which produces the fastest development. Clive McCay and his colleagues at Cornell have shown that sexual maturation of rats could be delayed for periods up to 1,000 days (longer than the normal life span) and that, after this period, survivors were capable of resuming growth and starting reproduction, thus considerably increasing their total life span; the gain in further expectation of life, however, was not equal to the period of underfeeding and was greater in males than in females. Other workers have shown that life expectancy of a laboratory strain of mice can be doubled by severe underfeeding during growth. Albino mice which were fasted two days out of seven had an increase in life span of more than 50 per cent. Similar experiments on other strains bear out the general conclusion that the beneficial effect on the total life span of retardation of growth and sexual maturation is much greater than what could be achieved with *ad libitum* feeding during growth followed by avoidance of obesity in adulthood.

It has been estimated that if our mature population were to avoid obesity through dietary control and exercise, the gain in life expectancy could be no more than four to five years. (Lest this be minimized, such an increment is twice what the cure of cancer could bring.) Whether or not man, with his proportionately low growth rate and lengthy growth period, is similar to lower animals in being able to resume growth and sexual maturation after prolonged periods of consumption of a qualitatively complete but calorically inadequate diet in early life, and whether or not such treatment would prolong life by decades, has never been tested. It is difficult to see how such an experiment could be conducted. Yet this fascinating possibility may well offer the one way in which life expectancy could be spectacularly increased by nutritional means.

Because of the very fact that so few of the obese live to an old age, it is not surprising that undernutrition and resultant emaciation are more frequently seen in old age, particularly extreme old age. In fact, there appears to be general agreement that admissions to general hospitals with partial or serious malnutrition are more numerous in old patients than in young and middle-aged ones. But despite voluminous propaganda, vitamin deficiencies are not common in the aged. They are usually found in oldsters who are subsisting on monotonous and nondiversified meals. In many cases normal foods have been replaced by diet fads, perhaps supplemented by expensive "miracle preparations" or by too much alcohol. Norman Jolliffe and his colleagues in New York have described a condition seen exceptionally often in the aged which they named nicotinic acid deficiency encephalopathy (an organic disease of the brain). The onset is insidious and the earliest symptoms are vague (fatigue, irritability, depression, nervousness). Later, impairment of intellectual function supervenes, followed by stupor and coma.

There are physiological, psychological, and sociological factors involved in this kind of malnutrition. A combination of factors is often seen in the same person. Structural disease of the esophagus or stomach may cause discomfort and result in the patient's never eating adequate meals.

Lack of teeth may make proper mastication difficult and may be a very serious problem in the aged.

The fluoridation of water supplies, although its main physiologic effect is on the young, may have its most beneficial nutritional effect on the aged, in that conservation of teeth permits continued mastication and thus greater choice of foods. (It may also retard osteoporosis, the loss of calcium in the bones of the aged.)

Disinterest in eating because of loneliness is not infrequently observed, particularly in patients who live alone and are unable or unwilling to go through even cursory meal preparation. Economic factors are paramount in many cases. It has been estimated that in the United States at present, 75 per cent of the people over 65 have a cash income of less than $1,000 per year, and 15 per cent of those most in need of dietary improvement, less than $500 per year.

In many cases, the most important deficiency afflicting many of the aged is not a deficiency of protein, vitamins, or minerals, but of money.

Finally, an important factor in the determination of the diet of many older patients is food faddism. In an era of rising educational standards, older persons often function at a lower level of information than do young adults. Their often incurable ailments cannot be eliminated by medical treatment; in their search for relief they grasp at the irresponsible promises of wonder healers. The treatment of arthritis, for example, is infested by these quacks, and a great deal of the propaganda for youth elixirs, "nature" foods, and fad diets is directed toward the aged. Expenditures for such items may work great hardship on limited budgets and may be made at the cost of variety in the diet and proper medical care. Hospitalization, with particular attention to diet, often results in gains of up to 15 per cent in body weight or more in chronically emaciated persons. A number of ill-defined deficiency symptoms also disappear. Such treatment is by no means always successful; irreversible physiological and psychiatric conditions and often insurmountable social problems continue to restrict the intake of the patient. There is little doubt that lack of appetite is common in the aged. By weakening the patient and making him feel sick, his malnutrition may be self-perpetuating and even self-accelerating. Undernutrition not only decreases the enjoyment of life but may make the older patient more difficult to care for and less likely to resist infections or surgical traumas.

The possible relationship of fat content and kind of fat in the diet to heart disease is of obvious relevance to the problems of nutrition in the aging. This subject has received a great deal of popular attention recently and is reviewed in Chapter 8. There is general agreement that, by and large, saturated fatty acids, found in milk, butter, most margarines and shortenings, meats, and eggs, tend to elevate serum cholesterol, regarded as one of the main villains in coronary heart disease.

Recent studies mentioned in Chapter 8 emphasize also the possible influence of exercise in preventing heart disease, and the unfavorable effect of cigarette smoking. From a practical viewpoint, it appears reasonable to suggest that aging individuals and probably all adults, males in particular, should consume a diet not too high in fats (saturated fats especially) and should adopt methods of food preparation which will minimize the total saturated-fat content of the diet.

The advisability of a drastic decrease of salt intake in the treatment of many cardiovascular diseases—the salt-free diet—is well documented, and its practice is familiar to many readers. Available experimental data on rats and data on men are, however, at best suggestive that limitations of salt intake are useful in the prevention, rather than the treatment, of hypertension and coronary accidents. Prudent persons will try to limit their salt intake as they become older. This does not mean a salt-free diet, but simply cutting down on unnecessary salting of meals. Older women are notoriously prone to fluid retention, which often appears to nullify the effect on weight of a reducing diet. Salt restriction decreases the likelihood of such fluid retention.

R. C. Garry, Professor of Physiology at the Glasgow Medical School and an excellent gerontologist, has said,

> Above all, we must see the elderly in continuity with youth and middle age. We accept that the child is father of the man. We could equally well say the elderly person is the child of his youth and years of maturity. The elderly do not form a special isolated section of the community; we must continually hark back to the earlier years.

Nowhere is this more true than in the field of nutrition and in that of personal hygiene. Consumption of a varied diet, adapted in amount to the need of the moment, avoidance of dietary excesses, avoidance of an excessively fat diet, moderate salt intake, generous fluid intake, sufficient exercise and rest—these recommendations are as valid for old age as they are for young adults and the middle-aged.

chapter 11

The Science
of Nutrition

Even though the problem of obesity is one which transcends nutrition per se and also requires, to be grasped, some understanding of biochemistry, physiology, psychology and psychiatry, physical and cultural anthropology, and sociology, it is nevertheless true that an overall view of our thinking in nutrition generally is a *sine qua non* when dealing with obesity. Rather than presenting an ABC of nutrition couched in the usual textbook approach dealing with topic after topic, I have thought it more interesting to my readers to deal with nutrition on an historical basis, explaining the order in which the main ideas originated, and ending with an exposition of the lines of attack of present-day research, particularly as they deal with obesity and related subjects. In my historical exposition, I shall try to give some idea of the development of our social concepts of nutrition as well as of our scientific and medical concepts. The reader will see that the science of nutrition is very young. Even though man's main preoccupation has been food since the beginning of his existence as a species, nutrition as a science is less than two hundred years old. Casimir Funk, who coined the household word, *vitamin,* died in 1967. By contrast, while the stars are far away and exert, at most, an extremely indirect influence on the human species, astronomy became a science over 25 centuries ago. But then, modern experimental biology, and in particular, physiology, started only at the beginning of the seventeenth century when Harvey discovered the general circulation of blood.

Very broadly, the evolution of the science of nutrition can be divided into four periods:

(1) the prescientific period, extending from the dim beginnings of the Stone Age to the second half of the eighteenth century, following Lavoisier's introduction of heat-measuring concepts;

(2) the age when caloric and nitrogen balance were studied, the nineteenth century;

3) the era when the trace elements, vitamins, and essential amino acids were discovered, and the deficiency diseases studied, extending from the beginning of the twentieth century to the 1940's; and

4) the period since the end of World War II, with development of the study of nutrition's role in degenerative diseases and recognition of the fact that what is in the diet can be almost as important as what is missing from the diet.

Let us briefly review the history of these periods.

The prescientific period

An intricate knowledge of food is necessary for survival. In a long series of trials and errors—sometimes mortal errors—the number of animals and plants known to provide food was slowly extended. And the idea that food does more than assuage hunger is very old. Certain beliefs, such as the notion that consumption of the heart or flesh of brave or strong animals or enemies would confer the same virtues on the warriors of the tribe, appeared during the Stone Age. While some edicts may well have had something to do with the unwholesomeness of certain foods (e.g., the Biblical prohibition of pork may well have been based on the recognition of the occurrence of illness and even death from the consumption of swine now assumed to have been infested with *Trichinella*), most such beliefs seem to have had no basis in fact. Examples of such apparently pointless practices were the Egyptian prohibition of beef or chicken for kings and the Biblical declaration against hare.

Closely allied with the problem of taboos and superstitious beliefs was the search for foodstuffs which also would be remedies. Many herbs and parts of plants or animals were prescribed because of their shape, their color, or some other property unrelated to any demonstrable pharmacologic effect. But the common recommendations of the "Ebers Papyrus" (1600 B.C.), of Hippocrates, the founder of scientific medicine (fifth century B.C.), and of several medieval writers to the effect that liver was a "cure" for eye diseases and for night blindness, and of Cartier's Indians, who used evergreen needle infusions for scurvy, are early examples of prescriptions for deficiency diseases. Incidentally, Hippocrates paid considerable attention to nutrition in his writings. Many of his opinions are difficult to justify—for example, his belief that beef is more troublesome to digest than pork, or that fish should be roasted rather than boiled for feverish patients. But his abhorrence both of extreme abstemiousness and diet restriction, and of excessive intake without corresponding physical labor, is still good nutritional advice.

The age of study of caloric and nitrogen balance

Probably the greatest turning point in the history of biology and medicine was the investigation of combustion conducted by Lavoisier (1743–1794). He introduced measurements in biologic and chemical studies, and in his experiments laid the basis for our understanding of caloric expenditures and requirements.

Specifically, Lavoisier showed that oxygen was used by the body to burn foods. The smallest amount of oxygen was used when the individual was resting at a comfortable temperature, several hours after he had eaten. This is very close to what we call the condition of basal metabolism. The figures Lavoisier obtained for oxygen consumption, with primitive equipment, approximated the figures we now recognize as normal. Lavoisier showed, further, that consumption of food increased the oxygen consumption (and the heat loss) of his subjects, a phenomenon which we now call "Specific Dynamic Action" (SDA). He also showed that exposure to cold similarly increased heat loss, energy requirements, and oxygen consumption. Finally, he showed that increased muscular activity increased oxygen consumption and energy requirements. In fact, this could double or even triple Lavoisier's basal energy requirement.

Since Lavoisier's studies, a great deal of work has been done to get more precise figures for the energy cost of man's various activities and the energy cost of keeping body temperature constant under different climatic conditions. As an upshot of this work, we can ascribe a figure, in terms of calories, to all such human needs. We can calculate with great accuracy how many calories a particular man, woman, or child will require to live a particular type of life.

The findings of Lavoisier had to do with *amounts* of food. They told us how much an individual required. They did not reveal whether this food had to be of any particular nature. The next development in nutritional knowledge assured us that it did and, in a general way, indicated what the required nature was. It took place in the nineteenth century, with the discovery that all forms of calories are not equivalent. Protein, which provides the basis for the construction of the structural elements of the body, plays a very special role. While carbohydrates can replace fat, and, to a large extent, vice versa, from the point of view of calories available to the body, the same type of replacement cannot be made for protein. There *is* a minimum protein requirement.

Lavoisier's results were extended by the work of nineteenth-century physiologists and chemists. Such scientists as Vauquelin, Magendie, Prout, Mulder, and, pre-eminently, Von Liebig (1803–1873) developed concepts and methods of analysis permitting the establishment of food composition tables. These, as will be shown, are still the essential tool of the nutritionist. For any reassessment of the value of a diet and any dietary recommendations must be translated in terms of foods to be of practical use.

Boussingault (1820–1887) studied absorption and digestion of foodstuffs. The proportion of carbohydrate, protein, and fat, and their contributions to the caloric content of foods became the basis of nutrition, with only scant attention being given to the minerals and almost none to the nutritional factors present in small amounts which, as vitamins, essential amino acids, and essential fatty acids, we now consider to be indispensable to the maintenance of life, let alone health.

Atwater, who returned to this country in 1892 following a period of European study, tried to put all of practical nutrition on the basis of the financial cost of calories and protein. In effect, he advocated deriving the diet chiefly from cereals, peas, and beans because of their cheapness, and omitting fruits and garden vegetables, which he felt, ignoring qualitative nutrition, contributed little for their cost. Both Von Voit and Atwater recommended large amounts of protein for adults (approximately 150 grams per day), in spite of Chittenden's experiments in New Haven showing that men could live and work with less than one-third this amount.

Trace elements, vitamins, amino acids; deficiency diseases

The revolution in the thinking on nutrition which took place between 1905 and 1910 has rarely been paralleled. It was much like the change in our knowledge of infectious diseases after the discoveries of Louis Pasteur. The turning point came with the concept of *essential nutrients,* that is, substances necessary for growth, health, and maintenance of life. This was tantamount to recognizing that the human organism is a good, but not a perfect chemist. It can synthesize thousands of complicated molecules. It *cannot* synthesize a number of structures—vitamins and essential amino and fatty acids. Hopkins showed tryptophan, one of some twenty-two amino acids, the building blocks of proteins, to be one such indispensable nutrient. Osborn and Mendel demonstrated that the addition of tryptophan and lysine, another essential amino acid, considerably improved the biologic value of corn proteins; the chief corn protein, zein, is particularly low in these amino acids. McCollum and Davis showed that the minimum adequate diet for the rat must provide, in addition to the long-known nutrients, two unidentified factors which they called "fat-soluble A" and "water-soluble B." These were later shown to be complex: the fat soluble factors included vitamins A, D, E, and K; the water soluble factors included vitamin C and the several B vitamins.

It is remarkable that, while physicians—Linde, Trousseau, and Ejikman—first established nutrition as a factor in such diseases as scurvy rickets, and beriberi, it is to chemists—Hopkins, Mendel, McCollum, and others—that we owe the concept of deficiency diseases as clinical entities. It seems almost incredible that barely a century ago Charles Caldwell, one of the most prominent physicians of his time, was writing a 95-page pamphlet denouncing Von Liebig and proclaiming that chemistry had nothing to contribute to medical science!

It should be unnecessary to point out the extreme speed at which our understanding of the deficiency diseases, the characterization and synthesis of vitamins, and the translation of experimental nutrition into clinical advancement progressed between World Wars I and II. Rickets, once the most prevalent disease condition in cities of the Western world, was almost wiped out in ten years by the widespread use of fish liver oils and by the fortification of milk with vitamin D. Goiter was eliminated from entire populations by the addition of iodine to salt. Flour enrichment and diet improvement have so effectively dealt with pellagra that it has been impossible for several years to locate a pellagrous patient in the whole state of Georgia to demonstrate the once common signs of the disease to the students of the Medical College of the state university.

At the same time that our experimental and clinical knowledge improved, our sense of social responsibility increased. It came to be accepted that educated nations could not tolerate that easily preventable diseases should continue to kill and disable millions of human beings. In his famous book, "Diet, Health, and Income," John Boyd Orr showed that in Scotland poor growth and sickness were much more prevalent among the low-income classes than among the wealthy. Hazel Stiebling in this country and André Mayer in France conducted nutritional surveys which demonstrated that many children and adults, particularly in the poorer classes, were undernourished or malnourished. In the 1930's the League of Nations called together a committee of physiologists which promulgated the first set of recommended dietary allowances, as well as a practical handbook on the assessment of the nutritional status of populations. This impetus was further accelerated by the preoccupation with food problems during World War II.

Since the end of World War II

Scientific advisory bodies, such as the United States National Research Council Food and Nutrition Board, came into existence on several continents. More importantly, over sixty nations combined their efforts to improve nutrition all over the world. A number of additional nations have joined the organization since, bringing the total to the vicinity of 100. The Food and Agriculture Organization of the United Nations, the Nutrition Section of the World Health Organization, and the United Nations International Children's Emergency Fund are some of the healthy offspring of this great movement. In many regions the emergency measures taken by some of the "crisis committees" created by FAO averted the widespread starvation that would have followed the end of the war. UNICEF has started and encouraged child-feeding programs covering millions of children in Asia, Africa, and Latin America. FAO and WHO have initiated, supported, and publicized epidemiological and clinical studies of kwashiorkor—the most widespread deficiency syndrome found in poor areas—which apparently is due to lack of good-quality proteins in the diet during early childhood following weaning.

It would seem, on first view, that these considerations would not be germane to our main topic, obesity. But, in fact, the renewed interest in *undernutrition* during World War II which led to the creation of several international organizations resulted directly in an interest in *overnutrition*. Observers were struck by the drastic decrease in the number of patients hospitalized with conditions of the heart and blood vessels during the famine accompanying the siege of Leningrad. When the siege was broken and the famine relieved, the "refeeding" period was associated with an upsurge in such conditions. In the United States, statistics accumulated by life insurance companies emphasized, at the same time, though less dramatically, the positive correlation of excess weight and mortality, not only from cardiovascular diseases, but also from liver conditions, diabetes, increased operative risk, accidents, and other circumstances. This body of data in turn stimulated interest in the study of the causes and development of obesity, and its associative and causative links to disease.

Considerable interest also was generated by Keys' suggestion that the presence of a high proportion of fat in the diet was associated with a high level of blood cholesterol, atherosclerosis, and coronary disease. A lively and constructive experimental controversy still rages as to the relative influence on cholesterol levels of the proportion in the diet of animal and vegetable fats, the degree of saturation of the fat, the concentration of polyunsaturated (essential) fatty acids, and the presence of plant sterols (wax-like substances analogous to cholesterol, found in man and other animals). It has been seen (Chapter 8) that the bulk of the evidence shows that the higher the serum cholesterol level, the higher the risk of cardiovascular catastrophe. Furthermore, it is now agreed that, in general, polyunsaturated fatty acids decrease, and saturated fatty acids increase, the cholesterol level. Putting coronary patients on a "high polyunsaturated" diet—while reducing the total dietary fat—drastically reduces the risk of a second cardiovascular accident. Because obese individuals are more prone to cardiovascular disease (we have seen in Chapter 8 that both association and causation may be involved), this is germane to the problem of obesity.

Another recent development was the recognition that the time factor should be accorded more attention in nutrition. For example, Best showed in experimental animals that certain deficiencies during growth may lead to hypertension in old age; many investigators produced congenital malformations by feeding pregnant animals deficient diets at certain crucial periods during pregnancy. The links between diet and degenerative diseases also pointed to the need for longer-term studies. For example, what is the difference in risk between life-long obesity and recent obesity? Is obesity more dangerous at certain ages?

Incidentally, this introduction of the factor of longer duration in nutritional problems re-emphasized the fact, known to experienced physicians since Hippocrates, that, to understand how a given disease affects a given patient at a given age, one must consider not only the disease agent, but also its duration of action and the patient's individual constitution. Other recent findings have also underlined the importance of studying the interaction of constitutional and nutritional factors. For example, it is becoming clear that there are strong genetic determinants in the ability of an organism to switch from a high-carbohydrate to a high-fat diet without accumulating excessive adiposity. We have seen also that there are demonstrated constitutional differences in the ability to regulate food intake at low exercise levels; in other words, the appetite of certain individuals is brought down proportionately when their activity is reduced to low levels, while others are constitutionally prone to overeat if their activity is too low.

There are many other nutritional problems which have been attacked vigorously since 1945, such as the relationship of diet to resistance to infection; to the effectiveness and risks of antibiotic therapy; to aging; to mental retardation; to physical and intellectual performance; to reproduction; and to the special nutritional problems of adolescence, arising in part from the recognition that iron deficiency anemia in this age group is widespread. (Again, we have seen that this situation too may have significance as regards obesity.) Intravenous and other nonoral nutrition, especially when prolonged, urgently raises the whole problem of nutritional requirements and of individual differences in requirements. The long-term maintenance of astronauts poses the same problem. Advances in general nutrition have also led to a critical re-examination of many of the classic special diets. Is the high-fat diet used for ulcer patients dangerous from the viewpoint of atherosclerosis? Is the rice diet used for hypertensive patients deficient in protein? What of electrolyte balance, the balance between minerals, in patients on a low-salt diet for a long time?

Postwar developments of cultural anthropology have placed emphasis on what may be called the non-nutritional aspects of foods. Certain food practices and certain dishes may have a symbolic significance which, through conscious and subconscious associations, is linked with the taboos of an earlier age, as well as with buried childhood memories. The possible relationship of alcoholism to nutrition has been critically examined, though results are ambiguous: in many cases alcoholism causes malnutrition; malnutrition may predispose to alcoholism. The addiction of many people to fad diets and "nature foods" causes an unnecessary strain on their budgets, often results in an unbalanced diet, and may be a symptom of more serious psychologic difficulties which can be understood only in terms of their general emotional background. Some research has been done on the cause of such addictions (often linked to resentment against intellectualism, expressed also in such attitudes as opposition to fluoridation), but much remains to be done in this field.

Nutrition remains an area of vigorous growth in our knowledge of man. It appears increasingly clear that, in order to control the old enemies of mankind—starvation and pestilence—and to combat such new enemies as heart disease and diabetes (the degenerative illnesses), or such miseries as mental retardation, which have accompanied man in the past and seem likely to stay with him for a long time, nutrition research will have to be expanded and the results rapidly (and intelligently) taught. That nutrition is poorly taught at present, not only to the public but also to the health professions, is a sad but incontrovertible fact. The cost of this neglect is daily mounting.

chapter 12
Diets
and Obesity

Nutrition is a matter of kind and *amounts* of nutrients. Any dietary prescription entails, therefore, the analysis of the present diet in terms of calories and nutrients, the determination of changes to be effected—in the case of the obese person this constitutes lessening the caloric intake while maintaining the nutritional balance—and a prescription expressing the nutritional changes in terms of altered pattern and/or altered amount of food to be consumed.

The place for an obese person to obtain a reducing diet is the office of a physician who is particularly concerned with that person and with the correction of his or her obesity; or a weight-reduction clinic which is applying sound nutritional principles under medical direction. The count-down on calories which has become more important to millions of Americans than the count-down at Cape Kennedy has bred too many "authorities" on the subject of nutrition in general and weight reduction in particular. Their pronouncements are often at best whimsical and at worst dangerous. The subject of nutrition is too extensive and too complex for even the wisest layman to attempt to acquire all the background he might desire for responsible self-treatment. Self-conscious and harassed teenagers, conscientious nursing mothers, busy executives, older people soon to be retired, practically every literate American should by now be convinced that the selection of a good diet is based in part on a large body of scientific information. For never has such a large percentage of any public been so emphatically and frequently informed of the importance of eating exactly what they should for health, slimness, long life, and happiness. What a good many people fail to recognize, however, is that no one particular diet is appropriate for everybody. Good but personally irrelevant diets and all quack diets would be forever ignored if each of us recognized the value of a varied diet, consisting of sufficient but not too much total content, tailored to individual needs.

How does a physician or a dietitian go about selecting the amount of food that you require? By determining a daily caloric intake that matches your daily activities and, in the case of a reducing diet, by cutting down the quantity to be consumed without endangering the supply of any of the necessary ingredients. Physiologists have determined how many calories are expended in each activity.

Even a state of complete rest is an expenditure, for you still need food to keep your vital organs working and to keep your temperature at the proper level. We have seen earlier that the energy required to perpetuate this comparatively quiet state under fasting conditions is called the *basal* metabolism. It is usually measured in a comfortably warm room, with the patient lying down, 14 hours after the last meal. If the metabolism is measured under conditions of normal nutrition (no fast), but again with the patient lying down at a comfortably warm temperature, it is called the *resting* metabolism.

When you decide to indulge in even the slightest amount of greater activity—such as whistling one chorus of a popular song—the energy expended requires you to eat a small but precise amount of extra food. If you make up your mind to get up and live actively—keep house, teach a college class, operate a chain of newspapers, grow a large garden, learn to play squash—you need more food. The exact amount depends upon your size, physical activity, and to a very minor degree, the climate where you live. A 25-year-old, 154-pound house painter who lives in Minneapolis (mean annual temperature: 50° F.) uses 3,300 calories a day, thus:

Working Activity (10 hours)
8 hours standing and painting (3 cal./min.)	1,450
2 hours gardening or sports (5 cal./min.)	600

Non-occupational Activity (6 hours)
1 hour washing, dressing, etc. (2.5 cal./min.)	150
4 hours driving, sitting, etc. (1.7 cal./min.)	400
1 hour domestic work (3.5 cal./min.)	200

Rest in Bed	500
TOTAL	3,300

On the other hand, a relatively inactive 53-year-old, 132-pound housewife who lives in the same city, uses up only 2,000 calories:

Working Activity (8 hours)
Domestic work (1.9 cal./min.)	910

Non-occupational Activity (8 hours)
1 hour washing, dressing, etc. (2 cal./min.)	120
1 hour shopping and driving (1.8 cal./min.)	100
6 hours sitting (1.3 cal./min.)	470

Rest in Bed	400
TOTAL	2,000

But a 21-year-old, 121-pound new mother in northern California (mean annual temperature: 68° F.) uses 3,200 calories a day—almost as many as the Minnesota house painter—largely because she is tending and nursing her baby:

Working Activity (10 hours)	
Domestic work, care of baby, etc. (2 cal./min.)	1,200
Non-occupational Activity (6 hours)	
1 hour washing, dressing, etc. (2 cal./min.)	120
1 hour walking at 3 mph. and shopping (3.2 cal./min.)	200
2 hours playing golf or gardening (3.0 cal./min.)	360
2 hours sitting (1.2 cal./min.)	140
Rest in Bed	400
Lactation allowances (600–700 cc. milk)	800
TOTAL	3,220

We are steadily increasing our knowledge of the number of calories needed by various types of people, engaged in various types of occupations. But despite the fact that these calories are widely referred to and clearly defined, their very definition is sometimes not completely understood. In scientific terms, the calorie is the amount of heat energy required to raise the temperature of one kilogram of water—somewhat less than a quart—by one degree Centigrade, from 14.5° to 15.5°. On the Fahrenheit scale, that represents a rise from 58.1° to 59.9°.

Various forms of energy are, of course, interchangeable. You can, therefore, measure in calories the energy you spend in activities of any sort and the energy you acquire in food of any kind (for the latter, see Appendix IVa). By matching the number of calories you take in with those you use up, your physician is able to plan for you a diet and activity program which will bring about the goal you want, in this instance a reduction in weight.

The principal sources from which we acquire calories are carbohydrates, fats, and proteins. Among the carbohydrates are sugar, starch, and the cellulose which forms most of our undigested roughage. (Cellulose furnishes no calories to man, but does to the cow whose rumen contains bacteria which break it down to usable fragments.) Typical fats are butter, lard, and olive oil. Proteins are found in meat, fish, and many vegetables. From the point of view of energy, carbohydrates, fats, and proteins are interchangeable in accordance with their "caloric equivalents." These equivalents were determined with great precision by the first American nutritionist, W. O. Atwater, at the turn of the century. He found, first of all, that the proteins, fats, and carbohydrates contained in various foods are not strictly equal, gram for gram, from the viewpoint of energy. For example, a gram of starch contains a little more energy than a gram of bread protein. But he also found that these differences are minute. In general, a gram of protein or of carbohydrate contains four calories, a gram of fat is equivalent to nine calories. After determining the relative proportion of each major constituent of a food, we can get an excellent approximation of the number of calories the food contains.

Food composition tables are prepared along these principles. To be immediately helpful, they should give caloric values in terms of common household units—slices, cupfuls, portions, etc. Appendix IVa, is such a table. It gives a good idea of the range of calories provided by various foods.

In order to use this table intelligently to calculate the caloric content of your ordinary diet or of a reducing diet, it is essential that you train yourself to evaluate the size of the portions you are consuming. There is a great difference between a three-ounce hamburger (about 320 calories) and a six-ounce hamburger (640 calories); and yet this is a variation encountered in the same family when two teenagers "cook themselves a hamburger," depending on their appetites (or what is left in the refrigerator). Martinis, depending on whether they are "small" or "large," will similarly vary from 150 to 300 calories; a punch cup of Christmas eggnog contains 340 calories, while an eggnog consumed in an ordinary glass by an enthusiastic participant in Yuletide festivities may well hold 600 or 700 calories—and so it goes. Left to himself, a patient will usually be very careful to mention whether he or she has had one poached egg (77 calories) or two poached eggs (154 calories), one banana (119 calories or two bananas (238 calories), one tangerine (35 calories) or two tangerines (70 calories), but will not attempt a quantitative description of the calorically more important foods described above. The method of preparation has to be described with equal accuracy. The same weight of potatoes (100 grams) is equivalent to less than 100 calories if it is baked and peeled after baking, about 300 calories if it is French fried, and close to 600 if it is potato chips! And, finally, the way in which the food is consumed is also important. Some careful dieters may decrease the 400 calories contained in an untrimmed slice of ham by as much as 100 calories by carefully trimming out the fat. I cannot emphasize enough that understanding of these facts is a prerequisite for success in reducing. If your physician is too busy to spend a great deal of time instructing you in these matters, he will probably refer you to the dietary outpatient department of the nearest large hospital. There the dietitian will help you visualize portion sizes by the use of realistic models of the common foods. She will also answer your questions about how the mode of preparation of dishes can influence the caloric content of your diet.

One of the comforting features of the science of nutrition is that so much of it makes clear and unencumbered sense. One would expect that a large person would need more calories than a small person and that is the way it is. The physically quite active person, as has been repeatedly affirmed, requires more calories to maintain his current weight than does the sedentary person. And anyone, large or small, busy or indolent, will need a few more calories in the winter, particularly if he lives in the northern part of the United States or in Canada, than he will in the summer.

Of these factors—relative activity, differing size, and contrasting temperature—the most important is physical activity. For example, if you are a medium-sized male executive, you will need about 2,400 calories daily; if you are an active farmer, 3,500; and if you are a lumberjack, 5,000. United States women need from 1,600 to 2,800 calories daily, depending on their routine. For information on the daily caloric requirements of men, women, and children of various ages and weight, see Appendix II.

Almost as much on the mind of the general public as calories is the subject of vitamins. Vitamins, as has by now become known to everyone within range of a radio or a television set, are necessary to the body's functioning. But the average person who has the good fortune to live and eat in the United States should not worry about obtaining the proper variety and quantity of vitamins. If he gets the appropriate supply of calories from sufficiently varied foods of animal and plant origins, he will almost always get the right amount of needed vitamins, too. You don't have to supplement your diet with vitamins unless your physician has determined that you do, in truth, have a deficiency; and your physician is the man to tell you what the specific deficiency is and how it may best be taken care of. Do not assume that vitamin supplementation is an automatic ingredient of a weight-reduction program, unless your physician so directs. (On the other hand, if your food habits are irregular, if for one reason or another there are certain classes of food that you have been directed by your physician to omit, if there is, in short, any reason to suspect the adequacy of your vitamin supply, then you will be advised to take vitamins. Similarly, if you have been put by your doctor, no doubt for good and sufficient reasons, on a fairly *drastic* weight-reduction diet, vitamin supplements may be part of your regimen. And, of course, infants and children do require vitamin D supplementation and sometimes other supplements as well.)

What is true of vitamins is true of the various mineral elements that the body requires in small quantities. The likelihood is great that these inorganic nutrients—particularly calcium, iron, and iodine—will be furnished by any really varied diet. The one conspicuous exception is the need of the young child for small quantities of fluoride to prevent excessive tooth decay. The most accessible source of fluoride is its presence in a water supply, either as a natural component or as an artificial supplement.

The belief that the young are, more than anyone else, entitled to adequate nourishment is not a casual one. After all, they are completely at the mercy of the dietary wisdom of their elders; and there is always the hopeful possibility that a new generation can be brought up with no bad dietary habits at all. The diet to fit the daily life of a growing child is one that allows for physical development and for a high degree of activity. In other words, boys and girls need good food and a lot of it. Diets geared exclusively to the young are, however, unnecessary. In fact, outside of vitamin D, healthy children need no special food or special preparation that is not a routine ingredient in the whole family's regular meals, even if the children are engaged in a truly rigorous physical regimen. (I am assuming, of course, that the family is eating regular meals, based on a sufficient variety of foods.) There is no basic nutritional need for a "training table," either in the home or elsewhere.

This basic law applies to growing children as well as to adults: the greater the energy expenditure, the greater the need for food intake. An inactive child will need less food than an active one; but it may also take a careful medical investigation to determine the cause of the child's inactivity. Under no circumstances should boys or girls be subjected to fad diets. Such diets can cut them off from sources of nourishment which are of vital importance. Many a plump girl may need no special diet at all. Her only requirement may be a little patience until she gets older and her physique comes to terms with itself. The same is true of the preteen boy's "puppy" fat. Their parents, however, should make sure that they get all the daily exercise they need.

Motherhood presents special nutritional problems. When the baby arrives, its best source of nourishment is its mother's milk. To manufacture this milk, the mother definitely has to eat more than she has been accustomed to. She must add first-quality foods to her diet, particularly protein foods and especially milk and cheese. The exact amount depends on the amount of milk she must produce. For example, she needs to eat 1,000 extra calories or more a day to produce a liter of milk, the normal requirement for a two-month-old baby. Unfortunately, the need for extra food during lactation is frequently forgotten. The lactating mother is likely to stop worrying about her own nutrition, even though the need for calories, for proteins, and for vitamins is much greater at this time than it is during pregnancy.

Finally, we have seen in Chapter 10 that old people do not require special diets any more than do children. In spite of the advertised claims of "gerontological" preparations, no special vitamins, iron, or other supplements are necessary. Your blood does not get "tired" simply because you are getting older. Caloric intake need not be limited simply because a person is getting old, provided the intake was not excessive in early middle age and provided the same schedule of activity is maintained. The relation between obesity and degenerative disease is, however, close enough to warrant considering prevention of obesity as a major nutritional measure in preparation for old age. The old should drink enough fluids. They should continue to avoid excessive fat intake and excessive smoking. They should continue to take regular moderate exercise which is not only good for the heart, but necessary for proper bowel movement. (An hour's walk is better and safer than a laxative.) These recommendations are valid for any age, but they should be followed particularly by the older individual whose capacity for physical adaptation is reduced. Actually, some of the greatest nutritional problems in the aged are caused by dental and social difficulties. It is important for oldsters to receive dental attention so that they will be able to chew properly. A denture is not just a cosmetic ornament. It is a necessity for good nutrition. Lack of companionship and of an incentive to prepare and eat a good meal constitute the second major nutritional handicap in the elderly. Grandmother will generally do better if she eats with her children and grandchildren than if she eats alone.

We have already alluded to the fact that, unfortunately, the elderly are the prime target and the most frequent victims of the food faddists and "health" merchants. Too much of their limited income finds its way into expensive "nature" foods and "programmed" supplements, instead of being spent in the supermarket on wholesome fish, meat, eggs, vegetables, and fruit.

Babies appear to live primarily to eat. Adults live for a multitude of other, often more noble, reasons. Nonetheless, as one of the pleasures of existence, eating can be worthwhile for all kinds of people. Well-chosen and well-prepared food, a little wine perhaps, relaxed mealtime conversation—these are the simple satisfactions that should be part of everyday existence and are pleasures which need not be denied to the obese.

chapter 13

The Treatment
of Obesity

The reduction of weight is a medical problem and a difficult one. No layman can estimate with any accuracy the degree to which he is obese and no layman can independently plan and follow a program aimed at the safe and successful removal of fat. The diagnosis and treatment of obesity are the responsibility of a physician, ideally one who is sympathetically aware of the intricacies of the condition and of the obstacles that loom in the way of its correction. The fat person who attempts to rid himself of fat by following the latest diet publicized in the periodical press is taking a dangerous course. For most such diets fail and some, if continued long enough, are a peril not only to health but to life itself. Even under the direction of a dedicated physician, many reducing efforts fail. Many fat people, in spite of the guidance of doctor or of clinic, do not lose a significant amount of their unwanted fat. And, of those who are victorious, a number sooner or later drift back to their original condition.

Lest this summation appear too discouraging, it is well to point out that these somewhat unhopeful declarations are based largely on the reports of specialized clinics. As Dr. Charlotte M. Young, the well-known Cornell nutritionist, has suggested, it is possible that "the more easily treated patients have been screened out" (and have not made their way into the medical literature), while it is the more difficult ones who have found their way to the clinics and, too frequently, to failure.

Certainly a major factor in effective fat loss is high motivation. The victim of obesity must deeply want to become and remain more lean. He must be firmly aware of the injury that obesity can bring to the quality and to the length of his personal life. He must know that obesity is a burden in more ways than the obvious one. For certainly, as I have attempted to show, the bill of particulars against obesity has received extensive and repeated confirmation.

Most literate Americans must know by now, as earlier chapters have indicated, that fat people are more likely to suffer from heart and kidney diseases, high blood pressure, diabetes, and many other afflictions. Surgery is more hazardous when the patient is obese. Accidents are more frequent for the fat man or woman. And the whole never-to-be-repeated-experience of being alive is dulled and deadened for the person who goes through his hours swaddled in pounds of unfriendly lipids.

Knowledge of these matters should fortify each individual's determination to reduce. His purpose should be strengthened also by awareness that both his social and his economic life may be benefited when he becomes more slim. He will look better and be more highly regarded by his family, friends, and employer, present or prospective. And, if he does rid himself forever of the fat that is doing him physical, psychic, and professional damage he will have achieved something that has been accomplished, as far as we know, by only a minority of people. Both he and his physician will rightly feel more than a little triumphant.

But, first of all, he will have reported to his physician and been declared obese. The doctor will have given particular attention to the evolution of the excessive body weight. For, as we have already indicated, the psychological aspects and prognosis are quite different in persons who become obese in their adult years and in persons who were obese as children or adolescents. The physician will understand that it is essential to know the age of the onset of obesity and its past course. Persons who were obese as youngsters are much more likely to be obsessively concerned with their self-image and to view their obesity as a badge of shame, rather than a medical problem which can be attacked by rather simple means. They are more likely to have failed repeatedly to control their weight in the past. They are more apt to be the victims of as yet little understood physiological or psychological abnormalities. While the classical "endocrine" abnormalities are rare, the possibility of endocrine disturbances—decreased thyroid function (hypothyroidism), excessive activity of the adrenals (hyperadrenocorticism), and, in men, decreased testicular function (male hypogonadism)—will be investigated by the physician. And the possible (though uncommon) occurrence of abnormal fluid retention will be considered.

Dietary habits will be thoroughly studied, together with their familial, psychological, and economic backgrounds. Patterns of hunger and satiety will be determined. They form the basis of decisions on distributing the calories allotted to the reducing diet over the proper number of meals and snacks, and are prerequisite to decisions on the possible use of appetite-depressing agents, their dosage, and the timing of administration.

The physician will want to know the actual time spent in activities which do not involve sitting or lying down and the vigor with which these activities are pursued. For these elements, together with the sex, size, and age of the patient, form the basis of the estimate of daily caloric requirements for energy balance. The physician may want to obtain serum iron data as well as hemoglobin as a possible indication of a tendency toward iron deficiency, a condition which seems much more prevalent among obese subjects than among the general population. Before searching for psychological factors which may have brought on or contributed to the bringing on and continuance of the obesity, the physician will want to evaluate the psychologic effects of obesity on the patient and weigh the psychological impact of any newly discovered disease condition (e.g., diabetes, hypertension) in terms of its possible effect on motivation. For one of the strongest factors in getting anyone, particularly an adult, to initiate and persevere in a weight-reduction campaign is the knowledge that his health is in peril.

The obese person by now must know that, outside of rare situations involving certain diseases and psychiatric problems, weight reduction is desirable in all obese individuals. The attitude that, in the absence of any clear and immediate reason for reducing, the obese person should leave his fat alone is unwise counsel which a physician would be unlikely to give. Should one wait for diabetes, or hypertension, or the immobilization consequent to the superimposition of excess weight on arthritis to do something about the problem? Furthermore, the general fitness of the patient is visibly improved when fat is banished; his employability is increased, both in government and industry; and, in a society which for better or worse puts a great deal of emphasis on appearance, his social acceptability (and in some cases his happiness) is improved.

We have seen in previous chapters that there are some serious conditions where the physician will find indications for weight reduction to be particularly pressing. Among these are certain respiratory difficulties. The work of breathing is increased if considerable additional weight is carried on the chest wall. Excessive adipose tissue also adds to the problem of keeping the whole body oxygenated. Obese people have, accordingly, a diminished exercise tolerance, and may show greater difficulty in normal breathing, particularly in the presence of any—even mild—respiratory infection. At the extreme, very marked obesity may lead to the "Pickwickian syndrome" where, through decreased ventilation, accumulation of carbon dioxide in the blood leads to lethargy and somnolence. Lower oxygenation of arterial blood may lead also to reactive polycythemia (an abnormal increase in the number of red cells), which may compound the possibility of thrombosis and abnormal blood clotting. Cardiac enlargement and congestive heart failure may also result from pulmonary difficulties due to extreme obesity. The removal of obesity is essential to the treatment of the Pickwickian syndrome. It can aid greatly in the treatment of congestive heart failure.

Another condition where weight reduction is urgent is hypertension. For there is a significant association between obesity and hypertension. In general, hypertension is more prevalent among the obese than among the nonobese, and the obese hypertensive show a greater illness and death rate and, in particular, a greater risk of coronary heart disease than nonobese hypertensives or obese nonhypertensives. The results of weight reduction on hypertension are by no means universally striking, but, when there is a change, it tends to be favorable, with the drop in blood pressure a function of the drop in body weight. Recent experience shows that in large groups of hypertensives, at least half—and in some instances, as many as 75 per cent—of the patients had significant decreases in blood pressure (20 mm. systolic or 15 mm. diastolic, measured respectively at the high and the low of blood pressure measurements) if they lost at least 15 pounds. While certain authors have claimed that the most important factor in weight reduction regimens for hypertensive patients was the curtailment of salt which accompanied the caloric restriction, it appears that this is only one of the variables involved. There is no doubt that, whatever the mechanisms involved, hypertension in an obese patient is a compelling indication for weight reduction. The favorable effect of weight reduction on the survival of postcoronary patients is well documented. While improvement in cases of angina pectoris is always difficult to measure, it seems certain that weight reduction is a favorable factor in this condition also.

Endocrine and metabolic disturbances are also helpfully treated by weight reduction. Hirsutism (the appearance of excessive, coarse hair on various body sites) and menstrual irregularities, much more frequent among obese women than among nonobese, can often be mitigated by sufficient weight loss. There are somewhat conflicting reports on the association of obesity with high serum cholesterol levels and other serum liquids (triglycerides, or fat, properly speaking, and fatty acids). It is probable that such conflicts are the result of failure to differentiate the phase of obesity (whether active weight gain or static obesity) and our inability at present to differentiate between various forms of obesity. It can be stated broadly that, while abnormal serum lipid levels frequently fail to respond to weight reduction, any response which does take place, particularly in blood cholesterol level, tends to be favorable. That is, the abnormally high lipid level is decreased temporarily or permanently.

Among obese subjects there is a high prevalence of impaired glucose tolerance (i.e., blood glucose takes longer to get back to normal after a large dose of sugar has been administered) and, in many cases, of hyperglycemia or high blood sugar. This type of "maturity-onset diabetes," which often responds dramatically to weight reduction, may be less likely to lead to vascular degeneration than juvenile "nonobese" types of diabetes. Nevertheless, avoidance of need for insulin, prevention of skin and other infections related to hyperglycemia, and the elimination of acidosis risk, lead the physician to call for the immediate institution of weight reduction programs for such patients. After suitable weight reduction, insulin can frequently be replaced by oral hypoglycemic agents—the various new pills which can lower blood sugar without the need for a daily injection. In many cases, the need for pharmacologic agents to control blood sugar may be eliminated altogether. For example, in a large eries of obese diabetics, normal glucose levels were resumed in nearly 75 per cent of the subjects who achieved the desired weight reduction, and improved glucose tolerances were seen in about half the remainder.

There are other pathological conditions which will influence the physician to advise immediate weight reduction. As regards pregnancy, the risk of toxemia and of delivery problems can be decreased if the weight of the woman is controlled, preferably by reduction before the beginning of pregnancy, or by cutting down on the weight gain during pregnancy. Infertility in obese men may be the result of the excessively high temperature of the scrotum because of its being surrounded by folds of adipose tissue. The situation as regards gall-bladder disease is more complex: while there is a significant association between obesity and gall-bladder disease, there is *as yet* no documented evidence that, once the disease is present, it is ameliorated by weight reduction.

Obesity, because it restricts normal heat loss by the body, tends to promote excessive perspiration. Contact or friction between moist skin areas in adjacent folds often leads to rashes, inflammation, and boils. While obesity probably does not per se cause varicose veins, weight reduction considerably lessens the risk of ulcers and other skin complications in patients who have varicose veins.

There are a number of bone and joint diseases greatly improved by weight reduction, which decreases the pressure on the damaged structure and facilitates mobility. Among these are rupture of intravertebral discs, osteoarthritis, and intermittent claudication (limping). In spite of steady advances in anesthesia and in surgical techniques, obese patients still face an increased risk in operations, and the physician will strive if possible to reduce the obese person before optional surgery.

Finally, particularly in adolescents, but also in many obese adults, especially women, the adverse psychological effects of obesity—"losing one's looks," anxiety about its effects on marital relationships, etc.—may by themselves constitute a pressing medical indication for weight reduction.

On the other hand, there are a few conditions in which weight reduction is not only unwise, but actually dangerous, and the physician will strongly advise against attempts to reduce people suffering from them. While certain diseases, in particular tuberculosis, gout, and diverticulitis, used to be (and sometimes still are) quoted as examples of conditions in which weight reduction is contraindicated, it has been repeatedly shown that weight reduction under medical supervision can be accomplished safely in these diseases, if done very gradually with a sensible dietary regimen. Weight reduction is definitely contraindicated in Addison's disease, regional ileitis, and ulcerative colitis. Obesity, however, is rarely associated with these diseases.

Cases in which rapid weight loss was associated with profound depression or even acute psychosis have received wide attention and have frequently been cited as illustrating the dangers attendant on weight reduction. While such cases are indeed documented, the physician will also be aware of the following points: first, such untoward effects of weight reduction are very rare; secondly, the victims had manifestly unstable personalities before the reduction therapy, which clearly should not have been attempted; thirdly, treatment was usually aimed at rapid weight loss and was based on a drastic curtailment of food intake, rather than aimed at a slow loss with a combination of increased exercise and moderate diet used to create the caloric deficit necessary.

In practice, the physician will know from his patient's medical history of previous instances of successful weight loss by the patient. Even though the lower weight was not maintained, the physician will properly regard its achievement as a sign that the obese person can tolerate a course of weight reduction without incurring psychic damage.

Certainly, in the enormous majority of cases, the physician will not fear grave psychologic complications as the patient loses weight gradually. He will make regular checks of the patient's outlook, will carefully examine the degree of hunger and fatigue experienced by the patient, and will take proper remedial measures if either appears excessive.

The various methods of weight reduction we are going to discuss are not alternative methods. Diet and exercise are measures which complement each other in establishing the caloric deficit. The manipulation of the dietary schedule, the use of saccharin, of formula diet, and of appetite-depressing agents are all directed at making the limitation of caloric intake more acceptable. Salt restriction may help to provide a more even rate of reduction by avoiding excessive fluid retention. The physician who has prescribed these treatments will provide the patient with the psychological support that is always an essential element of any long-term therapy.

The mature patient will approach a program of weight reduction with an awareness that a proper diet must provide all necessary nutrients in sufficient amounts, be palatable, easily available from the viewpoints of economics and convenience, and be limited in calories so as to produce the desired caloric deficit. For ideally, the diet must be such as to help in the re-education of the patient so that, when the required weight has been obtained, it will, by increasing somewhat the size of the portions, provide a proper maintenance diet for the future.

The determination of the desired deficit is, of course, based on the fact that a pound of body fat is the equivalent of 3,500 calories. This, in turn, means that a daily deficit of 500 calories will lead, over a long enough period, to an average loss of one pound a week, and a deficit of 1,000 calories to an average loss of two pounds a week. Every obese person who aspires to reduce should be warned that this rate of two pounds a week is as much as should be lost by anyone not under extremely close, medical supervision. Guided by his physician, a very obese patient can safely obtain a greater rate of weight loss at least at the beginning of a reduction regimen, but the physician will urge drastic immediate reduction only when the reason for such a rapid rate is pressing, as for example impending surgery.

Once the rate of weight loss has been decided by the physician (e.g., two pounds per week, tantamount to a deficit of 1,000 calories per day), he makes an estimate as to the requirements for maintenance of the patient, given his or her size and pattern of activity. Let us assume that the experienced guess is of the order of 2,200 calories. The physician adds an hour of walking to the usual activity pattern, bringing the amount of calories required to keep the weight at its current level to 2,500. The diet he recommends is then geared to provide 1,500 calories. As the results of the trial become available over, say, a two-week period, he adjusts the intake to the precise number of calories needed to provide the 1,000-calorie daily deficit and no more.

Determining the caloric content of the diet is but one aspect of dietary prescription. Knowledge of his patient's familial and financial condition, his usual eating habits, his tastes, and the capabilities of the person who does the marketing and cooking are necessary before the choice of foods to be included in the diet can be made. The patient will always remember that the more varied a diet is, the greater are the chances that it will be nutritionally adequate, thus eliminating the need for nutritional supplements such as vitamin pills. The goal of any reducing program is not merely to lose weight, but to keep it off. The obese patient needs a thorough education in the caloric content of the various foods in various size portions. This is essential not only to the success of the weight reduction program, but to that of the maintenance program which will follow. Such expressions as an "average" potato, and an "average" serving of lean meat are understood by different individuals to mean widely different sizes. The patient will be well within his rights and responsibilities if he insists that his physician couch his instructions, in terms of specific and familiar quantities. Many physicians and most dietitians have available sized models of simulated food made of painted plaster, which can be very helpful to the patient's comprehension of "portion size" in the prescribed diet.

The distribution of the food into a number of meals and snacks is a matter which the physician will prescribe for each individual and with which he will experiment. A "good" reducing diet is one on which the patient does not become too hungry. With his knowledge of the normal pattern of hunger and satiety in his patient, the physician can shrewdly estimate the number of meals and snacks which will prevent the development of excessive hunger. If, nevertheless, this does come about, when caloric restriction is instituted, further fragmentation (five very small meals, perhaps, rather than the traditional three small or moderate-sized meals), of the daily food allowance may help to mitigate the problem. If this course is also unsuccessful, the physician will then prescribe appetite-depressing agents.

There is at present no evidence available which would support the idea that any of the more extreme diets recently popularized have any advantage over a calorically restricted, balanced "normal" diet. A low-protein, low-fat, "rice" type diet was popular a few years ago. It was followed by a very low-protein diet, dubbed the "Rockefeller" diet by its promoters. One trouble with the low-protein diets is that they usually do not supply the materials needed for proper nourishment in adequate amounts. A very high-protein, moderate-fat, moderate-carbohydrate diet has been recommended by a number of groups. Excessive reliance on the high-protein diet is based on a misconception about the magnitude of the specific dynamic action of proteins in a mixed diet (see Chapter 1). The advocates of the high-protein diet believe that metabolizing the diet brings about a much greater expenditure of wasted energy than it actually does.

The high-fat, low-carbohydrate (or carbohydrate-free) diet reappears every now and then under a variety of names, most recently the DuPont or Pennington diet and the Mayo diet. With alcohol added, it has become the "drinking man's" diet. Again, those who endorse these diets (and who are sincere) are apparently misguided on a number of counts. While it is true that a high-fat diet depresses fat *synthesis* (the production of fat in the body itself), it by no means prevents fat *deposition* (the accumulation of fat in the body) when fat is copiously available in the diet. Fat does, as contended, have "satiety" value, but so do other foods. After the consumption of a sufficient amount of anything, the urge to eat temporarily atrophies in normal people, or most of us would be more obese than we are. And while a carbohydrate-free, high-fat diet can cause an immediate weight loss (over and above the steady decrease due to caloric deficit which often is built into the diet), this is due to partial dehydration. It is of no lasting significance in a program designed to reduce adiposity and not simply to decrease fat per se over the short term. A diet high in fat, where calories and alcohol can be consumed at will—and some non-nutritionists have urged exactly that—not only tends to make the one who uses it fat and inebriated, but it may increase serum cholesterol and precipitate atherosclerosis.

A balanced diet, containing no less than 14 per cent of protein, no more than 30 per cent of fat (with saturated fats cut down), and the rest carbohydrates (with sucrose—ordinary sugar—cut down to a low level), is still the best diet. It contains all the nutrients needed for life-long nutrition; it does not, through excessively low carbohydrate content, introduce an additional cause of fatigue and irritability; it does not, through excessively high fat content, promote high cholesterol. At the same time, the protein and fat content are still high enough to promote long-term satiety (while the carbohydrates in the diet promote short-term satiety as well). A varied diet staying within this reasonable range is infinitely preferable to any of the fad diets mentioned above, and to their cousins, the grapefruit diet, the banana diet, the hard-boiled egg diet, and many others that have been forced on our attention.

Formula diets are something else. They have become very popular in the past ten years or so. Whether purchased in liquid form or as powders to be suspended in water, their main advantage is the fact that they provide strictly established amounts of food (three times 300 calories or four times 225 calories per day, in general), and this makes available a simple, rigid regimen which does not need to be based on any knowledge of foods and food values. Formula diets are often helpful at the beginning of the reducing period (first two to four weeks). Their use should not, however, be allowed to retard the dietary education which sooner or later is absolutely necessary to carry the dieting person over a prolonged weight reduction period and through the life-long maintenance phase. For the great majority of people who use a formula diet supplemented by other foods, the intrinsic value of a strictly measured diet is lost. Formula diets may, nevertheless, be found useful during maintenance as the exclusive replacement of one meal a day. We must remember that the human race has spent millennia habituating itself to solid food and it is not likely to change this preference pattern in any foreseeable future.

The very multiplicity of dietary fads and clinical fashions in the treatment of obesity testifies to our continued ignorance of the deeper causes of the many syndromes entailing prolonged positive energy balance and, hence, our continued ignorance of their rational treatment. The latest popular method of dealing with intractable obese patients (those in whom "self-control," bolstered by the doctor's most persuasive manner, has failed) is total, prolonged fasting. While it is true that daily weight losses in cases of total starvation are much greater than those seen in patients on restricted diets, this does not mean that total fasting causes much greater losses in body *fat,* which is, after all, the object of "weight" reduction. First, the fact that the central nervous system requires glucose as its exclusive fuel forces the fasting organism to provide glucose by the breakdown of protein for the purpose of providing carbohydrate. Inasmuch as one gram of adipose tissue is probably equivalent to eight calories, while protein yields only four calories per gram and each gram is accompanied in tissue by three grams of water, the breakdown of "protein tissue" will cause a weight loss many times—perhaps as much as eight times—greater than the loss of adipose tissue. This loss of protein —liver, muscle, kidney tissue—is, however, obviously undesirable.

In addition, many possible consequences of total fasting are still unknown. What is the effect of prolonged fasting on patients who are still growing? What types of personality may react to total fasting with serious psychiatric or psychosomatic disturbances? What is the composition of the tissue which is regained rapidly after fasting? Are there any pathologic consequences of the elevated blood ketones and dehydration seen in some totally fasted patients? What are the long-term effects on the liver and other organs of alternating total fasting and refeeding? And there are many other questions still unanswered.

Certain dangers of total fasting should, by all means, be kept in mind. First, as a result of the newspaper and magazine publicity given this procedure, a number of obese subjects will try—some are trying already —total fast as a method of weight reduction without hospitalization and, in fact, without consulting their physicians or changing their modes of life. The prospect of fasting obese teen-agers who must attempt to study or fasting subjects who drive automobiles is not a happy one. Secondly, unless careful instruction, supervision, and follow-up are available, the publicity given this procedure will lead once again to a widespread feeling that weight control can be an on-and-off business and that knowledge of the caloric content of foods along with establishment of proper dietary and exercise regimens, which alone can be effective over long periods, can be evaded.

Bulk-producing agents (such as methyl cellulose) designed "to fill the stomach" and to curb appetite have not been shown to have any special merit. Apples, celery, raw carrots, and salads are more palatable. They provide needed nutrients along with few calories and are more likely to become parts of a life-long dietary pattern. They are thus superior on all counts to artificial bulk producers. Work done in my laboratory suggests that bulky natural foods may be particularly valuable in a weight-reducing program not so much because of their stomach-filling role as because they slow down the course of a meal and provide time for satiety phenomena to take place. Artificial bulk-producing agents do not make a similar contribution to satiety.

The use of saccharin can be a helpful adjunct to reducing diets. Certainly there is little to say for the use of large amounts of sugar. It is an "empty" source of calories (the only nutrient it provides is carbohydrate). And when it is consumed in copious quantities, it may stimulate excessive insulin production and thus accelerate fat synthesis and the reappearance of hunger. A small amount of sucrose (e.g., *one* sourball once or twice a day at the end of a meal, as dessert, or as a snack if a meal is delayed) is welcomed by some dieters. But the use of sugar in the numerous cups of tea and coffee often consumed by reducers and the use of sugar-containing soft drinks should be strictly eliminated. If people who are reducing feel they need to drink a number of cups of black coffee and if the coffee has to be sweetened, the use of saccharin rather than other artificial sweeteners is encouraged. Incidentally, the consumption of large amounts of coffee (unless decaffeinated coffee is used) is a questionable practice, particularly for middle-aged obese diabetics. Preliminary results obtained in my laboratory suggest that caffeine may increase the severity of diabetes. There is also some statistical evidence that high consumption of coffee is accompanied by a higher risk of coronary attack.

The physician will prescribe significant restriction of salt only if the clinical picture warrants it. Less extremely, cutting down on the salt intake decreases the tendency to excessive fluid retention seen in many reducing persons. Among them are many middle-aged and older women as well as sedentary individuals. Decreasing salt intake may also have some effectiveness in the prevention of hypertension. Salt restriction is a much sounder and safer measure to prevent excessive water retention during weight reduction than the use of diuretics which, if prolonged, may cause kidney damage. It is regrettable that certain "reducing" pills containing such diuretics as ammonium chloride are still available for over-the-counter sale. Physicians invariably warn their patients against these preparations.

It is fortunate for many people who hope to reduce weight that anorexigenic agents—appetite-depressants—do exist. For though many persons can reduce effectively without them, many cannot. The main current anorexigenic agents are the amphetamines and related compounds. It is generally agreed that they act chiefly by stimulating the ventromedial (satiety) hypothalamic centers (see Chapter 1). They may, however, have accessory actions, including stimulation of spontaneous physical activity and, perhaps, some metabolic action as well. An individual who is reducing under medical direction should use, as in all chemotherapy, the particular dosage his physician has instructed and not the dosage some other physician has planned for another patient.

Ordinarily, the effective duration of amphetamine treatment is about a month to six weeks. It is most useful at the onset of a reducing program and with patients who have become obese only recently. Unfortunately, in many patients some side-effects are encountered: dry-mouth, restlessness, irritability, insomnia, and sometimes constipation. The superiority of some of the newer modifications of the classical amphetamines in terms of effectiveness and avoidance of side-effects is not yet established to the satisfaction of this observer, though one or two appear promising. Physicians have found supplementation of amphetamine therapy with sedatives or tranquilizers to be useful in some cases. And the physician will undoubtedly make clear to his patient that the use of anorexigenic agents does not lessen in any way the need to follow the prescribed diet and the exercise instructions. Actually, the chief value of anorexigenic agents is that they may "buy" the precious weeks during which the patient can be re-educated while his weight is going down and his appetite is lessened.

The value of exercise in the prevention of obesity and in the treatment of moderately obese persons of otherwise good health has been emphasized at length in Chapter 5. Its value in the prevention of heart disease has also been discussed. Let it be recalled simply that: First, exercise is the great variable in energy expenditure. Caloric equivalents of exercise of various types are given in Appendix III. The caloric expenditure due to exercise is proportional to the duration of exercise. It is also proportional to the weight of the subject. An obese person will thus use up proportionately more calories than a thin person to perform the same task. The caloric expenditure also increases rapidly with the intensity of the exercise. Second, exercise does not increase voluntary food intake in previously inactive subjects until it has reached a certain critical duration and intensity. Just where these points are varies with the individual.

While obviously a very obese person, even in good cardiovascular state as determined by his physician, should not suddenly commence a course of demanding exercise, it is well for him to begin walking every day and to increase the duration and eventually the intensity of the exercise as his weight reduction progresses. People accustomed to the constant use of automobiles and elevators should take advantage of every routine opportunity for walking and stair-climbing. The physician will remind them that the insulation provided by the excessive adiposity will restrict heat loss on hot days. The reducer will, accordingly, interrupt his exercise in the summer and in the tropics, and keep hydrated, preferably with water.

There is still too much thyroid hormone prescribed to obese patients (usually in the form of desiccated thyroid preparation). Such medication is based on the misconception—widely held by erroneously "knowledgeable" laymen—that many obese people have a low basal metabolism. This old notion originated from relating basal oxygen consumption to body weight, which is, of course, very high in the obese, rather than to the more appropriate denominator, body surface, which is proportionately far less increased. At present, sophisticated methods exist and should be used before a diagnosis of hypothyroidism is arrived at and acted upon. The administration of thyroid to a patient with a normal thyroid gland is to a certain extent self-defeating, anyway, as it depresses his own natural thyroid secretion. Moreover, reversal of this depression is a very slow process. If too high doses are given, acceleration of the heart rate (tachycardia), palpitation, nervousness, and insomnia appear, creating an unpleasant and a potentially dangerous situation.

For most obese patients, the success of reducing programs will depend solely upon their physicians and themselves. Relatives, friends, and associates will eagerly supply the reducer with information, most of it ridiculous, and with advice, much of it useless, irrelevant, or harmful. It is to the physician that the patient must turn both for technical advice and for tactical counseling. The physician and his auxiliary, the dietitian, in addition to their medical and nutritional knowledge, are well-informed about the psychology of becoming obese, being obese, and doing something to correct the obesity.

Anxieties and stresses, in someone otherwise predisposed to obesity by genetics or by constitution, may have caused overeating and immobilization, hence, weight accumulation. Once the individual is obese, particularly if the condition began in adolescence, we have seen that a galaxy of psychological traits develops which may tend to make the obesity self-perpetuating. These include: obsessive concern with self-image, passivity, expectation of rejection, and progressive withdrawal. The physician will urge the development of new interests which will ideally involve many other people and a considerable amount of purposeful activity, much of it physical. He will be able to ease much of the discomfort accompanying a prolonged period of caloric deficit. He will, far more wisely than the patient himself, be able to fix realistic short-term and long-term targets, the latter arrived at by clinical judgment and based on the actual body structure of the patient, his mode of life and his capabilities.

Obesity is not a sin. At most, it is the consequence of errors of omission, the result of not having kept up the life-long battle against an inherited predisposition and against an environment which combines constant exposure to food with the removal of any need to work for it physically. In the pilgrim's progress of the constitutionally plump, salvation demands more than the shunning of temptation. It requires a complete reaction against the form of life for which our society is geared and which it advertises, the shunning of constantly proffered self-serving misinformation, the adoption of an attitude almost stoic in its asceticism and in the deliberate daily setting aside of time for what will be often lonely walking and exercising.

Obesity is not a sickness in the literal sense of the term. The fat person may feel injured only in his self-respect. For most of his life, he is likely to function as well as his leaner contemporaries, as a private person, as a wage-earner, and as a citizen, except insofar as the modern prejudice against the obese may decrease his chances to succeed in his college aspirations and career advancement while lessening his stature as a romantic figure or leader. On the other hand, obesity *is* a *medical problem* of the first magnitude. In the increasing pandemic of cardiovascular and other degenerative diseases which in terms of life expectancy is threatening to nullify the results of medical advances in this generation, obesity plays a major contributing role. To the increased risk of morbidity and mortality from heart disease, diabetes, gall bladder disease, accidents, and a number of other conditions is added, particularly in the young, the psychologic hazards of being cast into a category of people which our society regards with distaste and contempt.

After close to twenty years of research in the somatic, the psychologic, and the social aspects of obesity, I am as aware as any man of the gigantic gaps in our knowledge—and of the likelihood that many of our present concepts may be erroneous. At the same time I trust that the facts which we do know and which I have presented will be found useful to the therapist, to the patient, and to his family. Only unmitigated quacks can pretend at present that they have a method of treatment which is at the same time safe and permanently effective for all. Yet success is possible in many cases if the advice given above is followed by the patient, working closely with his physician. Knowledge is not sufficient for cure, but its acquisition is a necessary step. And since the days of Hippocrates, life-long guilt—which I hope this book helps to remove—has not been felt by true healers to be a worthy tool of medicine.

appendix I
References

A. The following review articles will enable the reader to rapidly obtain a comprehensive bibliography on the problems of food intake regulation and obesity dealt with in this book:

Mayer, J., "Genetic, Traumatic and Environmental Factors in the Etiology of Obesity," *Physiol. Rev.*, 33 (1953), 472.

———, "The Physiological Basis of Obesity and Leanness," *Nutr. Abstr. Rev.*, 25, Parts I and II (1955), 597, 871.

———, "Obesity," *Ann. Rev. Med.*, 14 (1963), 111.

———, "Some Aspects of the Problem of Regulation of Food Intake and Obesity," *New Eng. J. Med.*, 274, Parts I, II, and III (1966), 610, 662, 722.

———, "Obesity, Cardiovascular Diseases, and the Dietitian," *J. Amer. Diet. Assoc.*, 52 (1968), 13.

——— and D. W. Thomas, "Regulation of Food Intake and Obesity," *Science*, 156 (1967), 328.

B. The following books on the regulation of food intake and the adipose tissue will give general information on nervous mechanisms and on fat metabolism:

Brain and Behavior, Second Conference. Brain Research Institute, University of California, Los Angeles. Washington, D. C.: American Institute of Biological Sciences, 1962.

Rodahl, Kaare and Bela Issekutz, Jr., eds., *Fat as a Tissue*. Proceedings of a Conference held at the Lakenau Hospital. New York: McGraw-Hill Book Company, 1964.

Blix, Gunnar, ed., *Occurrence, Causes and Prevention of Overnutrition*, Second Symposium of the Swedish Nutrition Foundation. Uppsala: Almqvist & Wiksells, 1964.

Renold, Albert E. and George F. Cahill, Jr., eds., *Adipose Tissue—Handbook of Physiology No. 5*. Washington, D.C.: American Physiological Society, 1965.

Adipose Tissue Metabolism and Obesity, Conference held at the New York Academy of Sciences, B. N. Brodoff, Chairman. New York: New York Academy of Sciences, 1965.

C. The following general textbooks give good reviews of the science of nutrition:

Davidson, Stanley and R. Passmore, *Human Nutrition and Dietetics*, 3rd ed. Baltimore: The Williams & Wilkins Co., 1966.

Wohl, Michael G. and R. S. Goodhart, *Modern Nutrition in Health and Disease*, 3rd ed. Philadelphia: Lea & Febiger, 1964.

appendix II

Recommended Dietary Allowances

RECOMMENDED DAILY DIETARY ALLOWANCES [a]

DESIGNED FOR THE MAINTENANCE OF GOOD NUTRITION OF PRACTICALLY ALL HEALTHY PEOPLE IN THE U.S.A.

The allowance levels are intended to cover individual variations among most normal persons as they live in the United States under usual environmental stresses. The recommended allowances can be attained with a variety of common foods, providing other nutrients for which human requirements have been less well defined.

Abbreviations: kg = kilogram; cm = centimeter; kcal = kilocalorie, commonly calorie; gm = gram; IU = International Unit; mg = milligram; μg = microgram; g = gram.

	Age [b] (years)		Weight		Height			Protein (gm)	Fat-Soluble Vitamins		
	From	Up to	(kg)	(lbs)	cm	(in.)	kcal		Vitamin A Activity (IU)	Vitamin D (IU)	Vitamin E Activity (IU)
Infants	0–1/6		4	9	55	22	kg × 120	kg × 2.2e	1,500	400	5
	1/6–1/2		7	15	63	25	kg × 110	kg × 2.0e	1,500	400	5
	1/2–1		9	20	72	28	kg × 100	kg × 1.8e	1,500	400	5
Children	1–2		12	26	81	32	1,100	25	2,000	400	10
	2–3		14	31	91	36	1,250	25	2,000	400	10
	3–4		16	35	100	39	1,400	30	2,500	400	10
	4–6		19	42	110	43	1,600	30	2,500	400	10
	6–8		23	51	121	48	2,000	35	3,500	400	15
	8–10		28	62	131	52	2,200	40	3,500	400	15
Males	10–12		35	77	140	55	2,500	45	4,500	400	20
	12–14		43	95	151	59	2,700	50	5,000	400	20
	14–18		59	130	170	67	3,000	60	5,000	400	25
	18–22		67	147	175	69	2,800	60	5,000	400	30
	22–35		70	154	175	69	2,800	65	5,000	—	30
	35–55		70	154	173	68	2,600	65	5,000	—	30
	55–75+		70	154	171	67	2,400	65	5,000	—	30
Females	10–12		35	77	142	56	2,250	50	4,500	400	20
	12–14		44	97	154	61	2,300	50	5,000	400	20
	14–16		52	114	157	62	2,400	55	5,000	400	25
	16–18		54	119	160	63	2,300	55	5,000	400	25
	18–22		58	128	163	64	2,000	55	5,000	400	25
	22–35		58	128	163	64	2,000	55	5,000	—	25
	35–55		58	128	160	63	1,850	55	5,000	—	25
	55–75+		58	128	157	62	1,700	55	5,000	—	25
Pregnancy							+200	65	6,000	400	30
Lactation							+1,000	75	8,000	400	30

[a] Source: National Research Council. Revised 1968.

[b] Entries on lines for age range 22–35 years represent the reference man and woman at age 22. All other entries represent allowances for the midpoint of the specified age range.

[c] The folacin allowances refer to dietary sources as determined by *Lactobacillus casei* assay. Pure forms of folacin may be effective in doses less than ¼ of the RDA.

Water-Soluble Vitamins							Minerals				
Ascorbic Acid (mg)	Folacin[e] (mg)	Niacin (mg equiv)[d]	Riboflavin (mg)	Thiamin (mg)	Vitamin B6 (mg)	Vitamin B12 (µg)	Calcium (g)	Phosphorus (g)	Iodine (µg)	Iron (mg)	Magnesium (mg)
35	0.05	5	0.4	0.2	0.2	1.0	0.4	0.2	25	6	40
35	0.05	7	0.5	0.4	0.3	1.5	0.5	0.4	40	10	60
35	0.1	8	0.6	0.5	0.4	2.0	0.6	0.5	45	15	70
40	0.1	8	0.6	0.6	0.5	2.0	0.7	0.7	55	15	100
40	0.2	8	0.7	0.6	0.6	2.5	0.8	0.8	60	15	150
40	0.2	9	0.8	0.7	0.7	3	0.8	0.8	70	10	200
40	0.2	11	0.9	0.8	0.9	4	0.8	0.8	80	10	200
40	0.2	13	1.1	1.0	1.0	4	0.9	0.9	100	10	250
40	0.3	15	1.2	1.1	1.2	5	1.0	1.0	110	10	250
40	0.4	17	1.3	1.3	1.4	5	1.2	1.2	125	10	300
45	0.4	18	1.4	1.4	1.6	5	1.4	1.4	135	18	350
55	0.4	20	1.5	1.5	1.8	5	1.4	1.4	150	18	400
60	0.4	18	1.6	1.4	2.0	5	0.8	0.8	140	10	400
60	0.4	18	1.7	1.4	2.0	5	0.8	0.8	140	10	350
60	0.4	17	1.7	1.3	2.0	5	0.8	0.8	125	10	350
60	0.4	14	1.7	1.2	2.0	6	0.8	0.8	110	10	350
40	0.4	15	1.3	1.1	1.4	5	1.2	1.2	110	18	300
45	0.4	15	1.4	1.2	1.6	5	1.3	1.3	115	18	350
50	0.4	16	1.4	1.2	1.8	5	1.3	1.3	120	18	350
50	0.4	15	1.5	1.2	2.0	5	1.3	1.3	115	18	350
55	0.4	13	1.5	1.0	2.0	5	0.8	0.8	100	18	350
55	0.4	13	1.5	1.0	2.0	5	0.8	0.8	100	18	300
55	0.4	13	1.5	1.0	2.0	5	0.8	0.8	90	18	300
55	0.4	13	1.5	1.0	2.0	6	0.8	0.8	80	10	300
60	0.8	15	1.8	+0.1	2.5	8	+0.4	+0.4	125	18	450
60	0.5	20	2.0	+0.5	2.5	6	+0.5	+0.5	150	18	450

[d] Niacin equivalents include dietary sources of the vitamin itself plus 1 mg equivalent for each 60 mg of dietary tryptophan.

[e] Assumes protein equivalent to human milk. For proteins not 100 percent utilized factors should be increased proportionately.

appendix III
Cost of Various Activities
(Over and Above Resting Metabolism)

Activity	*Calories per Hour*
A. Domestic Occupations	
(WOMEN, 120 LBS.)	
Sitting at rest	**15**
Standing relaxed	20
Mental work	5–8
Writing	10–20
Sewing	10–30
Dressing and undressing	30–40
Ironing (5-lb. weight)	50–60
Dishwashing	50–60
Sweeping	80–100
Polishing	100–175
B. Industrial Occupations	
(MEN, 150 LBS.)	
Bookbinding	80–100
Carpentry	150–300
Sawing wood	400–500
Stone masonry	300–400
Tailoring	40–80
Shoemaking	50–100
Housepainting	150–180
Locksmithing (light work)	100–125
Joinery (medium work)	150–200
Riveting	250–300
Coal-mining	125–350
(WOMEN, 120 LBS.)	
Work as seamstress	10–30
Work as seamstress (machine)	20–60
Work as laundress	125–250
Work as charwoman	80–180

C. Physical Exercise

(MEN, 150 LBS.)

Walking slowly (2.6 mph)	115
Walking moderately fast (3.75 mph)	215
Walking very fast (5.3 mph)	565
Running ⎤	800–1,300
Swimming ⎟	300–1,000
Rowing ⎬—dependent on speed	1,000–1,300
Cycling ⎦	150–600
Wrestling	600–1,000

Table of Food Values*

Values for prepared foods and food mixtures have been calculated from typical recipes. Values for cooked vegetables are without added fat. The following abbreviations are used: Gm. for gram; Mg. for milligram; I.U. for International Unit; Cal. for calories; Tr. for trace. Ounce refers to weight; fluid ounce to measure.

Food, and Approximate Measure	Food Energy Cal.	Protein Gm.	Fat Gm.	MINERALS		VITAMINS				
				Calcium Mg.	Iron Mg.	Vitamin A Value I.U.	Thiamine B_1 Mg.	Riboflavin B_2 Mg.	Niacin Value Mg.	Ascorbic Acid Mg.
A										
Apple, raw, 1 medium 2½" in diam.	76	.4	.5	8	.4	120	.05	.04	.2	6
Apple betty, 1 cup	344	3.9	6.7	34	.2	370	.13	.09	1.1	3
Apple butter, 1 tbs.	33	.1	.1	3	.1	—	Tr.	Tr.	Tr.	Tr.
Apple juice, fresh or canned, 1 cup.......	124	.2	—	15	1.2	90	.05	.07	Tr.	2
Applesauce, canned unsweetened, 1 cup...	100	.5	.5	10	1.0	70	.05	.02	.1	3
sweetened 1 cup..........	184	.5	.3	10	1.0	80	.05	.03	.1	3
Apricots, raw, three........	54	1.1	.1	17	.5	2,990	.03	.05	.9	7
canned, sirup pack, 4 medium halves, 2 tbs. sirup.	97	.7	.1	12	.4	1,650	.02	.03	.4	5
dried, uncooked, 1 cup (40 small halves)	393	7.8	.6	129	7.4	11,140	.02	.24	4.9	19
cooked, unsweetened, 1 cup (25 halves approx.).......	242	4.8	.3	80	4.6	6,990	.01	.14	2.8	9
cooked, sweetened, 1 cup (25 halves approx.).......	400	4.9	.3	78	4.6	6,860	.01	.13	2.9	10
frozen, 3 ounces..........	70	.6	.1	9	.3	1,410	.02	.03	.4	3
Asparagus, cooked, 1 cup cut spears.....	36	4.2	.4	33	1.8	1,820	.23	.30	2.1	40
canned, green, 1 cup cut spears........	38	4.2	.7	33	3.3	1,400	.11	.14	1.7	31
Avocado, raw, ½ peeled, 3½ × 3¼" diam.	279	1.9	30.1	11	.7	330	.07	.15	1.3	18
B										
Bacon, crisp, 2 slices........	97	4.0	8.8	4	.5	—	.08	.05	.8	—
Bananas, raw, 1 large, 8 × 1½"........	119	1.6	.3	11	.8	570	.06	.06	1.0	13
Barley, pearled, light, dry, 1 cup........	708	16.6	2.0	32	4.1	—	.25	.17	6.3	—
Bean sprouts, Chinese, 1 cup........	21	2.6	.2	26	.7	10	.06	.08	.5	14

* Adapted from "Composition of Foods—Raw, Processed, Prepared" United States Dept. of Agriculture, Handbook No. 8,

	230	14.6	1.0	102	4.9	—	.12	.12	2.0	—
Beans:										
Red kidney, canned or cooked, 1 cup...	230	14.6	1.0	102	4.9	—	.12	.12	2.0	—
Other (including navy, pea bean—raw), 1 cup...	642	40.7	3.0	310	13.1	—	1.28	.44	4.1	3
Baked—pork and molasses, 1 cup...	325	15.1	7.8	146	5.5	90	.13	.09	1.2	7
pork and tomato sauce, 1 cup...	295	15.1	5.5	107	4.7	220	.13	.09	1.2	7
Beans, lima immature, cooked, 1 cup...	152	8.0	.6	46	2.7	460	.22	.14	1.8	24
canned, solids and liquid, 1 cup...	176	9.5	.7	67	4.2	330	.09	.11	1.3	20
Beans, snap:										
green, cooked, 1 cup...	27	1.8	.2	45	.9	830	.09	.12	.6	18
canned, drained solids, 1 cup...	27	1.8	.2	45	2.1	620	.04	.07	.5	7
wax, canned, drained solids, 1 cup...	27	1.8	.2	45	2.1	150	.04	.07	.5	7
Beans, soya (See Soybeans)										
Beef cuts, cooked:										
Chuck, 3 ounces without bone...	265	22.0	19.0	9	2.6	—	.04	.17	3.5	—
Flank, 3 ounces without bone...	270	21.0	20.0	9	2.6	—	.04	.17	3.5	—
Hamburger: 3 ounces...	316	19.0	26.0	8	2.4	—	.07	.16	4.1	—
Porterhouse, 3 ounces without bone...	293	20.0	23.0	9	2.6	—	.05	.15	4.0	—
Rib roast, 3 ounces without bone...	266	20.0	20.0	9	2.6	—	.05	.15	3.6	—
Round, 3 ounces without bone...	197	23.0	11.0	9	2.9	—	.06	.19	4.7	—
Rump, 3 ounces without bone...	320	18.0	27.0	7	2.1	—	.04	.13	2.6	—
Sirloin, 3 ounces without bone...	257	20.0	19.0	9	2.5	—	.06	.16	4.1	—
Beef, canned:										
Corned beef hash, 3 ounces...	120	11.7	5.2	22	1.1	Tr.	.02	.11	2.4	—
Roast beef, 3 ounces...	189	21.0	11.0	14	2.0	—	.02	.19	3.6	—
Strained (infant food), 1 ounce...	30	4.9	1.0	3	1.2	—	Tr.	.06	.9	—
Beef, corned, canned:										
Lean, 3 ounces...	159	22.5	7.0	18	3.8	—	.01	.21	3.0	—
Medium fat. 3 ounces...	182	21.5	10.0	17	3.7	—	.01	.20	2.9	—
Fat, 3 ounces...	221	20.0	15.0	16	3.4	—	.01	.19	2.7	—
Beef, dried or chipped, 1 cup...	336	56.6	10.4	33	8.4	—	.12	.53	6.3	—
Beef, dried or chipped, 2 ounces...	115	19.4	3.6	11	2.9	—	.04	.18	2.2	—
Beef and vegetable stew, 1 cup...	252	12.9	19.3	31	2.6	2,520	.12	.15	3.4	15

Food, and Approximate Measure	Food Energy Cal.	Protein Gm.	Fat Gm.	MINERALS Calcium Mg.	Iron Mg.	VITAMINS Vitamin A Value I.U.	Thiamine B₁ Mg.	Riboflavin B₂ Mg.	Niacin Value Mg.	Ascorbic Acid Mg.
Beer (average 4 pct. alcohol), 8 ounces....	114	1.4	—	10	—	—	Tr.	.06	.4	—
Beets, red, raw, 1 cup diced.............	56	2.1	.1	36	1.3	30	.03	.06	.6	13
cooked, 1 cup diced...................	68	1.6	.2	35	1.2	30	.03	.07	.5	11
Beet greens, cooked, 1 cup..............	39	2.9	.4	1*171	4.6	10,790	.07	.23	.6	22
Beverages, carbonated:										
Ginger ale, 1 cup...................	80	—	—	—	—	—	—	—	—	—
Other, including kola type, 1 cup......	107	—	—	—	—	—	—	—	—	—
Biscuits, baking powder, 1–2½" diam. ...	129	3.1	4.0	83	.2	—	.02	.03	.2	—
Blackberries, raw, 1 cup...............	82	1.7	1.4	46	1.3	280	.05	.06	.5	30
canned, sirup pack, 1 cup.............	216	1.8	.5	45	1.8	460	.03	.05	.5	16
Blanc mange (vanilla cornstarch pudding), 1 cup...................	275	8.7	9.7	290	.2	390	.08	.40	.2	2
Blueberries, raw, 1 cup...............	85	.8	.8	22	1.1	400	.04	.03	.4	23
canned, sirup pack, 1 cup.............	245	1.0	1.0	27	1.2	100	.03	.03	.5	33
frozen without sugar, 3 ounces........	52	.5	.5	14	.7	200	.01	.01	.2	12
Bluefish, cooked, baked, 1 piece 3½ × 3 × ½"...................	193	34.2	5.2	29	.9	—	.15	.14	2.8	—
fried, 1 piece 3½ × 3 × ½".............	307	34.0	14.7	28	.9	—	.16	.16	3.1	—
Bouillon cubes, 1 cube.................	2	—	.1	—	—	—	—	.07	1.0	—
Brains, all kinds, raw, 3 ounces........	106	8.8	7.3	14	3.1	—	.20	.22	3.8	15
Bran (breakfast cereal almost wholly bran), 1 cup...................	145	7.2	2.0	56	6.2	—	.22	.23	11.5	—
Bran flakes, 1 cup....................	117	4.3	.8	24	2.0	—	.19	.09	3.5	—
Breads:										
Boston brown, unenriched, 1 slice 3 × ¾"	105	2.3	1.0	89	1.2	70	.04	.06	.7	—
Cracked-wheat, unenriched, 1 sl. ½" thick	60	2.0	.5	19	2.2	—	.03	.02	.3	—
French or Vienna, unenriched, 1 pound	1,225	36.8	12.3	109	3.2	—	.21	.28	4.2	—

1 * Calcium may not be available because of presence of oxalic acid.

Italian, unenriched, 1 pound	1,195	39.5	3.6	59	3.2	—	.23	.30	4.5	
Raisin, unenriched, 1 slice ½″ thick	65	1.6	.7	18	.3	Tr.	.02	.02	.2	
Rye, American, 1 slice ½″ thick	57	2.1	.3	17	.4	—	.04	.02	.4	
White, unenriched, 4 per cent nonfat milk										
solids, 1 slice ½″ thick	63	2.0	.7	18	.1	—	.01	.02	.2	
Toasted, 1 slice ½″ thick	63	2.0	.7	18	.1	—	.01	.03	.2	
Whole wheat, 1 slice ½″ thick	55	2.1	.6	22	.5	—	.07		.7	
Bread crumbs, dry, grated, 1 cup	339	10.5	4.0	98	2.3	—	.24	.19	2.7	
Broccoli, cooked, 1 cup	44	5.0	.3	195	2.0	5,100	.10	.22	1.2	111
Brussels sprouts, cooked, 1 cup	60	5.7	.6	44	1.7	520	.05	.16	.6	61
Buckwheat flour:										
Dark, 1 cup sifted	340	11.5	2.4	32	2.7	—	.56	.15	2.8	—
Light, 1 cup sifted	342	6.3	1.2	11	1.0	—	.08	.04	.4	—
Buckwheat pancake, 1 cake 4″ diam.	47	1.6	2.3	67	.3	30	.04	.04	.2	Tr.
Butter, 1 tbs.	100	.1	11.3	3	—	460 [1*]	Tr.	Tr.	Tr.	—
Buttermilk, 1 cup	86	8.5	.2	288	.2	10	.09	.43	.3	3
Buttermilk, 1 quart	348	34.2	1.0	1,152	.7	40	.35	1.74	1.1	13
C Cabbage, raw, 1 cup shredded finely	24	1.4	.2	46	.5	80	.06	.05	.3	50
cooked, short time, 1 cup	40	2.4	.3	78	.8	150	.08	.08	.5	53
Cabbage, celery or chinese:										
Raw, leaves and stem, 1 cup 1″ pieces	14	1.2	.3	43	.9	260	.03	.04	.4	31
Cooked, 1 cup	27	2.3	.6	82	1.7	490	.04	.06	.6	42
Cakes:										
Angel food, 2″ sector	108	3.4	.1	2	.1	—	Tr.	.05	.1	—
Foundation, plain, 1 sq. 3 × 2 × 1¾″	228	3.8	7.6	82	.3	100 [2*]	.02	.05	.2	—
With fudge icing, 3″ sector	314	4.0	10.4	88	.4	100 [2*]	.02	.07	.2	—
Fruit, dark, 1 piece 2 × 2 × ½″	106	1.6	4.1	29	.8	50 [3*]	.04	.04	.3	—
Cupcake, 1 2¾″ in diam.	131	2.6	3.3	62	.2	50	.01	.03	.1	—
Iced layer cake, 3″ sector	241	3.9	4.6	88	.3	70	.02	.05	.2	—

1* Year-round average.
2* If fat used is butter or fortified margarine, the Vitamin A value would be 350 I.U. per square and 520 I.U. per 2-inch sector iced.
3* If fat used is butter or fortified margarine, the Vitamin A value would be 120 I.U.

Food, and Approximate Measure	Food Energy Cal.	Protein Gm.	Fat Gm.	Calcium Mg.	Iron Mg.	Vitamin A Value I.U.	Thiamine B_1 Mg.	Riboflavin B_2 Mg.	Niacin Value Mg.	Ascorbic Acid Mg.
Cakes (*continued*):										
Iced cupcake, 1 2¾″ in diam.	161	2.6	3.1	58	.2	50	.01	.04	.1	—
Pound, 1 sl. 2¾ × 3 × ⅝″	130	2.1	7.0	16	.5	1*100	.04	.05	.3	—
Rich, 1 square 3 × 2 × 2″	294	3.8	13.3	79	.4	2*160	.02	.06	.2	—
Plain icing, 3″ sector	378	4.4	14.7	88	.5	170	.02	.07	.2	—
Sponge, 2″ sector	117	3.2	2.0	11	.6	210	.02	.06	.1	—
Candy:										
Butterscotch, 1 ounce	116	—	2.5	6	.5	—	—	Tr.	Tr.	—
Caramels, 1 ounce	118	.8	3.3	36	.7	50	.01	.04	Tr.	Tr.
Chocolate, sweetened milk, 1 ounce	143	2.0	9.5	61	.6	40	.03	.11	.2	—
Chocolate creams, 1 ounce	110	1.1	4.0	—	—	—	—	—	—	—
Fondant, 1 ounce	101	—	—	—	—	—	—	—	—	—
Fudge, plain, 1 ounce	116	.5	3.2	3*14	.1	60	Tr.	.02	Tr.	Tr.
Hard, 1 ounce	108	—	—	—	—	—	—	—	—	—
Marshmallows, 1 ounce	92	.9	—	—	—	—	—	—	—	—
Peanut brittle, 1 ounce	125	2.4	4.4	11	.6	10	.03	.01	1.4	—
Cantaloupe, ½ melon 5″ diam.	37	1.1	.4	31	.7	4*6,190	.09	.07	.9	59
Carrots, raw, 1, 5½ × 1″	21	.6	.2	20	.4	6,000	.03	.03	.3	3
Grated, 1 cup	45	1.3	.3	43	.9	13,200	.06	.06	.7	7
Cooked, 1 cup diced	44	.9	.7	38	.9	18,130	.07	.07	.7	6
Catsup, tomato, 1 tbs.	17	.3	.1	2	.1	320	.02	.01	.4	2
Cauliflower, raw, 1 cup flower buds	25	2.4	.2	22	1.1	90	.11	.10	.6	69
Cooked, 1 cup	30	2.9	.2	26	1.3	108	.07	.10	.6	34

1* If fat used is butter or fortified margarine, the Vitamin A value would be 300 I.U.

2* If fat used is butter or fortified margarine, the Vitamin A value would be 620 I.U. per square.

3* The calcium contributed by chocolate may not be usable because of presence of oxalic acid; in that case the value would be 11 mg. per ounce.

4* Vitamin A based on deeply colored varieties.

Celery, raw, 1 stalk, 8'' long, 1'' wide	7	.5	.1	20	.2	—	.02	.02	.2	3
Celery, raw, 1 cup diced	18	1.3	.2	50	.5	—	.05	.04	.4	7
Cooked, 1 cup diced	24	1.7	.3	65	.6	—	.05	.04	.4	6
Chard, cooked, 1 cup	47	4.6	.7	1*184	4.4	16,960	.07	.28	.5	30
Cheese:										
Camembert, 1 ounce	85	5.0	7.0	30	.1	290	.01	.21	.3	—
Cheddar, 1 ounce (1'' cube)	113	7.1	9.1	206	.3	400	.01	.12	Tr.	—
Cottage from skim milk, 1 cup	215	43.9	1.1	216	.7	50	.04	.69	.2	—
Cottage from skim milk, 2 tbs	25	6.0	.1	27	.1	10	.01	.09	Tr.	—
Cream cheese, 1 ounce	106	2.6	10.5	19	.1	410	Tr.	.06	Tr.	—
Limburger, 1 ounce	97	6.0	7.9	167	.2	360	.02	.14	Tr.	—
Parmesan, 1 ounce	112	10.2	7.4	329	.1	300	.01	.21	.1	—
Swiss, 1 ounce	105	7.8	7.9	262	.3	410	Tr.	.11	Tr.	—
Cherries, raw, sour, sweet, 1 cup pitted	94	1.7	.8	28	.6	960	.08	.09	.6	13
Canned, 1 cup	122	2.0	.8	28	.8	1,840	.07	.04	.4	14
Chicken raw, broiler 2*, ½ bird										
(8 oz. bone out)	332	44.4	15.8	31	3.3	—	.18	.36	22.4	—
Roasters, 4 oz. bone out	227	22.9	14.3	16	1.7	—	.09	.18	9.1	—
Hens, stewing, 4 oz. bone out	342	20.4	28.3	16	1.7	—	.09	.18	9.1	—
Fryers, 1 breast, 8 oz. bone out	210	47.0	1.0	28	2.2	—	.13	.18	21.1	—
1 leg, 5 oz. bone out	159	29.1	3.8	21	2.6	—	.14	.34	8.0	—
Canned, boned, 3 oz.	169	25.3	6.8	12	1.5	—	.03	.14	5.4	—
Chile con carne, canned, ⅓ cup										
(without beans)	170	8.8	12.6	32	1.2	130	.01	.10	1.9	—
Chili sauce, 1 tbs.	17	.5	.1	2	.1	320	.02	.01	.4	2
Chocolate, bitter, 1 ounce	142	1.6	15.0	1*28	1.2	20	.01	.06	.3	—
Sweetened, plain, 1 ounce	133	.6	8.4	1*18	.8	10	.01	.04	.2	—
Chocolate beverage, 1 cup (made with milk)	239	8.2	12.5	260	.5	350	.08	.40	.3	2
Chocolate sirup, 1 tbs.	42	.2	.2	1*3	.3	—	—	—	—	—
Cider—See apple juice										

1* Calcium may not be available because of presence of oxalic acid.

2* Vitamin values based on muscle meat only.

177

Food, and Approximate Measure	Food Energy Cal.	Protein Gm.	Fat Gm.	MINERALS Calcium Mg.	Iron Mg.	VITAMINS Vitamin A Value I.U.	Thiamine B₁ Mg.	Riboflavin B₂ Mg.	Niacin Value Mg.	Ascorbic Acid Mg.
Clams, raw, meat only, 4 ounces.........	92	14.5	1.6	109	7.9	120	.11	.20	1.8	—
Canned, solids and liquid, 3 ounces.....	44	6.7	.9	74	5.4	70	.04	.08	.9	—
Cocoa, breakfast, plain dry powder, 1 tbs.	21	.6	1.7	1*9	.8	Tr.	.01	.03	.2	—
Cocoa beverage made with all milk, 1 cup	236	9.5	11.5	298	1.0	400	.10	.46	.5	3
Cola beverage, carbonated, 1 cup......	107	—	—	—	—	—	—	—	—	—
Coconut, fresh, 1 piece, 2 × 2 × ½".....	161	1.5	15.6	9	.9	—	.04	Tr.	.1	1
Dried, shredded, 1 cup.............	344	2.2	24.2	27	2.2	—	Tr.	Tr.	Tr.	—
Milk only, 1 cup.................	60	.7	1.0	58	.2	—	Tr.	Tr.	.2	4
Cod, raw, 4 ounces edible portion......	84	18.7	.5	11	.5	—	.07	.10	2.5	2
Dried, 1 ounce...................	106	23.2	.8	14	1.0	—	.02	.13	3.1	—
Coffee, clear, 1 cup...............	—	—	—	—	—	—	—	—	—	—
Coleslaw, 1 cup..................	102	1.6	7.3	47	.5	80	.06	.05	.3	50
Collards, cooked, 1 cup............	76	7.4	1.1	473	3.0	14,500	.15	.46	3.3	84
Cookies, plain, 3" diam., ½" thick....	109	1.5	3.2	6	.2	—	.01	.01	.1	—
Corn, 1 ear 5" long...............	84	2.7	.7	5	.6	2*390	.11	.10	1.4	8
Canned, solids and liquid, 1 cup.....	170	5.1	1.3	10	1.3	2*520	.07	.13	2.4	14
Corn bread or muffins, 1, 2¾" diam.	106	3.2	2.3	67	.9	3* 60	.08	.11	.6	—
Corn flakes, 1 cup................	96	2.0	.1	3	.3	—	.01	.02	.4	—
Corn flour, 1 cup sifted............	406	8.6	2.9	7	2.0	4*370	.22	.06	1.6	—
Cornmeal (whole) cooked, white or yellow, 1 cup..................	119	2.6	.5	2	.5	5*100	.04	.02	.3	—
Corn sirup, 1 tbs.	57	—	—	9	.8	—	—	Tr.	Tr.	—
Crabs, canned or cooked, 3 oz. (meat only)	89	14.4	2.5	38	.8	—	.04	.05	2.1	—

1* Calcium may not be available because of presence of oxalic acid.
2* Vitamin A based on yellow corn; white corn contains only a trace.
3* Based on recipe using white corn meal, if yellow used, Vitamin A value is 120 I.U.
4* Vitamin A based on yellow corn flour, white contains only a trace.
5* Vitamin A based on yellow corn meal, white contains only a trace.

Food										
Crackers, graham, 4 small	55	1.1	1.4	3	.3	—	.04	.02	.2	—
Saltines, 2, 2″ square	34	.7	.9	2	.1	—	Tr.	Tr.	.1	—
Soda, plain, 2, 2½″ square	47	1.1	1.1	2	.1	—	.01	.01	.1	—
Cranberries, raw, 1 cup	54	.5	.8	16	.7	50	.03	.02	.1	13
Canned or cooked sauce, 1 cup	549	.3	.8	22	.8	80	.06	.06	.3	5
Cream, light, table, 1 tbs.	30	.4	3.0	15	—	120	Tr.	.02	Tr.	Tr.
Heavy or whipping, 1 tbs.	49	.3	5.2	12	—	220	Tr.	.02	Tr.	Tr.
Cress, garden, cooked, 1 cup	73	7.6	2.5	380	5.2	5,940	.11	.23	1.3	52
Cress, water, raw. 1 pound (leaves & stems)	84	7.7	1.4	885	9.1	21,450	.37	.71	3.6	350
Cucumbers, raw, 1, 7½ × 2″	25	1.4	.2	20	.6	—	.07	.09	.4	17
Currants, red, raw, 1 cup	60	1.3	.2	40	1.0	130	.04	—	—	40
Custard, baked, 1 cup	283	13.1	13.4	283	1.2	840	.11	.49	.2	1
D Dandelion greens, 1 cup cooked	79	4.9	1.3	337	5.6	27,310	.23	.22	1.3	29
Dates, fresh and dried, 1 cup pitted	505	3.9	1.1	128	3.7	100	.16	.17	3.9	—
Doughnuts, cake type, 1	136	2.1	6.7	23	.2	40	.05	.04	.4	—
E Eggs, boiled, poached, 1	77	6.1	5.5	26	1.3	550	.05	.14	Tr.	—
Omelet, 1 egg	106	6.8	7.9	50	1.3	640	.05	.17	Tr.	—
Scrambled, 1 egg	106	6.8	7.9	50	1.3	640	.05	.17	Tr.	—
Yolk, raw, 1	61	2.8	5.4	25	1.2	550	.05	.06	Tr.	—
White, raw, 1	15	3.3	—	2	.1	—	—	.08	Tr.	—
Endive, Escarole, 1 pound raw	90	7.3	.9	359	7.7	13,600	.30	.53	1.8	49
F Farina, cooked, 1 cup	104	3.1	.2	7	.2	—	.01	.02	.2	—
Fats, cooking (vegetable), 1 tbs.	110	—	12.5	—	—	—	—	—	—	—
See also Lard, Oils										
Figs, raw, 3 small, 1½″ diam.	90	1.6	.5	62	.7	90	.06	.06	.6	2
Canned, sirup pack, 3, and 2 tbs. sirup	129	.9	.3	40	.5	60	.04	.04	.4	1
Dried, 1 large	57	.8	.3	39	.6	20	.02	.02	.4	—
Fig bars, 1 small	56	.7	.8	11	.2	—	.01	.01	.1	—
Flounder, summer and winter, 4 oz. (raw) edible portion	78	16.9	.6	69	.9	—	.07	.06	1.9	—
Frankfurters, 1	124	7.0	10.0	3	.6	—	.08	.09	1.3	—
Frog legs, raw, 4 oz. edible portion	82	18.6	.3	20	1.2	—	.16	.29	1.3	—

Food, and Approximate Measure	Food Energy Cal.	Protein Gm.	Fat Gm.	Calcium Mg.	Iron Mg.	Vitamin A Value I.U.	Thiamine B₁ Mg.	Riboflavin B₂ Mg.	Niacin Value Mg.	Ascorbic Acid Mg.
Fruit cocktail, canned, 1 cup (solids & liquid)	179	1.0	.5	23	1.0	410	.03	.03	.9	5
G Gelatin, dry, plain, 1 tbs.	34	8.6	—	—	—	—	—	—	—	—
Dessert powder, ½ cup (3 ounce pkg.)	324	8.0	—	—	—	—	—	—	—	—
Dessert, ready-to-serve, 1 cup	155	3.8	—	—	—	—	—	—	—	—
Ginger ale, dry, 1 cup	80	—	—	—	—	—	—	—	—	—
Gingerbread, 1 piece 2 × 2 × 2″	180	2.1	6.6	63	1.4	50	.02	.05	.6	—
Gooseberries, raw, 1 cup	59	1.2	.3	33	.8	440	—	—	—	49
Grapefruit, raw, ½ medium (4½″ diam.)	75	.9	.4	41	.4	20	.07	.04	.4	76
Grapefruit, raw, 1 cup sections	77	1.0	.4	43	.4	20	.07	.04	.4	78
Canned in sirup, 1 cup solids & liquid	181	1.5	.5	32	.7	20	.07	.05	.5	74
Juice, fresh, 1 cup	87	1.2	.2	20	.7	20	.09	.05	.5	99
Juice, canned sweetened, 1 cup	131	1.3	.3	20	.8	20	.08	.04	.5	87
Juice, canned unsweetened, 1 cup	92	1.2	.2	20	.7	20	.07	.04	.4	85
Juice, concentrate, frozen, 1 can, 6 fluid ounces	297	3.8	.8	63	2.4	60	.24	.13	1.4	272
Grapes, raw—Concord, 1 cup skins & seeds	84	1.7	1.7	20	.7	90	.07	.05	.3	5
Malaga, Muscat, 1 cup (40 grapes)	102	1.2	.6	26	.9	120	.09	.06	.4	6
Grape juice, bottled, 1 cup	170	1.0	—	25	.8	—	.09	.12	.6	Tr.
Griddle cakes (wheat), 1 cake, 4″ in diam.	59	1.8	2.5	43	.2	50	.02	.03	.1	Tr.
Guavas, common, raw, 1	49	.7	.4	21	.5	180	.05	.03	.8	212
H Haddock, cooked, 1 fillet 4 × 3 × ½″	158	19.0	5.5	18	.6	—	.04	.09	2.6	—
Halibut, broiled, 1 steak 4 × 3 × ½″	228	33.0	9.8	18	1.0	—	.08	.09	13.9	—
Ham, See Pork										
Hamburger, See Beef										
Heart, beef, lean, raw, 3 ounces	92	14.4	3.1	8	3.9	30	.50	.75	6.6	5
Chicken, raw, 3 ounces	134	17.4	6.0	20	1.4	30	.10	.77	4.4	5

Herring, smoked, kippered, 3 ounces edible portion	180	18.9	11.0	—	56	1.2	—	Tr.	.24	2.5	—
Hominy grits, cooked, 1 cup	122	2.9	.2	—	2	.2	100	.04	.01	.4	—
Honey, 1 tbs.	62	.1	—	—	1	.2	—	Tr.	.01	Tr.	1
Honeydew melon, 1 wedge 2 × 7″	49	.8	—	—	26	.6	60	.07	.04	.3	34
I Ice cream, plain*, 1/7 of quart brick	167	3.2	10.1	—	100	.1	420	.03	.15	.1	1
J Jams, marmalades, 1 tbs.	55	.1	.1	—	2	.1	Tr.	Tr.	Tr.	Tr.	1
Jellies, 1 tbs.	50	—	—	—	2	.1	Tr.	Tr.	Tr.	Tr.	1
K Kale, cooked, 1 cup	45	4.3	.7	—	248	2.4	9,220	.08	.25	1.9	56
Kidney, beef, 3 ounces (raw)	120	12.8	6.9	—	8	6.7	980	.32	2.16	5.5	11
Pork, 3 ounces (raw)	97	13.9	3.9	—	9	6.8	110	.50	1.47	8.4	11
Lamb, 3 ounces (raw)	89	14.1	2.8	—	11	7.8	980	.44	2.06	6.3	11
Kohlrabi, raw, 1 cup diced	41	2.9	.1	—	63	.8	Tr.	.08	.07	.3	84
cooked, 1 cup	47	3.3	.2	—	71	.9	Tr.	.06	.06	.3	57
L Lamb:											
Rib chop cooked, 3 ounces without bone	356	20.0	30.0	—	9	2.6	—	.12	.22	4.8	—
Shoulder roast, 3 ounces without bone	293	18.0	24.0	—	8	2.2	—	.10	.19	3.9	—
Leg roast, 3 ounces without bone	230	20.0	16.0	—	9	2.6	—	.12	.21	4.4	—
Lard, 1 tbs.	126	—	14.0	—	—	—	—	—	—	—	—
Lemons, 1 medium	20	.6	.4	—	25	.4	—	.03	Tr.	.1	31
Juice, fresh, 1 tbs.	4	.1	—	—	2	—	—	.01	Tr.	Tr.	7
Lettuce, loose leaf 1 head	32	2.6	.4	—	48	1.1	1,200	.10	.18	.4	17
Lettuce, loose leaf, 2 large leaves	7	.6	.1	—	11	.2	270	.02	.04	.1	4
Limes, 1 medium	19	.4	.1	—	21	.3	—	.02	Tr.	.1	14
Juice, fresh, 1 cup	58	1.0	—	—	34	.2	—	.11	.01	.3	65
Liver, beef, 2 ounces cooked	118	13.4	4.4	—	5	4.4	30,330	.15	2.25	8.4	18
Calf, 3 ounces raw	120	16.2	4.2	—	5	9.0	19,130	.18	2.65	13.7	30
Chicken, 3 ounces raw	120	18.8	3.4	—	14	6.3	27,370	.17	2.10	10.0	17
Lamb, 3 ounces raw	116	17.8	3.3	—	7	10.7	42,930	.34	2.79	14.3	28
Liver, canned, strained, 1 ounce (infant food)	30	4.5	1.1	—	7	2.0	5,440	.01	.61	1.8	—

* Based on 5 pounds of ice cream to the gallon, factory packed.

Food, and Approximate Measure	Food Energy Cal.	Protein Gm.	Fat Gm.	MINERALS		VITAMINS				
				Calcium Mg.	Iron Mg.	Vitamin A Value I.U.	Thiamine B_1 Mg.	Riboflavin B_2 Mg.	Niacin Value Mg.	Ascorbic Acid Mg.
Lobster, canned, 3 ounces	78	15.6	1.1	55	.7	—	.03	.06	1.9	—
Loganberries, raw, 1 cup	90	1.4	.9	50	1.7	280	.04	.10	.4	34
M Macaroni, enriched, cooked, 1 cup (1" pieces)	209	7.1	.8	13	1.5	—	.24	.15	2.0	—
Macaroni & cheese baked, 1 cup	464	17.8	24.2	420	1.1	990	.07	.35	.9	Tr.
Mackerel, canned 1*, 3 ounces solids & liquids	153	17.9	8.5	221	1.9	20	.02	.28	7.4	—
Mangos, raw, 1 medium	87	.9	.3	12	.3	8,380	.08	.07	1.2	55
Margarine, 1 tbs.	101	.1	11.3	3	—	2*460	—	—	—	—
Marmalade, 1 tbs.	55	.1	.1	2	.1	Tr.	Tr.	Tr.	Tr.	1
Mayonnaise, 1 tbs.	92	.2	10.1	2	.1	30	Tr.	Tr.	—	—
Milk, cow: fluid, whole, 1 cup	166	8.5	9.5	288	.2	390	.09	.42	.3	3
Fluid, nonfat (skim), 1 cup	87	8.6	.2	303	.2	10	.09	.44	.3	3
Buttermilk, 1 cup	86	8.5	.2	288	.2	10	.09	.43	.3	3
Canned, Evaporated (unsweetened), 1 cup	346	17.6	19.9	612	.4	1,010	.12	.91	.5	3
Condensed (sweetened), 1 cup	981	24.8	25.7	835	.6	1,300	.16	1.19	.6	3
Dried, whole, 1 tbs.	39	2.1	2.1	76	—	110	.02	.12	.1	1
*Dried, nonfat solids (skim), 1 tbs.	28	2.7	.1	98	—	Tr.	.03	.15	.1	1
Malted beverage, 1 cup	281	12.4	11.9	364	.8	680	.18	.56	—	3
Half & Half (milk and cream), 1 cup	330	7.7	29.0	261	.1	1,190	.08	.38	.2	3
Chocolate flavored, 1 cup	185	8.0	5.5	272	.2	230	.08	.40	.2	2

1* The vitamin values are based on drained solids.

2* Based on the average Vitamin A content of fortified margarines. Most margarines manufactured for use in the U.S. have 15,000 I.U. of Vitamin A per pound; minimum Federal specifications for fortified margarine require 9,000 I.U. per pound.

* When a tablespoon or two of dry milk is added to a cup of skim milk, it makes the latter more pleasant to taste, and a good substitute for cream. Adds additional protein, vitamins and minerals too.

Milk, goat, 1 cup	164	8.1	9.8	315	.2	390	.10	.26	.7	2
Molasses, cane, light, 1 tbs.	50			33	.9		.01	.01	Tr.	
Medium, 1 tbs.	46			58	1.2				.4	
Blackstrap, 1 tbs.	43			116	2.3		.06	.05		
Barbados, 1 tbs.	54			99	.3		.01	.04	.2	
Muffins, plain, 1, 2¾″ in diam.	134	3.8	4.0	26	.7	50	.02	.06	.5	
Mung bean sprouts, raw, 1 cup	21	2.6	.2	17	2.0	10	.06	.08		14
Mushrooms, canned, 1 cup solids & liquid	28	3.4	.5	31	.7		.04	.60	4.8	
Muskmelon, ½ melon 5″ diam.	37	1.1	.4			6,190	.09	.07	.9	59
Mustard greens, cooked, 1 cup	31	3.2	.4	308	4.1	10,050	.08	.25	1.0	63
N Noodles, unenriched, containing egg, 1 cup (dry)	278	9.2	2.5	16	1.5	140	.15	.08	1.7	
Cooked, 1 cup	107	3.5	1.0	6	.6	60	.05	.03	.6	
Nuts:										
Almonds, shelled, 1 cup	848	26.4	76.8	361	6.2		.35	.95	6.5	Tr.
Brazil, shelled, 1 cup (32 kernels)	905	20.2	92.3	260	4.8	Tr.	1.21			
Cashew, roasted, 1 ounce	164	5.2	13.7	13	1.4		.18	.05	.6	
Peanuts, roasted, 1 cup medium halves	805	38.7	63.6	107	2.7		.42	.19	23.3	
Peanuts, roasted, 1 tbs. chopped	50	2.4	4.0	7	.2		.03	.01	1.5	
Pecans, 1 cup halves	752	10.2	78.8	80	2.6	50	.77	.12	1.0	2
Pecans, 1 tbs. chopped	52	.7	5.5	6	.2	Tr.	.05	.01	.1	Tr.
Walnuts, 1 cup halves	654	15.0	64.4	83	2.1	30	.48	.13	1.2	3
Walnuts, 1 tbs. chopped	49	1.1	4.8	6	.2	Tr.	.04	.01	.1	Tr.
O Oatmeal or rolled oats, 1 cup dry	312	11.4	5.9	42	3.6		.48	.11	.8	
Cooked, 1 cup	148	5.4	2.8	21	1.7		.22	.05	.4	
Oils, salad or cooking, 1 tbs.	124		14.0							
Okra, cooked, 8 pods, 3 × ⅝″	28	1.5	.2	70	.6	630	.05	.05	.7	17
Oleomargarine, 1 tbs.	101	.1	11.3	3		460				
Olives, green, 10 large	72	.8	7.4	48	.9	160	Tr.			
Ripe, Mission, 10 large	106	1.0	11.6	48	.9	40	Tr.	Tr.		
Onions, mature, raw, 1, 2½″ diam.	49	1.5	.2	35	.6	60	.04	.04	.2	10

Food, and Approximate Measure	Food Energy Cal.	Protein Gm.	Fat Gm.	MINERALS Calcium Mg.	MINERALS Iron Mg.	Vitamin A Value I.U.	VITAMINS Thiamine B₁ Mg.	VITAMINS Riboflavin B₂ Mg.	VITAMINS Niacin Value Mg.	Ascorbic Acid Mg.
Onions, mature, raw, 1 tbs. chopped.....	4	.1	—	3	—	Tr.	Tr.	Tr.	Tr.	1
Cooked, whole, 1 cup.............	79	2.1	.4	67	1.0	110	.04	.06	.4	13
Onions, young green, 6 small.........	23	.5	.1	68	.4	30	.02	.02	.1	12
Oranges, 1 medium, 3" diam.........	70	1.4	.3	51	.6	290	.12	.04	.4	77
Orange juice, fresh, 1 cup...........	108	2.0	.5	47	.5	460	.19	.06	.6	122
Canned, unsweetened, 1 cup.........	109	2.0	.5	25	.7	240	.17	.04	.6	103
Canned, sweetened, 1 cup..........	135	1.5	.5	25	.8	250	.18	.05	.6	105
Orange juice concentrate, canned, 1 ounce	65	1.2	.2	17	.5	140	.10	.02	.3	63
Frozen, 1 can (6 fl. oz.)........	300	5.5	1.4	69	2.0	670	.48	.11	1.5	285
Oysters, meat only, raw, 1 cup (13–19 med.)	200	23.5	5.0	226	13.4	770	.35	.48	2.8	—
Stew, 1 cup (6–8 oysters).........	244	16.6	13.2	262	7.0	820	.21	.46	1.6	—
P Pancakes (griddlecakes)										
Wheat, 1 cake, 4" diameter...........	59	1.8	2.5	43	.2	50	.02	.03	.1	Tr.
Buckwheat, 1 cake, 4" diameter.......	47	1.6	2.3	67	.3	30	.04	.04	.2	Tr.
Papayas, raw, 1 cup, ½" cubes........	71	1.1	.2	36	.5	3,190	.06	.07	.5	102
Parsley, common, raw, 1 tbs. chopped...	1	.1	—	*7	.2	290	Tr.	.01	.1	7
Parsnips, cooked, 1 cup..............	94	1.6	.8	88	1.1	—	.09	.16	.3	19
Peaches, raw, 1 medium..............	46	.5	.1	8	.6	880	.02	.05	.9	8
Peaches, canned, sirup pack, 2 medium halves, 2 tbs. sirup......	79	.5	.1	6	.5	530	.01	.02	.8	5
Strained (infant food), 1 ounce.......	17	.2	.1	2	.3	180	.01	.01	.2	1
Frozen, 4 ounces.................	89	.5	.1	7	.5	590	.01	.03	.6	5
Dried, cooked, no sugar, 1 cup, 10–12 halves, 6 tbs. liquid..........	224	2.4	.5	38	5.9	2,750	.01	.16	4.3	11
With sugar added, 1 cup, 10–12 halves, 6 tbs. liquid..........	366	2.4	.6	37	5.8	2,750	.01	.15	4.3	12

Peanut butter, 1 tbs.	92	4.2	7.6	12	.3	—	.02	.02	2.6	
Pears, raw, 1, 3 × 2½″ diam.	95	1.1	.6	20	.5	30	.03	.06	.2	6
Canned, sirup pack,										
2 medium halves, 2 tbs. sirup	79	.2	.1	9	.2	Tr.	.01	.01	.2	2
Strained (infant food), 1 ounce	15	.2	.1	3	.1	10	Tr.	.01	.1	Tr.
Peas, green, 1 cup	111	7.8	.6	35	3.0	1,150	.40	.22	3.7	24
Canned, 1 cup drained solids	145	7.2	1.0	51	3.4	1,070	.19	.10	1.6	15
Canned, 1 cup solids & liquid	168	8.5	1.0	62	4.5	1,350	.28	.15	2.6	21
Peppers, green, raw, 1 medium	16	.8	.1	7	.3	400	.02	.04	.2	77
Persimmons, raw,										
Seedless kind, 1, 2¼″ diameter	95	1.0	.5	7	.4	3,270	.06	.05	Tr.	13
Kind with seeds, 1, 2¼″ diameter	74	.8	.4	6	.3	2,570	.05	.04	Tr.	10
Pickles: Dill, 1 large	15	.9	.3	34	1.6	420	Tr.	.09	.1	8
Bread & butter pickles, 6 slices	29	.4	.1	13	.8	80	.01	.02	Tr.	4
Sour, 1 large	15	.7	.3	34	1.6	420	Tr.	.09	Tr.	8
Sweet, 1 average	22	.2	.1	3	.3	20	—	Tr.	Tr.	1
Pies: Apple, 4″ sector	331	2.8	12.8	9	.5	220	.04	.02	.3	1
Blueberry, 4″ sector	291	2.8	9.3	14	.7	160	.02	.04	.3	5
Cherry, 4″ sector	340	3.2	13.2	14	.5	530	.04	.02	.3	2
Custard, 4″ sector	266	6.8	11.3	162	1.6	290	.07	.21	.4	1
Lemon meringue, 4″ sector	302	4.3	12.1	24	.6	210	.04	.10	.5	1
Mince, 4″ sector	341	3.4	9.3	22	3.0	10	.09	.05	.4	1
Pumpkin, 4″ sector	263	5.5	12.5	70	1.0	2,480	.04	.15	.1	
Pimientos, canned, 1 medium	10	.3	.2	3	.6	870	.01	.02	.3	36
Pineapple, raw, 1 cup diced	74	.6	.3	22	.4	180	.12	.04	.4	33
Canned, sirup pack, 1 cup crushed	204	1.0	.3	75	1.6	210	.20	.04	.2	23
Canned, sirup pack, 1 large slice &	95	.5	.1	35	.7	100	.09	.02	.2	11
2 lbs. juice	97	.5	.2	16	.3	110	.07	.02	.2	22
Pineapple juice, canned, 1 cup	121	.7	.2	37	1.2	200	.13	.04	.4	22
Plums, raw, 1, 2″ in diam.	29	.4	.1	10	.3	200	.04	.02	.3	3
Canned, sirup pack, 1 cup (fruit & juice)	186	1.0	.2	20	2.7	560	.07	.06	.9	3
Popcorn, popped, 1 cup	54	1.8	.7	2	.4	—	.05	.02	.3	

Food, and Approximate Measure	Food Energy Cal.	Protein Gm.	Fat Gm.	MINERALS Calcium Mg.	Iron Mg.	Vitamin A Value I.U.	VITAMINS Thiamine B_1 Mg.	Riboflavin B_2 Mg.	Niacin Value Mg.	Ascorbic Acid Mg.
Pork, fresh:										
Ham cooked, 3 ounces without bone....	338	20.0	28.0	9	2.6	—	.45	.20	4.0	—
Loin or chops cooked, 1 chop....	293	20.0	23.0	10	2.6	—	.72	.21	4.4	[
Pork, cured:										
Ham, smoked, cooked, 3 ounces without bone....	339	20.0	28.0	9	2.5	—	.46	.18	3.5	—
Luncheon meat: Boiled ham, 2 ounces....	172	12.9	12.9	5	1.5	—	.57	.15	2.9	—
Canned, spiced, 2 ounces....	164	8.4	13.8	5	1.2	—	.18	.12	1.6	—
Pork sausage, links, raw, 4 ounces....	510	12.2	50.8	7	1.8	—	.49	.19	2.6	—
Pork, canned, strained, 1 ounce (infant food)	36	4.8	1.7	4	.5	—	.10	.08	1.3	17
Potatoes, baked, 1 medium, 2½" diam. ..	97	2.4	.1	13	.8	20	.11	.05	1.4	22
Boiled in jacket, 1 medium, 2½" diam. ..	118	2.8	.1	16	1.0	30	.14	.06	1.6	17
Peeled and boiled, 1 medium, 2½" diam.	105	2.5	.1	14	.9	20	.12	.04	1.3	17
French fried, 8 pieces 2 × ½ × ½"....	157	2.2	7.6	12	.8	20	.07	.04	1.3	11
Hash-browned, 1 cup....	470	6.4	22.8	35	2.3	60	.15	.11	3.3	14
Mashed, milk added, 1 cup....	159	4.3	1.4	53	1.2	80	.16	.10	1.7	14
Mashed, milk and butter added, 1 cup..	240	4.1	11.7	53	1.2	500	.15	.10	1.6	13
Steamed or pressure cooked, 1 medium..	105	2.5	.1	14	.9	20	.12	.05	1.5	18
Canned, drained solids, 3-4 very small..	118	2.8	.1	16	1.0	30	.11	.05	1.3	18
Potato chips, 10 medium, 2" diam.	108	1.3	7.4	6	.4	10	.04	.02	.6	2
Pretzels, 5 small sticks....	18	.04	.2	1	—	—	Tr.	Tr.	Tr.	—
Prunes, dried, uncooked, 4 large....	94	.8	.2	19	1.4	660	.03	.06	.6	1
Cooked, no sugar added, 1 cup....	310	2.7	.7	62	4.5	2,210	.07	.20	2.0	2
Cooked, sugar added, 1 cup....	483	2.9	.6	64	4.4	2,200	.09	.18	1.8	3
Prunes, canned, strained, 1 ounce (infant food)....	28	.3	.1	7	.4	210	.01	.01	.2	1
Prune juice, canned, 1 cup....	170	1.0	—	60	4.3	—	.07	.19	1.0	2
Prune whip, 1 cup....	200	3.8	.4	35	2.4	1,160	.05	.15	1.0	3

Food										
Pudding, vanilla, 1 cup	275	8.7	9.7	290	.2	390	.08	.40	.2	2
Puffed rice, 1 cup	55	.8	.1	3	.3	—	.06	.01	.8	—
Puffed wheat, 1 cup	43	1.3	.2	6	.4	—	.01	.02	1.2	—
Pumpkin, canned, 1 cup	76	2.3	.7	46	1.6	7,750	.04	.14	1.0	5
R										
Radishes, raw, 4 small	4	.2	—	7	.2	10	.01	Tr.	.1	10
Raisins, dried, 1 cup	429	3.7	.8	125	5.3	80	.24	.13	.8	Tr.
Raisins, dried, 1 tbs.	26	.2	—	8	.3	Tr.	.02	.01	Tr.	Tr.
Cooked, sugar added, 1 cup	572	3.2	.6	112	4.7	60	.18	.12	.6	Tr.
Raspberries, black, raw, 1 cup	100	2.0	2.1	54	1.2	—	.03	.09	.4	32
Red, raw, 1 cup	70	1.5	.5	49	1.1	160	.03	.08	.4	29
Frozen, 3 ounces	84	.7	.3	24	.5	70	.01	.03	.2	14
Rhubarb, raw, 1 cup diced	19	.6	.1	1* 62	.6	40	.01	—	.1	11
Cooked, sugar added, 1 cup	383	1.1	.3	1*112	1.1	70	.02	—	.2	17
Rice, brown, raw, 1 cup	784	15.6	3.5	81	4.2	—	.66	.10	9.6	—
Cooked, 1 cup	204	4.2	.2	14	.5	—	.10	.02	1.9	—
White, raw, 1 cup	692	14.5	.6	46	1.5	—	.13	.05	3.1	—
White, cooked, 1 cup	201	4.2	.2	13	.5	—	.02	.01	.7	—
White, precooked, dry, 1 cup	420	9.7	.2	4	.5	—	.02	.02	.1	—
Wild rice, parched, raw, 1 cup	593	23.0	1.1	31	.9	—	.73	1.03	10.0	—
Rice, flakes, 1 cup	118	1.8	.2	6	.5	—	.02	.03	.3	—
Rolls, plain, pan rolls, unenriched (12 per pound), 1	118	3.4	2.1	21	.3	—	.02	.04	.4	—
Sweet, unenriched, 1	178	4.8	4.3	35	.3	—	.03	.07	.6	—
Rutabagas, cooked, 1 cup cubed or sliced	50	1.2	.2	85	.6	540	.08	.11	1.1	33
Rye flour, light, 1 cup sifted	285	7.5	.8	18	.9	—	.12	.06	.5	—
Rye wafers, 2	43	1.6	.2	6	.6	—	.04	.03	.2	—
S										
Salad dressings:										
Commercial, plain (mayonnaise type) 2*, 1 tbs.	58	.2	5.5	1	.1	20	Tr.	Tr.	—	—
French, 1 tbs.	59	.1	5.3	—	—	—	—	—	—	—

1* Calcium may not be available because of presence of oxalic acid.
2* Minerals and vitamins are calculated from a recipe.

	Food Energy Cal.	Protein Gm.	Fat Gm.	MINERALS		Vitamin A Value I.U.	VITAMINS			Ascorbic Acid Mg.
Food, and Approximate Measure				Calcium Mg.	Iron Mg.		Thiamine B_1 Mg.	Riboflavin B_2 Mg.	Niacin Value Mg.	
Mayonnaise 1*, 1 tbs.	92	.2	10.1	2	.1	30	Tr.	Tr.	—	—
Salad oil, 1 tbs.	124	—	14.0	—	1.4	—	—	—	—	—
Salmon, broiled, baked, 1 steak 4 × 3 × ½"	204	33.6	6.7	—	1.4	—	.12	.33	9.8	—
Canned, solids and liquid:										
Chinook or King, 3 ounces	173	16.8	11.2	2*131	.8	200	.02	.12	6.2	—
Chum, 3 ounces	118	18.3	4.4	2*212	.6	50	.02	.13	6.0	—
Coho or silver, 3 ounces	140	17.9	7.1	2*197	.8	70	.02	.15	6.3	—
Pink or humpback, 3 ounces	122	17.4	5.3	2*159	.7	60	.03	.16	6.8	—
Sockeye or red, 3 ounces	147	17.2	8.2	2*220	1.0	200	.03	.14	6.2	—
Sardines: Atlantic type, canned in oil:										
Solids and liquid, 3 ounces	288	17.9	23.0	301	3.0	—	.01	.12	3.3	—
Drained solids, 3 ounces	182	21.9	9.4	328	2.3	190	.01	.15	4.1	—
Pilchards, Pacific type, Canned, solids and liquid										
Natural pack, 3 ounces	171	15.1	11.5	324	3.5	20	.01	.26	6.3	—
Tomato sauce, 3 ounces	184	15.1	12.6	324	3.5	20	.01	.23	4.5	—
Sauerkraut, canned, 1 cup drained solids	32	2.1	.4	54	.8	60	.05	.10	.2	24
Sausage: Bologna, 1 piece 1 × 1½" diam.	467	31.2	33.5	19	4.6	—	.37	.40	5.7	—
Frankfurter, cooked, 1	124	7.0	10.0	3	.6	—	.08	.09	1.3	—
Liver, liverwurst, 2 ounces	150	9.5	11.7	5	3.1	3,260	.10	.63	2.6	—
Pork, links or bulk, 4 ounces (raw)	510	12.2	50.8	7	1.8	—	.49	.19	2.6	—
Vienna sausage, canned, 4 ounces	244	17.9	18.6	10	2.7	—	.11	.14	3.5	—
Scallops, raw, 4 ounces edible muscle	89	16.8	.1	29	2.0	—	.05	.11	1.6	—
Shad, raw, 4 ounces edible portion	191	21.2	11.1	—	.6	—	.17	.27	9.6	—
Sherbet 1*, ½ cup	118	1.4	2.0	48	—	—	.02	.07	—	—

1* Minerals and vitamins are calculated from a recipe.

2* If bones are discarded, calcium content would be much lower. Bones equal about 2% of total contents of can.

3* Based on 6.9 pounds to the gallon of ice cream.

Sh[ortbread], 2 squares, 1¾ × 1¾									—	—
Shredded wheat, 1 large biscuit, plain...	102	2.9	.7	13	1.0	—	.06	.03	1.3	—
Shrimp, canned, 3 ounces drained solids...	110	23.0	1.2	98	2.6	50	.01	.03	1.9	—
Sirup, table blends (chiefly corn sirup), 1 tbs..............	57	—	—	9	.8	—	—	Tr.	Tr.	—
Soups, canned: 2*										
Bean, ready-to-serve, 1 cup............	191	8.5	5.0	95	2.8	—	.10	.10	.8	—
Beef, ready-to-serve, 1 cup............	100	6.0	3.5	15	.5	—	—	—	—	—
Bouillon, broth, and Consomme, ready-to-serve, 1 cup.........	9	2.0	—	2	1.0	—	—	.05	.6	—
Chicken, ready-to-serve, 1 cup.........	75	3.5	2.5	20	.5	—	.02	.12	1.5	—
Clam chowder, ready-to-serve, 1 cup...	86	4.6	2.3	36	3.6	—	—	—	—	—
Cream soup—asparagus, celery, mushroom, 1 cup............	201	7.0	11.7	217	.5	200	.05	.20	.1	—
Noodle, rice or barley, 1 cup...........	117	6.0	4.5	82	.2	30	.02	.05	.7	—
Pea, ready-to-serve, 1 cup............	141	6.4	2.0	32	1.5	440	.17	.07	1.2	5
Tomato, ready-to-serve, 1 cup.........	90	2.2	2.2	24	1.0	1,230	.02	.10	.7	10
Vegetable, ready-to-serve, 1 cup.......	82	4.2	1.8	32	.8	—	.05	.08	1.0	8
Vegetable, strained, 1 ounce (infant food)	12	.7	.1	7	.3	700	.02	.02	.1	Tr.
Soybeans, whole, mature, dried, 1 cup.	695	73.3	38.0	477	16.8	230	2.25	.65	4.9	Tr.
Soybean flour, medium fat, 1 cup stirred..	232	37.4	5.7	215	11.4	100	.72	.30	2.3	—
Soybean sprouts, raw, 1 cup...........	49	6.6	1.5	51	1.1	190	.24	.21	.9	14
Spaghetti, dry, unenriched, 1 cup 2" pieces	354	12.0	1.3	21	1.4	—	.09	.06	1.9	—
Cooked, 1 cup................	218	7.4	.9	13	.9	—	.03	.02	.7	—
Spinach, raw, 4 ounces edible portion.....	22	2.6	.3	[1*] 92	3.4	10,680	.13	.23	.7	67
Cooked, 1 cup................	46	5.6	1.1	[1*] 223	3.6	21,200	.14	.36	1.1	54
Strained (infant food), 1 ounce........	4	.5	.1	[1*] 22	.4	1,190	.01	.03	.1	2
Squash, summer, cooked, 1 cup diced.....	34	1.3	.2	32	.8	550	.08	.15	1.3	23
Winter, baked, mashed, 1 cup..........	97	3.9	.8	49	1.6	12,690	.10	.31	1.2	14
Winter, canned, strained, 1 ounce (infant food)..............	8	.3	.1	9	.1	560	.01	.02	.1	1

1* Calcium may not be available because of presence of oxalic acid.

2* All ready-to-serve soups are calculated from equal weights of the condensed soup and water except cream soup which was based on equal weights of the condensed soup and milk.

	Food Energy Cal.	Protein Gm.	Fat Gm.	MINERALS Calcium Mg.	Iron Mg.	Vitamin A Value I.U.	VITAMINS Thiamine B₁ Mg.	Riboflavin B₂ Mg.	Niacin Value Mg.	Ascorbic Acid Mg.
Food, and Approximate Measure										
Starch, pure (corn), 1 tbs.	29	—	—	—	—	—	—	—	—	—
Strawberries, raw, 1 cup capped	54	1.2	.7	42	1.2	90	.04	.10	.4	89
Frozen, 3 ounces	90	.5	.3	19	.5	30	.02	.04	.2	35
Sugars:										
Granulated, cane or beet, 1 cup	770	—	—	—	—	—	—	—	—	—
1 teaspoon	16	—	—	—	—	—	—	—	—	—
1 lump 1⅛ × ⅝ × ⅛″	27	—	—	—	—	—	—	—	—	—
Powdered, 1 cup (stirred before measuring)	493	—	—	—	—	—	—	—	—	—
1 tbs.	31	—	—	—	—	—	—	—	—	—
Brown, 1 cup (firm-packed)	813	—	—	2*167	5.7	—	—	—	—	—
1 tbs.	51	—	—	2* 10	.4	—	—	—	—	—
Maple, 1 piece 1¾ × 1¼ × ½″	104	—	—	—	—	—	—	—	—	—
Sweet potatoes, baked, 1, 5 × 2″	183	2.6	1.1	44	1.1	3*11,410	.12	.08	.9	28
Boiled, 1, 5 × 2½″	252	3.7	1.4	62	1.4	3*15,780	.18	.11	1.3	41
Candied, 1 small	314	2.6	6.3	63	1.6	3*10,940	.07	.07	.9	16
Canned, 1 cup	233	4.4	.2	54	1.7	19,300	.12	.09	1.1	31
Swordfish, broiled, 1 steak 3 × 3 × ½″	223	34.2	8.5	25	1.4	2,880	.06	.07	12.9	—
T Tangerine, 1 medium	35	.6	.2	27	.3	340	.06	.02	.2	25
Juice, unsweetened, 1 cup	95	2.2	.7	47	.5	1,040	.17	.06	.6	75
Tapioca, dry granulated quick cooking, stirred, 1 cup	547	.9	.3	18	1.5	—	.08	.06	.8	—
Tomatoes, raw, 1 medium, 2 × 2½″	30	1.5	.4	16	.9	1,640	.08	.06	.8	35
Canned or cooked, 1 cup	46	2.4	.5	27	1.5	2,540	.14	.08	1.7	40
Juice, canned, 1 cup	50	2.4	.5	17	1.0	2,540	.12	.07	1.8	38
Tomato catsup, 1 tbs.	17	.3	.1	2	.1	320	.02	.01	.4	2

2* Calcium based on dark brown sugar; value would be lower for light brown sugar.

Food										
Tomato puree, canned, 1 cup	90	4.5	1.2	27	2.7	4,680	.22	.17	4.5	69
Tongue, beef, medium fat, raw, 4 ounces	235	18.6	17.0	10	3.2	—	.14	.33	5.7	—
Tortillas, 1, 5″ diameter	50	1.2	.6	22	.4	1*40	.04	.01	.2	—
Tuna fish, canned, 3 oz. solids & liquid	247	20.2	17.8	6	1.0	180	.04	.08	9.1	—
Tuna fish, canned, 3 oz. drained solids	169	24.7	7.0	7	1.2	70	.04	.10	10.9	—
Turkey, medium fat, raw, 4 oz. edible portion	304	22.8	22.9	26	4.3	Tr.	.10	.16	9.1	—
Turnips, raw, 1 cup diced	43	1.5	.3	54	.7	Tr.	.07	.09	.6	38
Cooked, 1 cup diced	42	1.2	.3	62	.8	Tr.	.06	.09	.6	28
Turnip greens, cooked, 1 cup	43	4.2	.6	376	3.5	15,370	.09	.59	1.0	87
V Veal, cooked, cutlet, 3 ounces without bone	184	24.0	9.0	10	3.0	2*	2*.07	2*.24	2*5.2	—
Shoulder roast, 3 ounces without bone	193	24.0	10.0	10	3.1	—	.11	.27	6.7	—
Stew meat, 3 ounces without bone	252	21.0	18.0	9	2.6	—	.04	.20	3.9	—
Veal, canned, strained, 1 ounce (infant food)	24	4.5	.5	4	.5	—	.01	.09	1.6	—
Vinegar, 1 tbs.	2	—	—	1	.1	—	—	—	—	—
W Waffles, 1	216	7.0	8.0	144	.8	270	.05	.14	.3	—
Watercress, raw, 1 pound (leaves & stems)	84	7.7	1.4	885	9.1	21,450	.37	.71	3.6	350
Watermelon, ½ slice ¾ × 10″	45	.8	.3	11	.3	950	.08	.08	.3	10
Wheat flour, whole, 1 cup stirred	400	16.0	2.4	49	4.0	—	.66	.14	5.2	—
Wheat products:										
Breakfast flakes, 1 cup	125	3.8	.6	16	1.0	—	.03	.06	1.7	—
Puffed, 1 cup	43	1.0	.2	6	.4	—	.01	.02	.6	—
Rolled, cooked, 1 cup	177	5.0	.9	19	1.7	—	.17	.06	2.1	—
Shredded, plain, 1 small biscuit 2½ × 2″	79	2.0	.6	10	.8	—	.05	.03	1.0	—
Whole meal, cooked, 1 cup	175	6.6	.7	22	1.7	—	.25	.08	2.3	—
Wheat germ, 1 cup stirred	246	17.1	6.8	57	5.5	—	1.39	.54	3.1	—
White sauce, medium, 1 cup	429	10.0	33.1	305	.3	1,350	.09	.41	.3	1
Wild rice, parched, raw, 1 cup	593	23.0	1.1	31	—	—	.73	1.03	10.0	—
Y Yeast, dried, brewer's, 1 tbs.	22	3.0	.1	8	1.5	—	.78	.44	2.9	—
Yogurt, commercial made with whole milk, 1 cup	170	11.0	8.0	560	.2	380	.10	.45	—	3

1* Vitamin A value of tortillas made from yellow corn; tortillas made from white corn have no Vitamin A value.

2* Data assumes cut to be prepared by braising or pot roasting.

appendix IVb
Caloric Content
of Alcoholic Beverages

Drink	Quantity (ounces)	Calories
Beer	12	150
Rum	1½	150
Whiskey	1½	110
Grasshopper	2	200
Manhattan	2	160
Martini	2	160
Old-fashioned	2	170
Whiskey sour	2	140
Liqueur	1	100
Wine, dry, 20%	4	160
Wine, light dry, 12%	4	100
Wine, sweet, 20%	4	180

appendix V
Some Questions
and Answers

)ver the years I have spoken to a large number of lay groups and been
t the radio station end of the telephone in a number of question-and-
nswer radio programs. The following are typical of questions I have
een asked. Physicians, dietitians, and other health professionals among
he readers will be, I hope, interested in what would-be reducers have
n their minds. Laymen may find some of the answers useful comple-
nents to the preceding essays. The questions are not in any particular
rder (any more than questions at meetings or on radio programs usually
re). The answers largely cover material already dealt with in the main
ext, but the emphasis is often different and in some cases additional
letails are given.

1. Are steam baths of value in a reducing program?
   There has never been any scientifically validated evidence that
   steam baths are of value in a reducing program. They cause a quick
   loss of weight through quick loss of water by sweating. When the
   individual drinks, the water is regained and, with it, the weight.

2. Are short fasts, long fasts, any fasts at all useful in fighting obesity?
   It is difficulty to give a "yes" or "no" answer to this question.
   Certainly very long fasts, while effective in causing weight loss, entail serious medical and psychological risks and should be conducted
   only in a hospital under constant supervision. Short fasts (of the
   order of two or three days) have been used by some physicians as a
   starting point in reducing programs. My own impression is that such
   fasts are not, in fact, necessary in the majority of cases, although, I
   would agree that a few days of dieting at a very low caloric level
   (e.g., 600 or 800 calories per day) can often be useful at the start of
   a reducing regimen, the level being brought afterwards to 1,000,
   1,200 or whatever number of calories the physician thinks adequate
   for the longer pull.

3. Does the skin of a successfully reduced person invariably form ugly
   folds at areas where much fat has been eliminated?

Unless individuals are young, with a very elastic skin, rapid weight loss will usually cause the appearance of wrinkles which, however, are usually eliminated after a while. If individuals were extremely obese and have lost a lot of weight (e.g., 100 to 250 pounds and more) large folds of skin may appear, for example, on the abdomen; these may have to be removed surgically. In general, the older people are the less elastic their skin is and the more time it takes for the skin to adjust to the new size.

4. How true is the contention that "you need to eat fat if you are to be slim"?

There is no evidence at all that eating fat will make you slim. Eating too many calories will make you fat whatever nutrient the calories are from. After all, hundreds of millions of Indians are very thin on a diet very low in fat. In the United States, it appears that there is very little statistical difference in the food choices and the proportion of the diet represented by fat between very thin, normal and fat individuals.

5. How accurate is the statement, "The more oil you drink, the more body fat you will burn"?

There is no basis for this statement. Safflower oil, soybean oil and corn oil are prescribed to individuals with high blood cholesterol because these oils, rich in polyunsaturated fats, lower the blood cholesterol to less dangerous values. Drinking oil, however, does not help the body burn fat. Oils are fat and are equivalent to about 9 calories per gram.

6. Is it generally accepted that "unrestricted calorie, high-fat, high-protein diets will get weight off the obese more effectively than any other kind of regimen"?

No. Unrestricted calories in any form will not reduce a patient. A pound of body fat is worth 3,500 calories. Over a sufficient period, a deficit of 500 calories per day will cause a weight loss of a pound a week, whatever the nature of the diet. Similarly, a deficit of 1,000 calories per day will cause a weight loss of two pounds a week. The diet should be nutritionally adequate and the proportion of fat, particularly of saturated fat, in the diet, should not be excessive (preferably not above 30 per cent). The less the number of calories, the greater the need for quality in the diet and the higher the proportion of protein ought to be. A good source of protein without much fat is cottage cheese. In a calorically restricted diet, the proportion of foods high in vitamins and minerals should also be high. Cottage cheese is high in calcium, but low in iron. Fruits and leafy vegetables are high in vitamins and minerals, including iron.

7. Is it useful for a dieter to include in his feeding program such things as wheat germ and brewer's yeast?

Wheat germ and brewer's yeast are useful foods, but have no particular magic virtue. A good diet with a sufficient variety of foods is going to be balanced without such exotic supplements. Live yeast, incidentally, may use up more vitamins in the intestine than it actually provides, and thus its consumption may be self-defeating.

8. Some authorities have urged that fish should be a major part of a reducing diet. Should it?

Fish has the advantage over meat of generally being lower in fat, and also higher in the polyunsaturated fats and lower in the saturated fats, according to present evidence. Replacing meat by fish should thus have a favorable effect on blood cholesterol. Inasmuch as, in obese individuals, the dangers of a high blood cholesterol are increased, stepping up fish consumption is a sound measure.

9. Some people advocate deep breathing as a method of "using up calories." Is it worthwhile?

There is nothing wrong with deep breathing, and it may be good exercise for the chest muscles, but it doesn't appreciably use up calories.

10. Is body resistance lowered by dieting?

Body resistance to infectious diseases is not lowered by *sensible* dieting, if a person needs to reduce. *Excessive* dieting leading to undernutrition and underweight, particularly by adolescents, a group more vulnerable to tuberculosis than other groups, should be discouraged as it may induce susceptibility to this disease.

11. If, as is claimed, "protein is consumed at a lower rate" and thus "postpones hunger," should much of a reducing diet be protein?

It is, in fact, difficult to vary the proportion represented by protein in a balanced diet by more than a few percentage points. For instance, cereals and beans contain a higher proportion of protein than the public often realizes—about 10 per cent for cereals and bread and about 20 per cent for beans. By contrast, meat contains a smaller proportion of protein than the general public believes, particularly in this country where we have become used to meat containing a very high proportion of the calories as fat. Meat is far from being "pure protein." Excellent cuts of meat made tender by fat "marbleization" contain a very high proportion of calories as fat. The net effect is that most diets will vary between 13 and 16 per cent of the calories coming from protein, and only heroic efforts at consuming a great deal of cottage cheese will push it much higher to, say, 18 per cent or a little beyond. While protein is important to health, forcing the protein consumption above the usual levels has not been shown to be particularly effective in reducing diets. Protein and fat are digested more slowly than sugar and their inclusion in the diet increases the duration of satiety. High-sugar, low-protein snacks are undesirable because, while they stop hunger, they often don't stop it for very long.

12. How useful is massage in a weight-reduction program?

Massage may make you feel good, but it has never been shown t have any particular virtue in weight reduction.

13. It has been alleged that "the body has no need for carbohydrates." Is this true?

No, it is not true. To the best of our knowledge, the exclusive fue of the brain is glucose (blood sugar), a very important carbohydrate In fact, there is a very complex mechanism in the body to insur that the carbohydrate supply to the brain remains uninterrupted Every hormone known to affect sugar metabolism except one (insulin is designed to increase the supply of carbohydrates. If carbohydrate are not available from the diet, the body breaks down its own protein (*not its fat*) to make carbohydrate for the brain. Again, this does no mean that large amounts of sugar ought not to be avoided by dieters But *some* bread, *some* potatoes (preferably baked or boiled) are ac ceptable components of a reducing diet.

14. What, if any, is the relationship between consuming great quantitie of liquids and getting and remaining fat?

There is no relationship between liquid consumption and gettin and remaining fat—unless, of course, the liquid contains calories such as sugar in soda pops, alcohol in beer and other beverages, and fat, proteins, and carbohydrates in milk. Drinking enough water every day is a sound hygienic practice. There is no need to curtail it be cause your weight is too high.

15. Is the use of sweets in small quantities an appetite-depressant and, therefore, an aid to a reducing program?

Many people find that one (*one!*) piece of candy at the end of a small meal or snack gives them a feeling of immediate satiety which would not exist without it. As long as the amount of sugar consumed is small and as long as it is kept under control and does not begin to grow on you, there is no objection to consuming it. Some individuals, however, do just as well at losing weight without this source of sugar

16. Should milk in an adult diet be whole, skim, buttermilk, or cottage cheese?

Skim milk, buttermilk, and cottage cheese are much lower in fat than whole milk. This means not only that a source of calories has been eliminated, but also a source of saturated fats. Saturated fats are, of course, involved in the development of atherosclerosis, a form of hardening of the arteries. Certainly, the average adult who has a weight problem, and for that matter the average adult American male who is very vulnerable to atherosclerosis, will do well to re place milk by buttermilk or skim milk.

17. Is there any merit to the practice of "eating slowly"?

The process of satiety takes a little time and it makes a considerable amount of sense for individuals who almost systematically tend to overeat whenever they eat fast to chew their food and eat slowly.

Thus, the various mechanisms involved in metering the food ingested will be given time to come into play, and the patient will feel satiated without having eaten as much. (Patient, incidentally, is a particularly apt subject for this last sentence.)

18. Has it been established that it is "being fat," rather than "being heavy," that is harmful?

The answer is a qualified "yes." Most of the evidence we have is based on weight rather than fatness and shows very clearly that being overweight is harmful. People who are very overweight are, in general, also overfat. The question is more delicate as regards people who are moderately overweight, some of whom may have just a very large bone and muscle mass without being too fat. The great heavyweight boxers, by and large, would all have been considered overweight by life insurance tables, yet at their fighting best they certainly were not and are not fat. The linemen of the Green Bay Packers had a very difficult time getting into the United States Navy because they were overweight, and it was only after Dr. Behnke, then serving as a medical officer at the Great Lakes Naval Station, had weighed them under water and shown that, while they were overweight, they were not overfat, that they were accepted. There is no doubt that people who are very light for their height have a better life expectancy than people who are on the moderately heavy or heavy side. In the intermediate category, it is difficult to know what is the contributing part of the fat and what may be a difference in the mortality associated with all different body types. One suspects that excessive fatness is bad in all cases, but may be particularly bad for certain body constitutions or types. One of the lines of research we are undertaking at present is the study of a very large number of adults, categorized as to body types, weighed, and with their skinfolds measured as a method of determining fatness. These individuals are being followed for long durations so as to find out what the effect of weight as such and the effect of fat as such are on these body types. None of this is to be construed as meaning that obesity is not a bad thing; it may mean that the constitution of the body under the fat is also very important.

19. Are the benefits of reducing, beyond the obvious aesthetic ones, really established?

In a great many conditions, there are well established favorable effects of weight reduction. For example, in middle-aged individuals with maturity-onset diabetes who are generally fat, weight reduction may make the use of insulin unnecessary and may allow patients to control their diabetes through pills. In some cases, drastic weight reduction may make all medications unnecessary. Hypertension also often responds favorably to weight reduction. A large percentage of arthritic patients are made mobile again by weight reduction, a great benefit to the patient. There are a number of other conditions which are helped by weight reduction, such as the Pickwickian syndrome, a condition arising from the difficulty an obese patient has in breathing adequately. With the exception of a very few medical and psychiatric situations, weight reduction can be shown to have favorable effects, either curative or preventive.

20. Are there any specific "necessary" foods? If so, what are they?

There are no specifically "necessary" foods, there are only necessary nutrients. The one exception is milk for small babies. Even in infancy, milk is not a complete food; it is low in copper, iron, and vitamin C. Small children who drink milk to the exclusion of anything else often become obese and anemic, so that even in their case a more varied diet is advisable. In older children and in adults, the secret of good nutrition is a varied diet, sufficient but not excessive in amounts. The more varied the diet, the greater the chance it will not be deficient in any necessary element. In Western countries, malnutrition generally results from reduction in the number of foods consumed because of lacking teeth, poverty, and food faddism in the elderly, or food faddism and inappropriate dieting in the young. When whole classes of foods are eliminated, unless the patient knows quite a bit about nutrition, there is a chance he will become deficient in some nutrient. When a patient is on a reducing diet, variety must be conserved and particular attention must be given to the quality of the diet.

21. A prominent entertainer has been quoted as saying, "I never eat starches and protein together. It confuses the stomach." Does it?

No. There is no basis for not mixing proteins and fats. In fact, proteins are not properly utilized unless there are a sufficient number of calories from other sources consumed at the same time.

22. Are there any useful and harmless appetite-inhibiting products available without prescription?

No. By and large, the amounts of drug compounds necessary for a significant inhibition of appetite are larger than can be sold over the counter without prescription. If you need an appetite depressant that will work, it has to be prescribed by your doctor.

23. Are mechanical vibrating devices of any help in removing fat deposits?

I have never seen convincing evidence that any of the mechanical vibrating devices help to remove fat deposits.

24. Is there any effective way of taking off fat in a particular part of the body?

Common observation suggests that exercise is instrumental in remolding the shape of the body. Excessive fat accumulated on the derrière will be eliminated more satisfactorily by a combination of weight reduction and sufficient walking or bicycling than by weight reduction alone.

25. Would it be worthwhile for a serious reducer to keep a meal-by-meal diet diary and, similarly, a day-by-day record of exercise engaged in, its nature, and degree of difficulty?

The answer is an enthusiastic "yes." As a further help, a serious attempt at determining the amount of foods actually consumed, the precise duration of energy engaged in, and a calculation of their caloric equivalents is invaluable to the dieter. Remember that if you find in the table the caloric equivalent of a three-ounce hamburger, and you eat a four-ounce hamburger, you multiply the value by 4/3. If the cost of walking at 3 mph. is given for a 150-pound man and you weigh 200 pounds, you again multiply the value by 4/3, as the cost of moving your body is proportional to your body weight.

26. Should vitamin supplements be consumed by each person on a reducing diet?

Vitamin supplements are not unlike an insurance policy against poor nutrition. On a nonreducing diet of sound nutritional value, most individuals will not need supplements. On the other hand, if you are on a calorie-restricted diet, it may be more difficult to obtain a sufficient amount of vitamins daily, and, unless your diet has been carefully analyzed and found acceptable by a dietitian or an internist, vitamin supplements may be needed. If the brand is a reputable one, with the amounts of vitamins not excessive, it will not do any harm. The advantage of having your diet analyzed is that a specialist is aware of any deficiency in substances such as iron or calcium, and can therefore prescribe the amounts of vitamins and minerals needed much more accurately.

27. Is there any limit to how fat a person can get?

We don't really know. It appears that certain body types just don't get fat. It is quite possible that they don't have enough fat cells to get obese. Getting fat is first of all a matter of filling up fat cells with fat, rather than putting fat everywhere, although in extreme obesity fat appears in cells other than fat cells. In the light of present knowledge, it seems that the number of fat cells is determined at birth or at least in early infancy. This number does not determine how fat you will be (this depends on how much you eat and how much you exercise), but it may determine how fat you *can* be.

A few years ago, there was an interesting article in the French medical literature about several individuals who wanted to become members of the "Cent Kilos Club," an organization whose membership is restricted to restaurant owners weighing 100 Kilos (220 pounds). These men were very anxious to belong to this élite group, but in spite of their efforts, could not get beyond 97 to 98 kilos. The physician reporting these cases suggested that there was as much resistance to weight gain above a certain limit as there is to weight loss in some other subjects. We can influence our weight through modifying the energy balance, but within a broad range, the limits are set by genetic potentialities.

28. Are laxatives useful in a reducing program?

They have been fashionable at times among some individuals (as has been the practice of tickling one's throat after a meal to throw up), but there is no evidence whatsoever that laxatives are of any value in a reducing program. Their repeated use may do considerable harm to the gastrointestinal system.

29. Is it true that the one element of temperament that most obese people have in common is passivity?

The answer is probably "no." Such obese individuals as Winston Churchill, Stalin, Tito, Franco, etc., cannot by any stretch of the imagination be considered passive. On the other hand, there is good evidence (which we have reviewed in the appropriate chapter) that in a society which is very punitive towards fat people, obesity, particularly in adolescent girls, causes individuals to feel that they are victims of a fate they can do little about. This feeling of helplessness does, in turn, often lead to a feeling of passivity. It thus seems that, when passiveness is a trait found in the obese patient, it may be as much the result as the cause of obesity.

30. Does drinking vinegar have a slimming effect?

No. There is no truth in the saying, "Fat will melt in vinegar." (And there is even less truth in the belief that fat will melt in alcoholic beverages.)

31. How true is the statement, "Most excess weight is salt water"?

Most excess weight in the obese is *fat*. There is a small amount of water and protoplasm that accompanies the laying down of fat, but over 80 per cent of the adipose tissue is fat. Very often, when people lose fat, the water is retained in the space freed by the disappearance of fat and thus it may be several days, and in some cases several weeks, before the water gets excreted and the actual weight is lost. This phenomenon of water retention on reducing diets is most often seen in inactive older women.

32. Does alcohol stimulate the appetite?

The answer is generally "no." What is generally true is that, when people are tense, their appetite is temporarily suspended. Any factors which help them to relax may help them to regain their appetite. Moderate amounts of alcohol may come under this category. It is useful to remember, however, that alcohol contains 7 calories per gram (about 200 calories per ounce). These calories should be counted as part of a person's intake.

33. What determines the particular spot where fat accumulates in the body of an obese person?

There are a number of factors. First, the sex of the person—men and women do not put on fat in the same places. Second, genetics of body type. Third, the pattern of muscular activity. Fourth, the pattern of endocrine secretion. (For example, steroid hormones will promote the development of the so-called "bull neck" obesity, with a lot of fat around the belt and particularly in the back of the neck.)

34. Is there any danger in following a low-protein diet?

The answer is "yes," particularly if the protein intake is very low and the individual is still growing. A lot of the anemia we see in adolescent girls is self-inflicted. At a time when the demands are relatively high, many of our teen-age girls place themselves on low-protein and low-iron diets.

35. Are home-exercising machines of any value?

The answer is "yes," if they are used long enough and with sufficient energy. A great deal has been said in this book about the value of exercise in weight control. It is well to underline the statement that exercise of short duration but high intensity, leading to pulse rates of 120 and up, has a very useful effect on the cardiovascular system. In individuals with some narrowing of the coronary, it may promote development of enough collateral circulation to save one's life when the coronary becomes completely occluded. Ideally, a person should exercise moderately (say, walk) for 3/4 of an hour or more every day and exercise very vigorously on a bicycle ergometer or rowing machine for no less than 15 minutes, at least three times a week.

36. Is hunger drive reduced by consuming such products as saccharin?

So far, there is no basis for thinking that it is.

37. Is it true that there are few obese people among the aged?

Actually, the peak incidence of obesity in the United States is probably in the 40-to-60-year age bracket. Over the age of 50, the obese population decreases, probably to a large extent because a greater proportion of the obese than of the nonobese have been eliminated by premature death.

38. Is obesity a world-wide problem?

We don't have very good data on the prevalence of obesity throughout the world. Obesity is reasonably common among the better-off classes of poor countries, so that it is at least potentially universal. Of course, there are areas where fattening oneself up every year in anticipation of a very "lean" period (caused by drought, poor methods of food conservation, etc.) is a life-saving procedure. I have observed this practice in the dry areas of West Africa bordering on the Sahara Desert.

39. Is it proper to regard obesity as a disease? If so, what justification do the nonobese have for treating the obese—as they do—with open contempt?

Obesity is probably not a disease as such, but a symptom common to a great many conditions which lead to a positive energy balance (relatively increased food intake or relatively decreased exercise). Mild obesity, particularly in the middle-aged, is in many ways a social disease brought about by the type of life which more and more middle-class urbanized Americans are leading. Certainly, if there is any theme to this book, it is that obesity is a medico-social problem, not a moral problem, and that there is no justification for looking down on the obese.

40. Is it true that obese people are subject to discrimination when seeking employment?

There have been a number of instance of individuals threatened with dismissal from their jobs unless they lost weight. This has been true even in such tenured positions as the armed forces. We have found that there is real discrimination against obese subjects, particularly against girls. It seems reasonable, though it is hard to document, that there is fairly widespread discrimination in employment against obese people. As regards college admissions, a study I conducted shows that obese girls have a much harder time getting into a high-ranking college than their thinner contemporaries with equal grades; or, again with equal grades, getting into college at all. Discrimination against obese boys is somewhat less.

41. Are there such things as "fat-blasting" enzyme foods that "dissolve" body fat tissue?

No.

42. Does honey have any advantages for the obese over any other carbohydrate food?

It tastes better.

43. Should vitamins be consumed while undertaking an otherwise "total" fast?

I am not in favor of total fasting, but if one does, vitamins in sensible amounts would not do any harm. The need for some of the vitamins B is reduced in fasting. Total fast of long duration should never be undertaken except in a hospital at the direction of a physician.

44. What motivation to become less obese seems to be the most effective?

The fear of immediate death in an individual afflicted with a serious degenerative disease and the desire to be attractive to the other sex are probably the most effective motivating factors.

45. Is it possible to be, at the age of 50, the same weight one was at the age of 22, and yet be as much as a third fatter?

The answer is "yes," particularly if one had a large muscle mass at age 22. On the other hand, there *is* a slow replacement of muscle by fat, even in thin people who keep their weight constant.

46. Is it true that protein more rapidly "appeases the appetite"?

The answer is "no." In very small amounts easily diffused sugars like sucrose (ordinary sugar) have the greatest effect on calming down hunger contractions quickly. For longer periods, protein and fat have a more lasting effect. Fat slows down stomach emptying and protein is absorbed slowly. People are unequally sensitive to the satiety effect of a sweet dessert (or a hard candy at the end of a meal). All in all, a small, complete meal is probably the best way to take care of both the immediate and the longer-term satieties.

47. At any given age, are women likely to contain more fat than men or about the same?

Women do contain more fat than men, so that a thin woman is actually fatter than a thin man.

48. Is smoking an appetite curb? Is there a tendency to gain weight when one stops smoking?

Smoking is an appetite curb, particularly in some people, but, generally, it is not as powerful a curb as people think. The majority of subjects gain about five to seven pounds when they stop smoking, but very often go on to lose it slowly. A few people do tend to gain a greater amount of weight when they stop smoking. It is well to remember, however, that heavy cigarette smoking is much more injurious to health than marked obesity. Depending on the age, a pack of cigarettes per day may have statistically the same deleterious effect as 50 to 100 pounds of excess weight.

49. Is it of value while reducing to cut the number of meals from three to two or even to one?

No. If you get too hungry, you not only eat rapidly, you tend to eat in order to relieve what has become an intractable hunger and thus more than make up for the deficit. You feel so virtuous after cutting out two meals that you will feel entitled to a very large one. Dividing the restricted number of calories among a larger number of small meals or snacks is a more effective method of reducing.

50. Is it true that nervous people "consume their blood sugar"?

There is very little doubt that patterns of glucose utilization vary from one individual to another, and it is not impossible that some people when under stress oversecrete insulin and tend to become hungry as a result. In most people, however, nervousness has the opposite effect of cutting down hunger, perhaps through the increase in secretion of such hormones as epinephrine, which tend to reduce the utilization of blood sugar by muscles and tissues other than the brain.

51. Can the frame type of one's body be determined by wrist measurement? If so, what is the formula—for men, for women?

Actually, it takes more than just the wrist measurement to determine body type. A complicated formula developed by Dr. Albert Damon of Harvard in 1965 is based on weight, height, upper arm circumference, upper arm skinfold, the skinfold taken below the shoulder blade, and hand grip strength measured by an instrument called the hand dynamometer. The term "frame" as used in insurance tables has never been defined and is completely ambiguous. Obese individuals, on the average, have heavier skeletons than the average for the population as a whole.

52. Why is hot weather usually more difficult for the obese than for the nonobese?

A layer of fat is a good insulation, but it functions in both directions. It insulates against cold (Channel swimmers have to be reasonably fat to endure seven to eight hours in cold water). It also makes heat loss difficult and hot weather is, because of this, hard on the obese.

53. Does the distended abdomen that accompanies much obesity constitute a health menace in itself?

The pressure on the diaphragm in excessive obesity is one of the factors in the Pickwickian syndrome, a condition due to difficulty in breathing and consequent accumulation of carbon dioxide (and drowsiness). In extreme cases it may lead to congestive heart failure. A very fat abdomen also increases surgical risk.

54. Has it been clearly established that weight reduction leads to longevity?

Thinner people live longer than fat people, and there is some evidence obtained by the Metropolitan Life Insurance Company that individuals who were obese and have reduced have a longer life expectancy than obese people who haven't.

55. Do bulk-producing products such as vegetable cellulose lessen the appetite?

Some people are helped by them, but the effect is temporary.

56. Does a vegetarian diet have anything to recommend it as a weight-reducer?

No. Some rice eaters, for example, manage to get very fat.

57. Is there more obesity among Americans today than there was a generation ago?

Yes. The statistics obtained by the United States Public Health Service show that the increase in weight of the American people has been more rapid than the increase in height.

58. Is a moral approach to obesity—the flat defining of it as a direct by-product of gluttony—effective as a reducing agent?

I hope that the whole tenor of the book has indicated that I am dead-set against this approach. It is particularly dangerous in adolescents, who gain from it an unfavorable self-image which may haunt them all their lives.

59. Increasingly over the past decade, millions of dollars worth of low-calorie foods have been sold and consumed in the United States. Has their use helped many people reduce and remain reduced?

The answer should be a qualified "yes." There is very little doubt that, if people have to watch their weight, they do much better when they can get the nutritive value of useful foods without having to absorb at the same time a lot of sugar or fat which bring nothing but calories. For example, a so-called dietetic fruit salad or serving of cut-up fruits is vastly preferable for anybody who watches his or her weight (and, for that matter, probably for everybody) than similar fruits preserved in heavy syrup. If people are going to have a large consumption of soft drinks, it is better for their teeth and probably their figures if these are made with sugar substitutes rather than with sugar. On the other hand, three notes of warning must be sounded. First, a number of so-called low-calorie foods really represent only a small decrease in the absolute number of calories. Second, a number of people get a feeling of false security out of the term "low-calorie," which they interpret as meaning "calorie-free." Third, the long-term safety of saccharin is well established, but that of the artificial sweetener, cyclamate, is still in doubt. Excessive amounts of cyclamate should be avoided, until its long-time safety is confirmed.

60. Have liquid diets, so popular in this country just a few years ago and apparently less so now, brought many people the weight reduction they sought?

Liquid diets are useful to some people for a limited amount of time. They have taught obese patients that quantity as well as quality of food is important. On the other hand, they are rarely useful for very extended periods. After two or three weeks during which they were the exclusive nourishment, they have been used most successfully as a substitute for one meal out of three.

61. Are there significantly more fat children and adolescents than there were a short time ago?

Our data would tend to show that at least in suburban Boston there is a steady increase in obesity among adolescents.

62. Is a regular program of group exercising—in the YMCA, the YMHA, the Health Club—likely to be more effective than exercising done in private?

The answer is probably "yes, at the beginning," because it forces individuals to adhere to a schedule of exercise. The value of group exercising is highly dependent on the ability of the teacher to make the individual exercise vigorously, steadily, and for a sufficient period of time. The lasting value of group exercise should be, however, that it instills habits of fitness which lead the individual to exercise on his own.

63. Are there other prosperous countries where obesity is less of a problem? If so, why?

The United States is particularly bad as regards the enormous prevalence of obesity, possibly because our urban areas (with the exception of San Francisco and some restricted areas of other cities) are unattractive and, as a result, people walk very little in American cities. Suburbs are so spread out—usually with no sidewalks—that walking there is also restricted. Finally, the habit of family walking or walking on vacations seems to have largely disappeared in this country. In many European countries where the standard of living, including the number of cars, is approaching that of the United States, there is still a tradition of physical exercise which has persisted longer than it has here. A friend of mine—a well known economist with a sense of humor—once said in my presence that "the United States, for obvious geographic reasons, was the first country in the world to become Americanized. The rest of the world is now following suit and becoming Americanized as well. We can hope that it is now time for the United States to become de-Americanized." The reinitiation of walking would be a good way to start as far as weight control and health generally are concerned.

64. The late Alexis Carrel stated that "fasting purifies and profoundly modifies our tissues." Does current research support this view?

A number of people have experienced lightheadedness and quasi-mystical experiences while fasting. Some people feel that their thinking becomes clearer after a 24-hour fast. There are changes in metabolism as a result of fasting (the organism runs out of carbohydrate stores and burns its fat and protein). Actually, what psychological changes are documented as a result of starvation are very unfavorable in terms of performance, and it is very doubtful that starvation can be considered a constructive experience for anybody.

65. Can a carbohydrate-free diet be damaging to the brain?

On a carbohydrate-free diet, the body has to provide carbohydrates for the brain by breaking down some of its own protein. A carbohydrate-free diet is also a high-fat diet and, hence, undesirable because it may promote high blood cholesterol and arteriosclerosis.

66. Does fat insulate against heat loss and thus tend to the accumulation of more fat?

Some recent work suggests that the decrease in heat loss due to insulation by fat is a small but steady contribution to the positive energy balance which eventually causes obesity.

67. Is common salt in excessive quantity a health menace? Is the consumption of too much salt a factor in obesity?

There is some indication that the habitual consumption of excessive amounts of salt is associated with a greater risk of high blood pressure. Americans have become used to more salting of their food than many other nations. To a large extent the taste for salt is a self-accelerating one. Cutting down on salt by omitting to salt previously salted food is a useful health measure and the body quickly ceases to notice any loss in taste.

There is no particular known relationship between salt-intake and obesity. If people lose weight rapidly, they often accumulate fluid. This hides the fact that they are losing fat because their weight may stay temporarily at the same level. Fluid retention is very much less likely to happen if the intake of salt is cut down.

68. Will increasing the proportion of protein in the diet increase the rate at which the body burns up food, and accordingly, help in reducing?

Actually, no. The idea that increasing the proportion of protein in the diet increases the rate at which food is burned stems from a misunderstanding of the physiological concept known as "specific dynamic action." Specific dynamic action, or SDA, is the cost of handling a particular nutrient or food. If pure carbohydrate (starch or sugar) is given to an individual who has been fasting, about 6 per cent of the energy contained in the carbohydrate is used in the handling of the carbohydrate by the body.

In the case of pure fat, the SDA is of the order of 4 per cent. In the case of pure protein, it is about 30 per cent. However, when the various types of nutrients are fed together, as happens in practice, the specific dynamic action of the meal is not the arithmetical sum of the SDA corresponding to the various nutrients; it is, instead, about 6 per cent. In other words, when protein is fed with carbohydrate or fat (as is the case if the protein is in the form of meat, milk, eggs, cheese, fish, etc.), it is handled much more effectively and the specific dynamic action of the meal is only about 6 per cent. A low-protein meal contains about 10 per cent protein (this is the protein content of dry wheat). A high-protein meal contains 15 to 18 per cent protein. Even if the protein intake is upped to 25 per cent, the specific dynamic action is essentially not increased. The *caloric* content of the diet is thus much more important than the *nature* of the diet in determining the energy balance. Obviously, as a nutritionist, I want everybody to eat as varied and balanced a diet as possible. I wish I could recommend a certain specific diet composition which would make it much easier to reduce, but there is neither theoretical nor empirical evidence for such a prescription.

69. Is there any correlation between obesity and stupidity?

In studies which we conducted on a large number of high school seniors in a suburban school system, we could find no significant difference in I. Q. or school performance in any subject (except physical education) between obese and nonobese youngsters. There is thus no association between obesity and lack of intelligence.

On the other hand, as has been described in other chapters of the book, we and others have found that obesity has an effect on people's views of themselves, and hence, sometimes on their performance—at least in a society which, like ours, holds fairly punitive views toward the obese. It does have a marked effect, as has been mentioned above, on college admissions, particularly for girls.

70. Is there a pituitary extract that safely reduces weight by increasing metabolic rate?

No. Every few years somewhere in the world a hitherto unknown physician comes up with a hormonal extract that will cure obesity in a few easy injections. So far these rumors have always been short-lived and unfounded.

71. Is it true that the less food one eats, the greater the nourishment one derives from it?

The answer is "no." Underfeeding eventually does lead to certain adjustments—decreased body weight and, hence, decreased requirements for maintenance and motion of the remaining body weight—but basically the same proportion of food is absorbed and metabolized whether one eats little or much.

72. The statement is frequently made that the human body is about two-thirds water. Is the water content of an obese person higher?

Actually, the human body contains two-thirds water only in childhood and the proportion of water tends to go down as people grow older. The total proportion of body weight represented by water is very much less in obese than in nonobese individuals because the adipose tissue contains very little water as compared to muscle, liver, brain, etc.

73. Hippocrates advised the obese to subsist upon well-fed pork boiled with vinegar. Is there any merit in the idea?

No.

74. Has it been proved that repeated fluctuations in weight, resulting from temporary successes of weight reduction attempts followed by failures, may be more harmful than a continuing condition of being moderately obese?

We have evidence that in at least one strain of obese and diabetic mice, the repeated practice of weight gain and weight loss (which I have called elsewhere the "rhythm method of girth control") leads to a shorter life expectancy than maintenance of an obese weight. On the other hand, reducing them and keeping them reduced does significantly increase their life span.

75. Are passive exercises—such as those that purport to achieve low voltage stimulation of the muscles—useful in fighting obesity?

No.

Index